PERVERSE CITIES

PERVERSE CITIES
Hidden Subsidies, Wonky Policy, and Urban Sprawl

Pamela Blais

UBCPress · Vancouver · Toronto

20 19 18 17 16 15 14 13 12 11   5 4

Printed in Canada on FSC-certified ancient-forest-free paper
(100% post-consumer recycled) that is processed chlorine- and acid-free.

Library and Archives Canada Cataloguing in Publication

Blais, Pamela
    Perverse cities: hidden subsidies, wonky politics, and urban sprawl / Pamela Blais.

Includes bibliographical references and index.
ISBN 978-0-7748-1895-7 (bound); ISBN 978-0-7748-1896-4 (pbk.)

    1. City planning – Economic aspects. 2. Cities and towns – Growth – Economic aspects. I. Title.

HT166.B53 2010   307.1'216   C2010-904778-8

---

e-book ISBNs: 978-0-7748-1897-1 (pdf); 978-0-7748-1898-8 (epub)

Canadä

UBC Press gratefully acknowledges the financial support for our publishing program of the Government of Canada (through the Canada Book Fund), the Canada Council for the Arts, and the British Columbia Arts Council.

This book has been published with the help of a grant from the Canadian Federation for the Humanities and Social Sciences, through the Aid to Scholarly Publications Program, using funds provided by the Social Sciences and Humanities Research Council of Canada.

UBC Press
The University of British Columbia
2029 West Mall
Vancouver, BC V6T 1Z2
www.ubcpress.ca

TO ELIZABETH AND EDMOND

Contents

Preface

As a city planning consultant during the 1990s, I worked on many plans, policies, and studies, researching patterns of urban development and developing policies that aimed to shift these patterns to something more sustainable economically, environmentally, and socially. Research reports, official plans, city plans, regional plans, innovative zoning policies: as the documents produced began to take up an alarmingly high number of linear feet on my bookshelf, I became more frustrated by what I saw as a lack of progress on the ground. The plans produced, ostensibly governing development patterns, seemed to say all the right things. We should create compact, liveable, mixed-use, vibrant, and less auto-dependent communities. And yet, when I looked around in the suburbs, things seemed little changed. The Toronto region, where I live, was (and is) growing by about 100,000 people every year, equivalent to a small city. Forty thousand new homes are needed annually just to keep up with demand, not to mention retail, office, and industrial development. Hectare upon hectare of new suburbs were being built every year, casting the die and entrenching urban form for many, many years to come.

Yet, for the most part, these new suburbs seemed to be being built more or less as they always had been. True, the lots had often become narrower, somewhat increasing residential densities, though with negative consequences for the streetscape as the inevitable double garages now dominated even more than they had before. And there were a significant number of townhouses. But the suburban street patterns remained the same (arterial, collector, local, cul de sac), land uses were still fanatically separated, and the corner "convenience" plaza was the only place nearby to buy a litre of milk (more often than not still requiring a hop into the car). And these were some of the most progressive new suburbs in North America. Some suburban Toronto municipalities had been among the first to apply the principles of "new urbanism" when creating new communities, but ambitious plans were frequently scaled back. Each of these suburban municipalities had a planned urban centre, which was to be a focal point for the community, with civic uses and a denser, mixed-use, walkable core offering services and concentrated employment. Yet, these seemed to be precisely the places where development was not occurring.

In the core of the region, reurbanization was taking place. High-rise condominiums were being built, and former factories were being converted into residential lofts. New neighbourhoods emerged on former industrial lands. But outside of the core there was virtually no reurbanization taking place, even within communities that had relatively older urban areas. When I looked around in these other areas, I saw opportunity. I saw underutilized land in many forms: parking in front of the two-storey strip malls that lined Toronto's arterials, low-density development around subway stops or at major intersections, large expanses of surface parking at shopping centres or in industrial areas, and the suburban "town centres" that were less dense than the suburbs they served. It seemed to me that new growth offered an opportunity to vastly improve these areas; to diversify the activities, services, and shopping available; to improve the quality of the public realm; to better balance employment and residential uses; to put more transit riders within walking distance of stops and stations (or, better still, to allow residents to walk or cycle to work).

And there was no lack of pressure to do so, as the official plans recognized. The loss of valuable farmland and natural areas at the edge of the urban area, rising levels of traffic congestion, an increasing number of smog-alert days every summer, and concern about greenhouse gas emissions and climate change were just a few of the pressing issues. I became concerned not only that we were building the equivalent of a small city every year at the urban fringe (and in a way that was of questionable sustainability) but also that, at the same time, we were building a massive future liability – an inefficient, inflexible urban form ill-suited to meeting future challenges, such as rising oil prices, financial market instability, or the productivity and competitiveness of businesses.

So, there were mounting pressures to change the development pattern, plentiful development opportunities existed, and the planning regime seemed to explicitly support more sustainable, compact urban forms. Why wasn't it happening? Of course, I was aware of the usual reasons given: zoning policies and engineering standards that still restricted compact development, planning approvals processes that were too arduous, NIMBYism, and banks that were loathe to take a gamble by financing "new" urban forms. Certainly these were factors. But I felt that something else had to be propelling these patterns. Early on, I had recognized that the structure of development charges was biased against reurbanization. I began to look further: in what ways, exactly, did this occur? I found that there were many. What about other financial instruments? Did they exert distorting pressures on development patterns? It became apparent to me that these and many other financial instruments, at all levels of government, represented adventures in mis-pricing that, from an urban development point of view, were critical to shaping development patterns. However, they consistently did so in a way that contradicted the planning objectives. While the city planners were busily envisioning a more compact, mixed-use urban form that would curb sprawl, and developing policies and regulations to secure it, down the hall the finance advisors were concocting financial instruments that would encourage and subsidize sprawl. The mis-pricing that these tools embodied was providing a powerful financial incentive to create more inefficient urban development. Not that they did this on purpose, but this was the unintended consequence of the financial instruments that they proffered. A situation was created in which planning and pricing policies were at loggerheads, with the latter actively undermining the former.

I came to recognize the critical importance of pricing to planning. I did so reluctantly as I was not keen to make myself into a student of pricing. I did not expect my planning career to bring me to the point where I am trying to decipher a pile of CRTC decisions written in tele-code in order to figure out how the hell local telephone rates are determined. But the role of pricing was, to me, incontrovertible. What is clear to me now is that, if the plans and policies aimed at creating more sustainable urban communities are to have any significant effect, it is fundamental that mis-pricing be addressed.

So, *Perverse Cities* is an attempt to explain why, after decades of planning, there seems to be so little tangible progress on the ground in curbing urban sprawl. It explores in some detail how mis-pricing acts to undermine planning policies aimed at creating more compact, mixed, sustainable communities. How can we identify instances of mis-pricing? How, exactly, do they operate to encourage sprawl? And how can we go about fixing these flaws in order to create accurate price signals and a level playing field? In short, how can planning do a better, more efficient and effective job of creating communities that meet the challenges of today and tomorrow?

Perverse Cities would not have been possible without the assistance of others, whom I would like to sincerely thank for their roles. Readers of drafts, including John van Nostrand and two anonymous peer reviewers, provided insightful comments and feedback that helped shape this book for the better. Michel Molgat Sereacki provided expert and enthusiastic research assistance. At UBC Press, Melissa Pitts was a thoughtful reviewer and patient guide through the publishing process, while Joanne Richardson's surgical copy editing smoothed out the many rough spots. Last and most, I thank Marvin, Oliver, and Audrey, who generously gave me the support, space, coffee, and considerable time needed to complete this project.

Of course, I remain far from being an expert on pricing, so any errors that may appear herein – on that score or on any other – are solely my responsibility.

PERVERSE CITIES

The Price of Sprawl

Sprawl has been lamented for decades. It is usually discussed in terms of its costs, and there is a long list of these: more expensive road, sewer, and water networks; loss of farmland and natural open space; air pollution and related illnesses, such as childhood asthma; excessive commuting and obesity; car accidents; policing; inner-city decline; socioeconomic segregation; isolation of non-drivers; unattractive landscapes; and more. However costly sprawl has been in the past, the stakes are even higher today and into the future. This is because, first, the scale of sprawl itself is increasing; second, the impacts per unit of sprawl are also increasing; and third, the world is changing in a way that makes sprawl issues even more critical now than they have been in the past.

As in other countries, population growth in Canada is increasingly concentrated in cities and, especially, the largest urban regions. Nearly 90 percent of the nation's population growth between 2001 and 2006 occurred in metropolitan areas.[1] Now almost half of Canada's population is concentrated in its six major urban regions.[2] The vast majority of population and employment growth is taking place in outer suburbs, in the form of low-density, single-use suburbs on former farms or natural areas. The amount of land required for each person and job has been increasing. The Canadian urban population grew 45 percent between 1971 and 2001.[3] The amount of urbanized land grew 96 percent during the same period, indicating that we are using more and more land per person.[4]

Levels of car ownership are rising, along with distances driven per car. The number of motor vehicles in Canada has increased from about 11 million in 1975 to almost 19 million in 2004.[5] In the Toronto area alone, it is projected that the number of vehicles will increase by almost 2 million, reaching 5.6 million by 2031.[6] Since 1989 in Canada, urban automobile use has increased by 16 billion passenger-kilometres, reaching 264 billion passenger-kilometres in 2000, while transit travel has remained fairly steady, at 23 billion passenger-kilometres.[7] And, even though fuel efficiency has improved, the move to larger vehicles and SUVs in recent decades, along with increases in truck traffic, has cancelled out these gains in efficiency. Emissions of most pollutants from motorized vehicles have continued to rise.

Moreover, some of the issues that are shaping up to play a major role in the twenty-first century are intimately related with sprawl. Water shortages are one example. Much urban growth is taking place in the very locations with the least water, such as the American sunbelt, while drought spreads across the agricultural centre of the continent. By disrupting natural hydrological cycles, sprawl contributes to drought. Access to a reliable, affordable water supply will become an ever more critical, city-shaping issue. Food security will be another. Maintaining productive farmland in close proximity to cities is fundamental to providing a secure, local food supply, while averting the substantial greenhouse gas (GHG) emissions associated with long-distance food transport.

Gas prices will continue to rise in the long term as cheaper oil sources become depleted. Rising gas prices intensify the strain on car-dependent neighbourhoods, households, and businesses. Many communities and business districts have been built in such a way that, other than by the automobile, there are very few means of access to and within them. Price peaks in 2008 provided a taste of the potential impact of high gas prices, causing many to rethink their travel, housing, and business location choices. The short-term repercussions of high gas prices were already evident: the decline in the demand for larger vehicles and the closing of the auto plants that produced them. Persistent high prices will see the next phase of altered decision making: people and businesses looking to reduce their need to drive by seeking out urban environments that support walking, cycling, and transit. That is made much more difficult by the kind of urban environment we have built over the last fifty years or so.

Last but not least is the related issue of GHG emissions and global warming. Interestingly, some of the most sprawling nations are those that are either far from meeting their Kyoto commitments (Canada) or did not sign on to the Kyoto Accord to begin with (Australia and the United States). The excessive vehicle travel associated with urban sprawl is a key contributor to GHG emissions. Yet, many government "greening" policies and programs are not addressing the biggest causes of GHG emissions related to cities and urban development. Much of the attention has been focused on programs that aim to reduce consumption within the home – energy-efficient appliances, windows, insulation, furnaces, and so on.

However, when it comes to reducing energy use and GHG emissions, the location of the home is far more important than are the green features of the house itself. This is because urban location and local context (such as the presence of nearby shops and services, schools and employment opportunities, and the presence of walkable, connected streets) determine how much travel occurs and by what mode. Household-related transportation creates significantly more GHGs than does the running of the home itself. Of the GHGs emitted directly by Canadian households (i.e., in household travel, home heating, lighting, and running appliances), almost two-thirds is related to transportation. Moreover, while the absolute amount of GHG emissions related to running the home has remained relatively constant since 1990, the emissions related to transportation have increased by about 25 percent.[8]

It has also been shown that even the greenest house located in the suburbs, with all the latest energy-saving features *and* an energy-efficient car, consumes more total energy than does a conventional house with a conventional car located in an accessible urban area.[9] This is due to the continued need to drive long distances from the suburban home.

Another study found that simply changing the location of a household from outer suburb to inner area (while holding everything else constant) reduced GHG emissions related to travel by 36 percent.[10] Altering the urban form alone and maintaining a suburban location reduced transportation emissions by 24 percent. But the household located in even the most compact mixed-use suburban neighbourhood still emitted more greenhouse gases than did one in the least compact inner-area neighbourhood. In other words, when it comes to reducing energy use and GHGs, location within the city and local context are critical determinants of GHGs and are substantially more important than are the features of the house. Yet, location and urban form are rarely addressed in GHG reduction strategies, where the focus has been squarely on introducing green features into the house itself.

For all of these reasons, it is increasingly necessary to refocus and redouble efforts to address urban sprawl (by directing growth to central and accessible locations) and to improve the local context of existing and new suburbs. This means retrofitting existing suburbs to diversify the mix of jobs and housing, improving the local accessibility of jobs and services, and increasing transit viability, walking, and cycling. It also means ensuring that newly built suburbs are mixed in terms of housing type and land uses, that they are compact, and that they are designed for modes of travel other than the automobile. Cities are expensive to build but slow and even more expensive to change. In an era of volatile energy costs, climate change, and water shortages, it is critical that new growth take a different tack. Otherwise, we continue to embed severe future problems by building sprawl that will be very difficult and expensive to mitigate.

Unfortunately, to this point, the record on dealing with sprawl is not particularly encouraging. For decades now, planners and others have been trying to put an end to urban sprawl. From the ecosystem planning of the 1970s to sustainable development in the 1980s and, most recently, "smart growth," governments have devoted considerable resources to altering the way in which cities grow. Had these approaches been successful, we ought by now to be living in the kinds of cities described in planning documents – that is, cities that are "healthy," "sustainable," "liveable," "compact," "transit-oriented," "walkable," "mixed use," and "efficient." Clearly, this is not the case.

In other words, planning is not curbing urban sprawl. Urban development continues along the same trajectory as it did before plans for more sustainable and compact development were adopted. Despite the spread of planning across communities, and its increased depth and focus on sustainable urban development patterns, it is not delivering results. Even some of the loudly trumpeted new approaches to city growth, such as new urbanism, have been criticized as merely producing "cuter sprawl."

The Sprawl Debate

Over recent decades, a substantial literature has accumulated on the issue of urban sprawl, focusing on its costs, its causes, and its remedies. It can be roughly divided into two camps: the first camp views sprawl as undesirable, while the second views it as benign and natural.

The first camp, which holds the prevailing view of sprawl, contends that it comes with many costs – social, economic, and environmental. Adherents of this view include planners, urban designers, and environmentalists.[11] Various movements, such as smart growth, new urbanism, and sustainable development fall within this camp, which sees sprawl as a problem because it comes with high social and private costs. Most often cited are the direct costs of a low-density development pattern at the urban edge, such as the loss of farmland and natural areas in proximity to the city. Other costs are attributed to the automobile dependency that is inherent in the low-density, single-use development pattern that characterizes sprawl. This includes driving costs, congestion, air pollution, climate change, health costs, accidents, policing, and road infrastructure as well as social costs incurred by those who are excluded because they cannot drive or cannot afford a vehicle, and by those who suffer lengthy daily commutes. The costs of other infrastructure, such as sewer, water, and utilities, are also raised on a per-dwelling-unit basis when density is low. According to the first camp, the current North American sprawl story began in the post-Second World War period, when it was supported by subsidies (such as federal housing programs for returning veterans and massive investments in highways) and then entrenched in an array of planning regulations and engineering standards.

Those in the first camp hold that the high costs associated with sprawl warrant a substantial intervention in order to turn these patterns around, creating instead more integrated, mixed-use, dense, and walkable neighbourhoods and districts. This can be achieved through better design and alternative forms of regulation, along with more strategic investment in infrastructure. This might include, for example, following the principles of "traditional neighbourhood development" put forward by the new urbanists, alternative engineering standards and forms of regulation, and more regional governance.

The second camp – which holds the minority view and comprises a relatively small group – takes a different approach to the issue of sprawl,[12] noting, among other things, that it was in evidence long before the Second World War.[13] This camp sees more recent urban development patterns as the result of economic and technological trends, expressed through a property market working to respond to consumer demand. In particular, the decentralization and suburbanization of recent decades is driven by rising real incomes and falling transportation costs, which have allowed homes and businesses to locate farther from central cities, typically consuming more land and floorspace per capita relative to central locations. In this view, sprawl is the natural and largely benign result of rising standards of living. If anything, the quality of people's lives has been improved with these advancements. According to this camp, what consumers demand is sprawl, which is what the market provides, and there is very little wrong with that. Holcombe and Staley sum up this view as follows:

Development patterns at the beginning of the twenty-first century are the result of market forces that respond to the demands of citizens, as residents, as workers and as consumers. If one understands the role that market forces have played in generating sprawling development patterns, several things become more obvious. First, it becomes apparent that regardless of the merits of altering current trends, it will be difficult for public policy to do so, because market forces will work in the opposite direction. Second, it is clear that there will be unintended secondary effects from anti-sprawl policies that may make people worse off. Third, these development patterns, responding to public demand, may not be so undesirable after all. And fourth, the way in which to design and implement land-use policy to further commonly held goals becomes clearer.[14]

Holcombe and Staley's fourth point gets us into the remedies proposed. Not surprisingly, this camp holds that few measures are needed, other than continuing to rely on the market, as the status quo is considered to be just about right. As an alternative to the smart growth strategies proposed by the first camp, the second camp recommends a laissez-faire approach, which is "guided by market forces, and foresees lower population densities and automobile travel as inevitable characteristics of the twenty-first century, and attempts to accommodate those market forces rather than to counteract them."[15] In practice, this means spending less on transit (where investment has inhibited road construction) and more on roads, which, by drawing traffic from existing roads, should reduce overall congestion. These roads should be paid for with user charges. Once the road building has been completed, then governments should retreat from land-use policy because the market will ensure the efficient use of land and minimize incompatible uses: "One might argue that this restriction in private property rights is justified to further the common good, but when one recognizes that the changes smart growth is trying to reverse are the result of market forces and personal choice, the arguments in favour of policies that fly in the face of these preferences lose their force."[16]

The Price of Sprawl
As I show in more detail in subsequent chapters, the evidence is overwhelming that sprawl incurs significant private and social costs across North American cities. One can't ignore these costs as do the sprawl advocates: they are real. But they have a good point when they assert that attempts to stop sprawl haven't worked at any meaningful scale;[17] however, they are

wrong about the reasons why this is true. Both the anti- and the pro-sprawl groups have failed to recognize a critical set of sprawl drivers – drivers that are the key to actually curbing sprawl. The focus of the debate has been on the cost of sprawl rather than on its price – that is, on what sprawl costs rather than on the price we actually pay for it.

Another way of looking at the issue is as follows. Sprawl is the result of a few key decisions that are made millions and millions of times every day across our cities by families, consumers, employees, businesses, developers, institutions, and governments. Together, these interdependent decisions relating to the use of land and travel ultimately determine how cities grow. Where to buy or rent a house – centre, inner suburb, new suburb, exurb? How big? What size of lot? What kind of neighbourhood – walkable and mixed use or car-oriented? How to get to work and do errands – bike, walk, transit, car? Where to locate my business? How much land? How much building? How will I and my employees get to work and conduct business travel? How will customers and suppliers get here? Will there be on-site parking?

These decisions are played out literally millions of times as cities grow and change. In recent years, about 500,000 homes are sold in Canada annually, and 250,000 new houses start construction.[18] In the United States, about 40 million people move house each year (of a total population of 290 million).[19] Every day, millions of people decide how and where to travel.

Ultimately, these four key intertwined decisions – regarding location, how much land, how much building, and mode of travel – are what shape urban development patterns. They are governed by many factors, such as proximity to family, work, employees, or suppliers as well as space needs. An important part of each of these decisions, however, is price. How much will a house cost depending on whether it is on a larger or smaller lot, on whether it is a larger or smaller house? How does the price of an inner-city location compare with that of a suburban property? These questions are critical components of the decision-making process.

Price is intended to give an accurate signal of the actual costs associated with the decision. This is a basic economic principle and one that, in economists' terms, ensures the efficient allocation of resources. In other words, an accurate price signal ensures that neither overspending on resources nor under-allocation of resources occurs. If prices are lower than costs, then consumers will consume too much of a good or service. Conversely, if the price is too high, too little of it will be consumed when compared to what is optimal and efficient.

With regard to development, when we talk about prices that accurately reflect costs, what is meant is that the actual costs associated with different locations and local contexts, different sizes of buildings and lots, and different modes and amounts of travel are accurately reflected in the prices charged for them. Only when accurate prices are charged – prices that reflect these cost variations – can efficient urban development patterns be achieved.

This applies not only to the prices of the property itself (i.e., the purchase price of a home or business property) but also to the prices of all of the other components that are considered when making a property decision. Given that location and transportation decisions tend to be made in tandem, transportation prices are very important, including vehicle costs, automobile insurance, gas, parking, and/or transit passes. Other costs considered include mortgage servicing, property taxes covering roads and other municipal services, natural gas (for heating), electricity, phone, and cable and internet access. In *Perverse Cities*, the phrase "urban goods and services" is used to refer collectively to this package of elements (including land, buildings, transportation, and services), which forms part of property-related decisions.

Unfortunately, with respect to the key decisions described above, the prices charged for the property and related services rarely if ever reflect their actual costs. Moreover, they act precisely in a manner that encourages the overconsumption of land, building, and transportation and discourages the efficient use of these resources. Inefficient development (such as low-density development or development that is distant from service networks) is priced at a discount, while efficient development (such as smaller lots or accessible locations) suffers from inflated prices. In other words, prices currently provide incentives to sprawl and disincentives to efficient development. And, to add insult to injury, it is usually the efficient development that is directly subsidizing the inefficient development. In other words, the owner of the Smart car is subsidizing the Hummer owner.

Why is it that prices charged rarely reflect actual costs and how do these cross-subsidies occur? As I show in *Perverse Cities*, a few common pricing and policy flaws are repeated over and over. One very common flaw is that prices are based on average costs, rather than on marginal costs as recommended by economists. This occurs when costs vary with location, density, context, or type of land use but prices do not. For example, in the case of network infrastructure and services such as water, sewer, or roads, extensive research has shown that lower densities mean higher infrastructure costs per unit.[20] But prices charged for these services rarely reflect the higher costs of servicing a larger or more distant lot; rather, prices based on average costs are used. In other words, costs are averaged across a range of different types of development associated with a range of actual costs. This leads inevitably to a situation in which those properties that incur lower-than-average costs pay more than their costs, while those properties that incur higher-than-average costs pay less than their costs. Thus, by definition, this form of mis-pricing leads to cross-subsidies.

Whether these distortions are evident in the price of services such as water or internet connectivity, or whether they become embedded in the price of the property itself (as they usually do in the case of development charges),[21] they create a set of "perverse subsidies" that provide financial incentives for inefficient development and disincentives for efficient development (see box). While subsidies are provided by the government to support a positive outcome that might not otherwise occur, perverse subsidies inflict negative, unintended consequences.

The difference between a twenty-foot-wide lot and a sixty-foot-wide lot may seem insignificant, and, if we were talking about one house or even a few, it might indeed be.[22] However, when the difference is multiplied, say, 762,000 times – which is a conservative estimate of the number of new single detached houses that will be needed in the Toronto area alone over the next thirty years[23] – it is easy to see the magnitude of the aggregate impacts. This includes more urbanized farmland and natural areas, more kilometres of roads, water and sewer pipes, gas pipes, and cables and conduits than would otherwise be needed as well as more auto travel and higher infrastructure costs.

In addition to prices based on average costs and the cross-subsidies they inevitably entail, there are yet other kinds of perverse subsidies and

Subsidies and Perverse Subsidies

Subsidies are an important tool of government and are used to promote an activity that is considered beneficial to the economy overall and to society at large – benefits that would not occur without this intervention. A perverse subsidy, on the other hand, is one that exerts adverse effects on the economy, environment, or society.[24]

Development Charges Distortions

Take the hypothetical case of two new homes of the same size on greenfields sites, one on a 20-foot lot and one on a 60-foot lot. They both incur the same development charge (DC), say $25,000. Yet, given the extra metres of road, sidewalks, pipes, cables, and wires, the actual costs associated with the wide lot are significantly higher than those for the narrow lot. The single detached house on a small lot is overcharged; the actual servicing costs it incurs are $15,000. The house on the wide lot is undercharged; its actual servicing costs are $35,000. Nevertheless, both houses are charged $25,000 by the municipality to cover services, and this $25,000 must be recouped in the house price. This means that the market price for the narrow-lot house will be higher than it would be if more accurate pricing prevailed, and the market price for the wide-lot house would be less than it really ought to be.

Under a more accurate pricing regime, while the wide-lot house may still be more expensive than the narrow-lot house because of its size, the price differential between the two would be greater. Say the larger lot and house are worth $125,000, and the smaller property is worth $100,000, excluding the cost of the DC. Adding in the cost of the DC under an average cost-based approach, the wide-lot property would be priced at $150,000, and the narrow-lot property at $125,000, a $25,000 spread.

If instead the DC reflected *actual* costs, the larger lot would be priced at $125,000 plus $35,000, or $160,000. The small lot would be priced at $100,000 plus $15,000, or $115,000 – a spread of $45,000.

The following table illustrates how the averaging of costs through the DC brings the prices of the two types of house closer together than they would be if actual costs were used. This provides a disincentive to purchase the smaller, more efficient lot, and an incentive to purchase the larger lot.

	Average cost DC		Actual cost DC	
	Narrow lot	Wide lot	Narrow lot	Wide lot
Lot and house	$100,000	$125,000	$100,000	$125,000
DC	$25,000	$25,000	$15,000	$35,000
TOTAL PRICE	$125,000	$150,000	$115,000	$160,000

mis-prices that occur – when prices are completely unrelated to costs precipitated, for example, or in the cases of direct subsidies or "bundled" goods and services. There are also poorly designed policies and programs that create market biases and mis-incentives. Many examples of each of these kinds of market distortion are detailed in subsequent chapters.

Together, these perverse prices, flawed policies, and market distortions undermine efforts to curb urban sprawl. A market that operates in this manner is the opposite of what planning calls for. Planning in its many guises – smart growth, new urbanism, sustainable development – has set about to achieve compact, mixed-use cities with efficient development and to curb urban sprawl. However, it has had very little success in doing so. And is this any wonder, when the very kinds of land use that it is trying to curb are subsidized and offered at discount prices, while the kinds it is trying to encourage are overpriced?

Planning has adopted a regulatory approach that has been blind to market flaws. The regulatory and design-oriented frameworks are fighting an uphill battle that is in direct opposition to powerful market forces and price signals that encourage sprawl. Indeed, many regulatory policies, such as zoning, that mandate minimum densities or separation of land uses are themselves often a source of sprawl.[25]

Sprawl advocates are right when they say that planners would do well to pay closer attention to market realities and dynamics. Now, with new pressures and realities, the case for pricing sprawl is more relevant than ever. However, their prescription to simply rely on the market in its current form is misguided. While planners may ignore the market, sprawl promoters ignore the fact that it is highly distorted in sprawl's favour. An unfettered market with accurate price signals would curb sprawl, not create it. The evidence and analysis I present address the sprawl proponents' view that natural market forces are at work and show why their view is fundamentally flawed.

Perverse Cities attempts to explain why planning efforts to curb sprawl, so intense and so long-lived, have delivered only weak results at best. In trying to find out why this is so, one is drawn out of the conventional realm of planning and into the realm of economics and fiscal policy, where one discovers that powerful levers are working in a manner that directly undermines the objectives of planning, smart growth, and the curtailment of sprawl. I attempt to uncover these largely hidden and undiscovered economic, fiscal, and financial drivers; to explain exactly how they undermine efforts to stop sprawl; and to lay out a course that, at least, corrects them and, at best, makes them over into strong drivers of efficient urban development patterns.

It is important to note up front that the type of market failure that is most often discussed with respect to sprawl – namely, the lack of pricing of externalities such as air pollution or loss of open space – is *not* my focus; rather, I address the pricing of the urban goods and services that comprise development decisions to which prices of some form are already attached, and that are currently paid for in the market – but are typically poorly priced. As such, my focus is on the *direct* costs related to urban development – of land, buildings, infrastructure, and related services – not external costs (such as air pollution) that, at present, are mostly unpriced. While the pricing of externalities is a valuable tool in the planner's repertoire, and can play an important role in curbing sprawl, a fairly extensive literature on this exists already. I leave it to others to continue to pursue this tack.

For my part, I detail the pricing and policy mis-incentives that are rarely discussed, especially in the planning literature. Addressing these flaws will, in and of itself, go a long way towards curbing sprawl. In fact, it is necessary to do this if one wants to have any significant success in curbing sprawl. At present, there is no economic imperative to build more efficiently; the right price signals are needed. It should be made clear, however, that dealing with these flaws alone will not be *sufficient* to curb sprawl. Other measures, such as good urban design, will be needed. Regulation still plays a role, but some strategic deregulation may also be necessary (such as removing or reforming planning policies that add to sprawl). But smart pricing must play a key role in achieving smart growth objectives.

In illustrating the arguments presented in *Perverse Cities*, and in explaining potential tools, I take many examples from the Toronto region, the Province of Ontario, and Canada as these are the areas with which I am most familiar. In many cases, research, data, and analyses pertaining to the topic of market distortions and their effect on urban development patterns are scarce. And when, as was often the case, suitable examples or case studies could not be found more locally, I ventured further afield – to the United States, the United Kingdom, and Australasia. The one proviso is that the context and its analysis had to be relevant and applicable to the North American and other market economies experiencing sprawl. Whatever the source of the example, the applicability of the analysis and the solutions is widespread. This is because sprawl is widespread, a serious and growing concern.

Perverse Cities is organized as follows. Part 1 explores how sprawl has been typically defined as a planning problem that has planning solutions (Chapters 2 and 3). Part 2 indicates the specific problems inherent in this approach, i.e., that the costs and benefits of planning are rarely sufficiently considered (Chapter 4), that planning approaches have not been particularly successful in their attempts to curb sprawl (Chapter 5), and that planning approaches have underemphasized the economic context in which cities evolve physically as well as, in particular, the important role of mis-pricing of urban goods and services and other policy mis-incentives (Chapter 6).

Part 3 provides detailed evidence of the existence of mis-pricing and policy mis-incentives for urban goods and services by looking at the following: in the municipal realm, development charges and property taxes (Chapter 7); the pricing of utilities and other network services (Chapter 8); and housing, infrastructure, and energy (Chapter 9). The few common and ubiquitous policy and pricing flaws that are uncovered in the preceding three chapters, and that are central to generating sprawl, are then discussed (Chapter 10).

Part 4 is concerned with finding practical and effective ways of dealing with the mis-incentives identified in Part 3. Chapter 11 lays out some basic principles to guide thinking and doing, while Chapter 12 provides a range of real world tools that can be implemented either to fix flawed policy and prices or to introduce new instruments. Chapter 13 returns to some of the key issues surrounding the sprawl debate, in light of the evidence pertaining to the role of price and policy mis-incentives, and suggests ways to promote the adoption of better policies and pricing.

PART 1

THE PLANNING PROBLEM

2

Sprawl
A Planning Problem

Conventionally, sprawl is seen primarily as a problem that stems from urban form, with planning and urban design providing the solutions. This chapter looks at how sprawl has been defined and approached as a planning (used here broadly to include urban design) problem. How is sprawl defined? What is thought to cause it? Why is it seen as a problem? And how have planners gone about solving it?

What Is Sprawl?

Though everyone intuitively understands what sprawl is, when it comes to defining it precisely there is a wide range of notions, even among those in the field (as is shown below). To some, the meaning of sprawl is relative, depending on context: Is suburbanization around Toronto really "sprawl" compared to that around, say, Atlanta (the answer, as is revealed in subsequent chapters, is yes)? How have planners and urban designers gone about answering this question?

Despite the large and growing body of literature on urban sprawl, the subject is surprisingly poorly defined. As Galster notes, this literature is a "semantic wilderness" in which sprawl has many competing meanings. Sprawl could be viewed as an aesthetic judgment, as the cause of an externality (e.g., auto dependence), as the consequence of an action or condition (e.g., exclusionary zoning), as a pattern of development, or as a process of development.[1] Needless to say, when there is little agreement on what the subject of the debate or study actually is, the result is a confusing debate and body of research. A clear definition is needed in order to identify and measure sprawl, to track its progress and compare cities, and to propose effective policy responses.

Most commonly, sprawl is defined as an urban landscape having certain characteristic physical elements. Definitions based on physical elements are especially attractive to planners, urban designers, and citizens as they are readily understood. There is little consistency with regard to what these elements are, however. Often cited are: leapfrog development, commercial strip development, low-density development, and single-use development on or near the urban fringe.[2] In a Smart Growth America (SGA) report, Ewing et al. define sprawl as follows:

> The landscape sprawl creates has four dimensions: a population that is widely dispersed in low density development; rigidly separated homes, shops, and workplaces; a network of roads marked by huge blocks and poor access; and a lack of well-defined, thriving activity centres, such as downtown and town centers.[3]

Galster defines sprawl as a pattern of land use "that exhibits low levels of some combination of eight distinct dimensions: density, continuity, concentration, clustering, centrality, nuclearity, mixed uses, and proximity."[4] Interestingly, he defines sprawl according to what it is lacking rather than according to what it is. Sprawl is also sometimes defined by its component parts: housing subdivisions, shopping centres and strip malls, business parks, "free-floating" civic institutions, and roadways.[5] Building on Ewing's definition, Gillham adds that sprawl "is the typical form of most types of late-twentieth-century suburban development,"[6] arguing that sprawl and suburbanization are, for all intents and purposes, synonymous.

Sprawl is also sometimes defined as a process, one "in which the spread of development across the landscape far outpaces population growth."[7] This definition involves comparing the rate of land development to the rate of population growth. If the rate of land development exceeds that of population growth, this suggests that land usage per person is increasing, and sprawl is said to be taking place. The drawback of this approach is that it is relative and says little about actual development patterns. Land urbanization rates could exceed population growth in a dense urban context, but this should not be considered sprawl. Except where noted, I adopt the common planning definition of sprawl – that it is a pattern of land use with some or all of the commonly cited physical characteristics and that not all suburban expansion or decentralization is necessarily sprawl.

Why Is Sprawl a Problem?

Some of sprawl's most vocal critics object to it on aesthetic and almost spiritual grounds, as illustrated by Duany, Plater-Zyberk, and Speck:

> It will be sprawl: cookie-cutter houses, wide treeless, sidewalk-free road-ways, mindlessly curving cul-de-sacs, a streetscape of garage doors – a beige vinyl parody of Leave It to Beaver. Or worse yet, a pretentious slew of McMansions, complete with the obligatory gatehouse ... Soulless subdivisions, residential "communities" utterly lacking in communal life; strip shopping centers, "big box" chain stores, and artificially festive malls set within barren seas of parking; antiseptic office parks, ghost towns after 6 p.m.; and mile upon mile of clogged collector roads, the only fabric tying our disassociated lives back together.[8]

But mainly, planners, environmentalists, urban designers, citizens, and others object to sprawl because this pattern of development is associated with high economic, social, and environmental costs (see Chapter 3). It is these high costs that provide the rationale for the many policy and other interventions aimed at curbing sprawl.

What Causes Sprawl?

A common planning explanation of urban sprawl begins in the post-Second World War period, when sprawl was kick-started by federal housing programs for returning veterans and massive investments in highways, thus promoting suburbanization. The suburbanization of population then precipitated the suburbanization of shopping and jobs, using techniques of standardization that created the classic suburban configuration – large lots and low density, winding cul-de-sacs, large expanses of single land uses. This pattern was then entrenched in an array of planning regulations and engineering standards that governed urban growth patterns for decades to come and that continues to this day.[9] This explanation emphasizes the role of government investment, subsidies, and regulation in causing sprawl.

Subsidies that are often seen as contributing to sprawl include direct grants for infrastructure (e.g., in the United States, heavy investment in a federal highway network in the 1950s) and tax breaks for homeownership (such as mortgage interest tax deductibility in the United States or capital gains exemptions).[10] These and other subsidies to urban development make land and housing cheaper than they would otherwise be (thus boosting consumption) and open up new fringe areas for suburbanization.

Subsidies are one example of a larger group of market failures. Ewing notes a number of other types of market failure that contribute to sprawl, including utility rate structures, negative externalities, and government regulation.[11] An emerging critique of zoning and other forms of conventional land-use regulation attribute sprawl, in part, to planning itself and, in particular, to zoning.[12] The idea is that overly uniform and restrictive zoning regulations lower densities and rigorously divide cities into districts according to land use and type of development. Examples of these regulations include minimum lot sizes and setbacks, maximum densities, and restrictive permitted use lists. It is argued that overzealous regulation has made desirable elements of town planning – such as the corner store or a granny flat at the rear of a property – illegal. In a study of US cities, Pendall found that land-use controls that mandated low densities increased levels of urban sprawl.[13]

Engineering standards have also come under attack for adding to sprawl. Standardized and over-generous road width and configuration standards, as well as parking standards, have been mandated by the Institute of Transportation Engineers and have become the norm across the North American continent. Add to these increasing schoolyard size standards and more stringent environmental protections: all raise the share of land devoted to servicing and infrastructure. Per hectare of land, a larger proportion is devoted to natural and engineered infrastructure and a smaller proportion to development, thus leading to lower overall ("gross") densities.

Fragmented urban governance is often cited as a cause of sprawl. For example, development can leapfrog to less regulated or unincorporated jurisdictions beyond the urban fringe in order to evade stringent development restrictions. In other cases, fragmented governance is more a condition that enables sprawl than something that directly drives it. In large cities comprised of multiple municipal governments, metropolitan-wide planning and growth management are difficult to implement. Research by Razin and Rosentraub shows that sprawling cities can be either more or less fragmented. Less fragmentation does not guarantee more compact development, but highly fragmented, compact cities are rare.[14] In other words, more integrated regional government may be a necessary but not a sufficient condition for curbing sprawl.

Knaap argues that sprawl is not just a matter of density but also involves the degree of mixed land use and the connectivity of the road network (high levels of which are associated with a low level of sprawl). Major structuring elements of the urban landscape are also important determinants of sprawl – in particular, the design of transportation networks, parks and open space, and the location of sewer networks.[15] In this view, poor design and coordination of these structuring elements has promoted sprawl in American cities.

Gillham notes the role that the low cost of land plays in producing sprawl. Large lots on suburban land are made easily accessible by a highway infrastructure, thus broadening affordability. Similarly, cheap land at the fringe, combined with a decreased need for clustering in many businesses, leads to the suburbanization of employment.[16] What Gillham is referring to is what economists call the "rent gradient," that is, the level of rent paid for land (or purchasing cost) as it varies with distance from the city centre. Urban economic models posit – and the real world confirms – that the farther from the city centre, the lower the cost of land. The emergence of polycentric cities may mean that there is not a consistent downward slope but, rather, that small price peaks are apparent where suburban nodes occur (though the overall trend still associates lower land costs with greater distance).

Sprawl opponents generally do not believe that sprawl is a result of consumer preference. To the argument that we have sprawl because it is what people want, planners respond that the perceived demand for sprawl is really more a reflection of supply. In other words, most housing "product" takes the form of conventional low-density development, and developers tend to repeat the same formula over and over. If a different type of supply were offered – more courtyard houses, small-lot houses, mixed use, new urbanist developments, and the like – people would make different choices. Planners cite consumer preference surveys that support the assertion that, while it is true that there is a strong preference for detached single-family dwellings, they do not necessarily have to take the form of sprawl.[17] In other words, consumers are much more open to alternatives to the norm than developers suppose, but the market does not provide them in any significant way. Thus, sprawl is attributed to quite a range of different potential causes. The planning view offers some consensus on what the alternative to sprawl might look like and how to achieve it.

Planning Solutions to Sprawl

In North America, as elsewhere, curbing sprawl has been the focus of a concerted campaign, with a plethora of policy initiatives. Since the 1970s, the approach has changed and evolved but the aim has remained the same – at the very least, to moderate the pattern of low-density, single-use growth at or beyond the urban fringe.

"Ecosystem planning" evolved out of the 1970s era of new enlightenment regarding environmental issues (see box). This approach gives equal

---

Approaches to Urban Growth

The *ecosystem approach* emerged in the 1970s with growing awareness of the impacts of human activity on the environment. Its central concept is that environment, economy, and society are interrelated, and that decisions in one area will affect those in all others. It is signified by the well-known three overlapping rings representing environment, economy, and society.

Sustainable development emerged from the influential 1987 Brundtland Report, *Our Common Future*. Building upon the ecosystem approach that aims to integrate social, economic, cultural, and environmental issues, the central and oft-quoted concept is that "sustainable development is development that meets the needs of the present without compromising the ability of future generations to meet their own needs." It has been applied to cities (in the sustainable cities movement) and to sustainable urban growth.

The International Centre for Sustainable Cities definition is: A sustainable city enhances the economic, social, cultural, and environmental well-being of current and future generations (www.icsc.ca).

Growth management is an approach to managing the growth of urban regions or large urban areas. It can mean many things, but at a minimum it usually includes the ideas of coordinating infrastructure investments with development and long-range comprehensive planning.

New urbanism is an approach that gained popularity starting in the 1980s, focusing on the design of neighbourhoods and calling for a return to traditional elements of city-building. It is now spearheaded by the Congress for the New Urbanism, which defines the movement in the following terms:

> We advocate the restructuring of public policy and development practices to support the following principles: neighborhoods should be diverse in use and population; communities should be designed for the pedestrian and transit as well as the car; cities and towns should be shaped by physically defined and universally accessible public spaces and community institutions; urban places should be framed by architecture and landscape design that celebrate local history, climate, ecology, and building practice.[18]

Smart Growth is a more recently evolved approach to growth management focusing on redressing the perceived costs associated with typical regional growth patterns. Principles include: creating a range of housing opportunities and choice; creating walkable neighbourhoods; fostering distinctive, attractive communities with a strong sense of place; mixing land uses; providing a variety of transportation choices; strengthening and directing development towards existing communities.[19]

Compact development describes a form of urban development that makes more efficient use of land than does sprawl. It usually implies higher density development in new communities at the urban fringe, as well as a greater emphasis on the redevelopment of already-urbanized areas.

consideration to environmental, social, and economic factors in making planning decisions, as represented by the familiar three interlocking circles. With the Brundtland Report in 1987, the concept of ecosystem planning tended to be supplanted by the concept of "sustainable development."

At the regional scale, the concept of "growth management" has more recently evolved into the concept of "smart growth." Smart growth is the planning regime du jour across North America and is at the forefront of the "war on sprawl." At the neighbourhood scale, "new urbanism" has been adopted in several newly planned communities across Canada and the United States. Smart growth is a particular form of growth management that emerged in the mid-1990s, with Maryland's Smart Growth and Neighbourhood Conservation Program.[20] While specific definitions are many and varied,[21] one is as follows:

In general, smart growth invests time, attention, and resources in restoring community and vitality to center cities and older suburbs. New smart growth is more town-centered, is transit and pedestrian oriented, and has a greater mix of housing, commercial and retail uses. It also preserves open space and many other environmental amenities.[22]

After reviewing a range of definitions of smart growth, Nelson finds that they share two features: (1) building where infrastructure and development already exist, as opposed to in greenfields, and (2) connecting land uses with transportation alternatives to the single-occupant car.[23] This is accomplished, in part, through using investment strategically so that it aligns with planning objectives, such as establishing priority investment areas or investing in transit rather than in highways. In other words, subsidies are redirected away from sprawl and towards compact development and redevelopment. The physical vision embodied in smart growth is generally consistent with compact growth, mixed uses, walkable neighbourhoods, an emphasis on transit over the auto, and so on.

The aim of new urbanism is to provide an alternative to sprawl based on a return to traditional town-building principles, such as narrower streets forming a connected grid, closer mixing of land uses, and an emphasis on the design of the public realm. These traditional urban forms are seen as flexible, socially mixed, and environmentally sustainable, providing opportunities for walking and cycling, for example. The main obstacle to achieving this alternate vision is overly restrictive zoning codes, which prohibit many of the elements that make up the new urbanist vision. Thus, as a solution to sprawl, new urbanism focuses on fixing zoning codes that prevent these urban forms from being built, and it embraces an alternative design vision.

New urbanists propose "form-based" zoning (dictating the form, placement, and design of buildings and other urban elements, while being flexible with regard to specific uses of buildings or land) as an alternative to conventional Euclidean zoning (which tends to restrict use and impose less precise parameters on the form of development). Form-based zoning has been formalized into a "SmartCode" – a model zoning code that defines the types of restrictions and design elements to be implemented. SmartCode requirements vary, depending on the type of area, according to the "transect." The transect is "a geographical cross-section of a region used to reveal a sequence of environments."[24] The transect is comprised of six types of "ecozones," from urban core to rural reserve, each with its own particular set of SmartCode requirements.

The SmartCode uses the same basic type of regulations as does conventional zoning, such as requirements for minimum or maximum building setbacks or height limits, only substituting different numbers to create different urban outcomes. For example, most suburban codes require a significant front-yard setback, pushing the house back from the street. A new urbanist code might stipulate a minimum and a maximum front-yard setback, requiring that houses be brought close to the street. Though using the same basic toolset as does conventional zoning, SmartCode zoning manages to be more prescriptive, utilizing greater precision and intending a more tightly defined physical outcome.

In essence, the SmartCode exchanges one vision of development (conventional postwar suburbia) for another vision (new urbanism). This is accomplished by exchanging one set of land development regulations for another (albeit, more elaborate) set. The new urbanist approach is arguably more highly and tightly regulated than is its conventional alternative. New urbanism tends to focus on the creation of new suburbs and neighbourhoods, often on greenfields sites – that is, on the individual pieces of the urban puzzle. What about the whole puzzle – that is, the city-region?

Calthorpe argues that one cannot focus on sprawl in isolation, that solving sprawl is equally dependent on what happens in the inner city and in mature suburbs. In *The Regional City: Planning for the End of Sprawl*, he argues that a solution would be complex and multifaceted, relying on both design and policy. Design is based on the principles of diversity, conservation, and human scale. At the regional scale, the building blocks are centres, districts, preserves, and corridors. The physical design is supported by policy, in particular, the use of regional boundaries, along with integrated land use and transportation planning. As well, the related social and economic aspects must be addressed through actions such as regional tax base sharing and urban educational reform.

Tools of the Trade

Approaches to sprawl have evolved over time, incorporating ideas about environmental protection and sustainability as well as recognizing that sprawl cannot be dealt with in isolation – either from what goes on in other parts of the city region or from economic, social, and environmental factors. The vision of the desirable urban (or, more usually, suburban) form has also evolved (or perhaps reverted, in the case of new urbanism). Smart growth aimed to lever investments in infrastructure and facilities in order to support more efficient development patterns. However, for the most part, the tools used to achieve the desired form have remained fairly constant.

Overall, the focus of the planning approach has been on using the twin pillars of regulation and design to curb urban sprawl. Regulation can be divided into two broad categories: containment and planning. Containment involves policies aimed at imposing physical limits to urban expansion. The use of urban growth boundaries (UGBs) is viewed as perhaps the most direct solution to sprawl. A boundary is drawn around the urban area, beyond which the city will not expand. Use of this tool is still fairly rare in North America, assuming a UGB is taken to mean a permanent perimeter that does not actually expand outward as the pressure for growth builds. Portland,

Oregon, is the most famous example in the North American context. Green-belts are also sometimes used as a tool to contain urban growth as well as to protect sensitive environmental areas at the urban fringe.

Planning tools are aimed at coordinating growth and infrastructure investment in order to ensure that the necessary facilities are in place to serve new urban development as well as to ensure the orderly development of the urban area (e.g., preventing leapfrogging). Here the tools include the formation of regional or metropolitan planning agencies; the use of comprehensive, long-range regional or city plans; master planning of new communities or subdivisions; and zoning and subdivision control. In Canada, all major cities will, at a minimum, have a comprehensive long-range plan, master planned new subdivisions, and zoning and subdivision control. In the United States, regional planning is not as universal as it is in Canada, and the control of urban growth often falls more heavily on local plans and zoning.

The most au courant approaches to sprawl – smart growth and new urbanism – rely heavily on these tools, as did their predecessors. In other words, these newer approaches have been implemented primarily through a program of re-regulation. They still rely upon zoning, but the content of the regulations has changed. Some might argue that the level of precision demanded by some new urbanist projects borders on hyper-regulation, adding to the rigidity of the planning framework and creating new layers of regulation.

In short, over the past decades, efforts to control sprawl have been expanding in both geographic reach and intensity. They are being replicated across the thousands of cities and towns in North America and elsewhere, as planning has become more widely accepted and implemented. State, provincial, and federal governments have become involved. At present, about one-half of all US states are implementing or improving state-wide planning reforms, while nearly one-third are actively pursuing their first major state-wide planning reforms.[25] Much of the interest has to do with finding a means of reducing the high costs of sprawl, which are outlined in the following chapter.

3   The Costs and Benefits of Sprawl

Sprawl is seen as a problem because it is associated with a long list of undesirable outcomes, ranging from endless repetition of big box stores and strip malls to air pollution to loss of farmland to rising obesity rates to overly costly infrastructure to the deterioration of city centres. Different commentators will emphasize different aspects of the problem: urban designers say that sprawl is unsightly and dysfunctional; economists say that it is wasteful and inefficient; environmentalists say that it disrupts natural hydrological and biological cycles; planners say that it comes with all of the above issues.

Whatever the specific viewpoint, there is wide agreement that sprawl is a problem because it incurs a range of costs that are both broad and significant. Furthermore, it is generally understood that urban form underlies these high costs. In other words, these costs result from the particular way in which our cities have been growing: primarily on greenfields sites, with low densities, and with different types of land uses religiously separated from one another. The range and magnitude of these costs is reviewed below.

The Costs of Sprawl

Sprawl costs are usually thought of as falling into three categories: environmental, social, and economic. On the environmental front, sprawl is linked to a range of undesirable impacts, including: the loss of viable farmland, natural habitats, and open space, along with the disruption of hydrological systems and the exacerbation of drought. It is estimated, for example, that the amount of imperviousness created by converting natural or farm land to low-density development amounts to billions of litres of water not being infiltrated every year. In Atlanta alone, the water converted to runoff as a result of urbanization would be enough to supply 1.5 million to 3.6 million people per year.[1] With global warming increasingly contributing to drought conditions across vast areas of North America and elsewhere, serving urban centres with an adequate water supply is a front-and-centre issue.[2]

The most severe environmental impacts of sprawl, however, occur because sprawl patterns generate higher levels of car ownership per household; more auto travel; a smaller share of trips by transit, walking, and cycling; higher numbers of trips; and longer trips.[3] Differences can be seen at the level of whole metropolitan regions. The most sprawling urban regions have more cars per household on average than do more compact regions, and average distances driven are greater.[4] In the most sprawling US cities, the average person travels 27 miles per day by car, compared to 21 miles in the most compact cities. And there are 180 cars per 100 households in the most sprawling cities, compared to 162 in the least sprawling. Two percent of commutes were by transit in sprawling centres, compared to 7 percent in more compact cities.[5]

Because these figures reflect whole urban regions, the differences tend to be less dramatic than is the case when different urban settings within a given city are examined. It is at the intra-urban level that the role of density, mix of uses, and access to transit come clearly into evidence. In the Toronto area, for example, it has been shown that the number of autos owned and vehicle-kilometres travelled increases systematically with distance from the city centre, while transit modal shares fall as densities decline (see Table 3.1).[6] These travel patterns generate high levels of energy use and emissions, resulting in air pollution, smog, and GHGs that are linked with climate change.

Related health issues include increasing asthma and obesity rates, and a greater risk of fatal crashes in sprawling areas.[7] In Riverside, California – the most sprawling city included in a study by Ewing et al. – the rate of fatal car crashes was more than double that in less sprawling cities: 18 per 100,000 residents compared to 8 per 100,000.[8] The Ontario College of Family Physicians notes: "Evidence clearly shows that people who live in spread-out, car-dependent neighbourhoods are likely to walk less, weigh more, and suffer from obesity and high blood pressure and consequent diabetes, cardiovascular and other diseases, compared to people who live in more efficient,

Table 3.1

Transport and urban form, Greater Toronto Area, 2001

	Core	Core ring	Inner suburbs	Outer suburbs
Number of trips per day per person	2.08	2.31	2.34	2.67
Auto/walk, bike, transit split (%)	40/60	64/36	76/24	87/13
Motorized kilometres travelled per person	10.5	13.6	16.6	23.7
Households with no car (%)	51	29	17	5
Residential density (persons per square kilometre of urbanized area)	9,900	6,100	3,100	2,500

Source: Centre for Sustainable Transportation, *Sustainable Transportation Performance Indicators Project,* 66.

higher density communities."[9] Mental stress from time spent commuting and traffic congestion are also noted. In addition, some cancers (such as leukemia in children) have been linked to exhaust toxicants.[10]

Sprawl is also associated with a number of social issues. Living and working in a low-density sprawl environment means relying on the use of an automobile. When even getting a litre of milk at the "convenience" store calls for a trip in the car, those who do not have access to a car or who cannot drive are excluded from many activities due to difficulty of access. Those affected tend to include the young, the old, women, the poor, and the disabled. As well, sprawl is linked with increasing socioeconomic segregation within cities, as those with the economic wherewithal and ability are able to leave central areas and their perceived problems for more homogeneous, controlled suburban environments, often supported by exclusionary zoning.[11]

Most studies of the costs of sprawl focus on the economic costs associated with different development patterns. The emphasis is on public infrastructure costs, such as roads, water and sewer, transit, and fire protection services. In addition to these network infrastructure costs, some studies also assess costs of community facilities such as schools and community centres. The costing can include capital costs as well as operating and maintenance. Some external costs are also sometimes estimated, such as the costs of air pollution or health costs related to transportation emissions.

There is a long history of attempts to quantify the costs of sprawl, with studies dating back to the 1950s.[12] These early studies examine the effects of urban form factors such as density, size of urban area, location, and

Types of Urban Infrastructure

Network infrastructure: infrastructure that takes the form of a linked network extending over urban territory, such as roads, sewer, and water. Also included are quasi-public network infrastructure such as hydro, gas, cable and internet, and telephone.

Community facilities: urban infrastructure that consists of a facility or group of facilities that are not physically linked with one another, occurring more as discrete "points," such as community centres, recreation centres, or schools.

On-site infrastructure: facilities located within a particular development, community, or subdivision, usually related to local infrastructure, such as local roads or parks.

Off-site infrastructure: facilities associated with a particular subdivision or community, but that are located outside the development itself, for example, regional roads or water treatment facilities.

development pattern on infrastructure costs and other impacts. They use hypothetical constructs of different urban patterns as a basis for their analysis and consistently find that significant potential infrastructure savings result if developers move away from sprawl patterns and towards denser, contiguous development. In 1955, Wheaton and Schussheim, for example, found that a 41 percent saving in infrastructure capital costs resulted from increasing densities from eleven units per hectare to thirty-two units per hectare.[13]

Since that early period, there has been a profusion of studies that examine the costs of sprawl from many angles, using many different definitions of sprawl and a wide range of methodologies. With the rising popularity of smart growth, studies have been undertaken across the United States and Canada in order to assess the potential impacts on infrastructure costs of implementing smart growth legislation and policies. These studies typically project urban growth over twenty or thirty years within a "current trends," or "status quo," scenario and compare the outcomes with one or more compact development or smart growth alternatives. This can be done on a metropolitan, regional, state, or provincial level.

These studies find overwhelmingly that sprawl costs more than other, more compact, urban development patterns. For example, a range of studies conducted by Robert Burchell in various US urban regions find that compact

Types of Costs

Capital costs: the one-time costs associated with the construction of infrastructure, facilities, or buildings, including machinery and land.

Operating and maintenance costs: the ongoing costs associated with operating and maintaining infrastructure, facilities, or buildings.

Replacement costs: the costs of replacing infrastructure, facilities, or buildings once their useful life expectancy is reached.

Life-cycle costs: the costs for any particular infrastructure, facility, or building over its entire life cycle, that is, the sum of capital, operating, and maintenance and replacement costs.

External costs: costs associated with a good or service but to which no monetary value is attached or charged, so that these costs are "external" to the monetary transaction. Common examples are the costs associated with the loss of open space and air pollution.

On-site costs: the costs of facilities located within a particular development, community, or subdivision, usually related to local infrastructure such as local roads or parks.

Off-site costs: costs associated with the development of a particular subdivision or community but that are incurred outside the development itself, for example, regional roads or water treatment facilities.

Direct costs: costs that are directly attributable to a particular action or activity; for example, the direct costs of auto use include gas, insurance, and depreciation.

Indirect costs: costs that are precipitated by a particular decision or activity but are not paid directly by the actor, for example, the public costs of health care related to auto use, such as those related to accidents, asthma, or obesity.

growth results in public-private capital and operating cost savings of between 12 percent and 26 percent for local roads, and between 7 percent and 14 percent for water and sewer infrastructure.[14] A Florida study conducted by James Duncan finds that, when compared to sprawl patterns, compact development reduces capital costs of roads by 60 percent, of schools by 7 percent, and of utilities by 40 percent.[15] A study of the Minneapolis-St. Paul area finds that savings on local infrastructure costs of 57 percent per dwelling unit are associated with a smart growth alternative, as is a 29 percent savings on regional sewer and water infrastructure.[16] In the Toronto region, a study of growth alternatives also shows that considerable savings on infrastructure result from moving away from the existing growth pattern. Savings on capital and operating costs for transportation and utilities range between 18 percent and 29 percent, depending on how compact the growth.[17] Overall, based on Burchell's synthesis of several major studies, it was found that compact development typically saves 25 percent on local road costs, 5 percent on school costs, and 20 percent on utilities.[18]

Another major study, *Costs of Sprawl – 2000*, which looks at uncontrolled versus controlled growth across the United States, finds modest savings for controlled growth – about 3 percent.[19] This study, unlike the vast majority of other studies, completes the picture by also estimating the revenue side of the equation and showing how these also vary with urban form. New development not only incurs costs but also, once built, provides revenue to the municipality in the form of property taxes, user fees, and intergovernmental transfers. Looking at both the cost side and the revenue side, and determining the "net" result of a development decision or pattern, provides a much better indicator of its fiscal impact. The study finds that, when compared to the uncontrolled growth option, while costs are lower in the controlled growth option, revenues are very slightly higher.[20] The net result is that, though both scenarios produce a deficit, the deficit in the controlled growth case is 10 percent lower than it is in the unplanned growth case. A study of sprawl versus smart growth in Virginia Beach finds that the latter lowers infrastructure costs by 45 percent when compared to the former and that the net fiscal impacts are positive for smart growth ($5 million) but not for sprawl ($19 million deficit).[21]

Other studies measure the cost of sprawl on a per household basis. For the United States, the cost of providing services to a typical new single-family home is estimated at $20,000 to $30,000.[22] An Oregon study estimates the costs at $15,000 to $20,000 for neighbourhood infrastructure, and at an additional $15,000 to $30,000 for off-site infrastructure (e.g., arterial roads, sewer and water trunk lines and treatment plants, schools, fire stations).[23] This is in line with Canadian costs, as reflected in the development charges in place in many municipalities that cover most of the cost of new off-site infrastructure. The estimated costs for a new home in Oregon are shown in Table 3.2. Another study in Minnesota compares per unit costs of infrastructure within a sprawl versus a smart growth scenario. It is estimated that a new home built in a sprawl scenario incurs about $18,000 in infrastructure costs while one built in a smart growth scenario incurs $8,000.[24]

Table 3.2

Infrastructure cost summary for a typical new single-family house in Oregon, 1998

Facility	Cost ($)
Schools	11,809
Sanitary sewerage	1,660
Transportation facilities	4,430
Water system facilities	2,729
Parks and recreation facilities	2,915
Stormwater drainage	483
Fire protection facilities	298
Library facilities	441
Electric power generation and distribution facilities	8,494
Total infrastructure cost	33,259

Source: Fodor, "The Cost of Growth in Oregon."

Another type of study examines only the neighbourhood, or "on-site," costs of different development patterns or densities. Essiambre et al. compare a conventional development plan for a suburban neighbourhood with a denser, mixed-use alternative plan and find savings of 9 percent in lifecycle costs for the latter.[25] A similar study by the American Farmland Trust finds that increasing the density of development from 1 unit to 4 units per acre results in a 62 percent reduction in net municipal costs.[26]

It is difficult to make strict comparisons across studies as they tend to measure different types of costs and urban form. Most studies are not comprehensive in the types of costs they evaluate and so will tend to underestimate the total costs associated with inefficient development patterns. They might examine the costs of only some types of infrastructure, or only on-site costs, or only capital or operating costs, for example. A comprehensive assessment would measure all infrastructure costs that vary with the urban development pattern – both on-site and off-site, both capital and ongoing operating and maintenance costs – over the long term. In addition, external costs are rarely addressed. Though they can be substantial, these costs are usually not priced directly and paid for as part of the development equation; rather, they are either unquantified (e.g., the value of the loss of open space) or are paid indirectly by others (e.g., public health costs associated with air pollution from transportation).

Challenging Sprawl Costs

In contrast to this by now quite extensive research on the costs of sprawl, a small group of mostly conservative economists and planners dispute its negative effects.[27] They argue that the lower infrastructure costs associated with compact development have never been adequately demonstrated, taking exception to the prospective approach adopted by many costs-of-sprawl studies.[28] There are two studies in particular that are constantly referenced to back up their arguments, one by Helen Ladd and the other by Richard Peiser.

The Peiser study, which compares a theoretical planned development with a theoretical unplanned development, does show infrastructure savings for the former on the order of 1 percent to 2 percent.[29] Only "major" infrastructure costs are analyzed, for arterial roads, sewer, water, and drainage. Costs for roads are found to be higher for planned development than for unplanned development, and there are savings on the other infrastructure costs. Higher road costs resulted from the fact that roads in the planned community connected its different subdivisions, while the roads in the unplanned community did not and were therefore shorter in total length. The relatively small savings can be attributed to the fact that the urban form of the two communities did not vary in significant ways. While the distribution of uses and street layout varied, both the planned and unplanned communities had the same overall area, population, and jobs. In particular, density – a prime determinant of costs and benefits – was held constant across the two scenarios. As Peiser acknowledges, "Consequently, the valuation of benefits and costs may not be as favourable to planned development as they would be if density varied between the two types of communities."[30] The cost savings that did occur were more related to efficiencies gained from better coordination of facilities in the planned community than to urban form per se.

The Ladd study uses regression analysis to look at how local public spending varies with density.[31] The study is based on aggregate spending for 247 counties in 1985, accounting for about 60 percent of the US population. It looks at annual spending on services, capital spending, and public safety. Controlling for a number of variables, it finds that, for annual spending on services, the lowest spending occurs at a low density of 250 people per square mile. For densities below 250, costs fall as densities rise. Between densities of 250 and 1,250 people per square mile, costs continue to rise and then fall as densities increase to 1,750 people per square mile, then rise again in the highest density counties. This finding is often cited as providing proof that costs do not fall with rising density. There are several problems with making this interpretation.

First, the author concludes from this data that "the basic message is that beyond the relatively low density of 250 persons per square mile, the costs of providing public services increase with rising density," taking the form of a "U" shaped curve. But, at the same time, she acknowledges that the results do not exhibit this pattern. Even after checking and trying different density intervals to make sure that it was not a "quirk," she still finds a similar pattern of falling, rising, falling, and rising costs – more like a wonky "W" than a "U."

Second, the study focuses on total public spending by all local governments within a given county but does not give any information regarding the composition of that spending and how it might vary from county to county. Some kinds of annual spending we would expect to vary with density, especially network services like roads or sewer and water infrastructure, while others we would not, such as spending on schools or social services. Some counties may spend more on the former and less on the latter; some may have extensive and expensive transit systems, while others may have none. While critical to the results, these variations are not accounted for.

Finally, a central problem with this analysis from the planner's perspective is that it only looks at gross density at the county level. This means that any addition of population within the county's boundaries (which are fixed over time) leads to an increase in population density as measured. At this scale, gross population density says very little about development pattern. Two counties with identical gross densities can have very different development patterns – one may be very compact and efficient and be only partly urbanized, while the other may be entirely evenly developed. So this study says little about the relationship between local spending and development pattern – which is what planning aims to shape. Gross population density is useful as a measure only insofar as it says something about the development pattern; however, at the geographic scale used in this analysis, it does not. Furthermore, the results can be interpreted as merely showing some relationship between gross spending and gross density: they cannot be interpreted as showing any causal relationship. Other factors that are co-related with but not caused by density may be at work. If anything, this study makes clear the need to be specific about urban form when discussing sprawl and its potential costs.

A similar study by Cox and Utt uses regression analyses to assess the effects of a range of factors on municipal spending per capita.[32] Included are population density, population growth rates, and age of municipality. They use actual municipal spending data drawn from over seven hundred US municipalities. They find that all thirteen factors they analyze together explain only a small portion of variation in municipal expenditures and that the highest density, slowest-growing, and oldest communities do not have lower expenditures per capita. They conclude by suggesting that most of the variation is attributable to employee compensation levels – that newer (lower-density) municipalities have lower labour costs than do older (higher-density) municipalities. Interestingly, labour costs were not a factor they evaluated in their model. Little information is provided in their report regarding either the specific types of expenditures included or the physical and urban form characteristics of the municipalities studied. Without this information, it is very difficult to draw from their analyses any substantive conclusions regarding the urban form/cost relationship.

This group also takes exception to the other commonly acknowledged costs of sprawl. For example, they argue that, while the loss of agricultural land and open space on the fringe of expanding cities does occur, it is not a problem because (1) it represents such a small proportion of available farmland and (2) agricultural productivity is rising.[33] While this may be true at a national scale, having agricultural land close to urban centres where food is consumed is beneficial not only from a food safety and security perspective but also because it significantly reduces transportation costs and emissions. A study prepared for the UK Department of Environment, Food and Rural Affairs shows, for example, that food transport accounts for one-quarter of all kilometres driven by heavy goods vehicles as well as for a 12 percent increase in carbon dioxide emissions related to food-related transport generally.[34]

Those who do not view sprawl as a problem also argue that it does not necessarily lead to increased traffic congestion and travel time. Indeed, there is some evidence that this is true with respect to travel time. SGA's comparison finds that this is the sole indicator when there is little difference between more and less compact cities.[35] SGA finds that commute times are identical for more sprawling versus less sprawling cities, at twenty-six minutes on average. The reason given by some sprawl advocates is that trips by public transport take longer and usually occur in denser areas (e.g., European cities).[36] It is true that transit trips take longer on average, but in the case of US cities the proportion of trips taken by transit is so small that it is unlikely to have much bearing on overall average travel times. The more likely explanation is that, as Gordon and Richardson suggest,[37] over time employment has suburbanized, bringing jobs closer to suburban labour.

This involves an ongoing process of adaptation between living and work locations. The result regarding commuting times is not tied to sprawl per se (i.e., to a specific development pattern) but, rather, hinges on the jobs-housing relationship (i.e., the location of jobs in relation to the location of housing). A lack of increase in commute times cannot therefore be seen as a vindication of sprawl itself.

However, the SGA report also shows that those who live in sprawling cities drive greater distances on average (twenty-seven miles per person per day on average in sprawling areas, compared to twenty-one miles in more compact cities) and own more cars than do those who live in high-density cities.[38] It is difficult to conclude, when the overall body of evidence is weighed, that low-density development patterns do not aggravate traffic congestion more than do their compact alternatives.

With respect to the impacts of urban form on transportation and air pollution, the pro-sprawl group argues that denser areas produce higher local concentrations of air pollution. In other words, the production of air pollution per square kilometre is higher in denser areas than it is in sprawl areas. However, comparing two cities of the same population, one low density and one high density, the low-density city will, of course, be larger in area, so one cannot conclude that the less dense city has lower aggregate effects on total transport-related emissions and air pollution. In terms of the further impacts of emissions on global warming, sprawl proponents argue that reductions in emissions can be achieved from improved technologies.[39]

The pro-sprawl group also challenges the link between sprawl and health, denying, for example, that obesity is associated with sprawl. They claim that land patterns have not changed markedly during the period in which obesity has increased and, therefore, cannot be a cause.[40] While the causes of the obesity epidemic are admittedly complex, a reduction in activity related to increased amounts of driving per household, which has been documented, does not seem to be an implausible factor. And, while the overall pattern of urban growth may not have changed markedly in the last twenty-five years, ongoing suburbanization has meant that the proportion of the population living in low-density suburban environments has increased dramatically. In the postwar period, the vast majority of growth in US cities has been in their suburbs. By 2000, over 50 percent of the US population lived in suburbs.[41]

Benefits of Sprawl

To some, talking about the benefits of sprawl may seem oxymoronic. There are, however, those who suggest that sprawl is at least benign, if not beneficial.

Their main argument is that the usually cited costs of sprawl are either not real or are over-emphasized.[42] Peter Gordon and Harry Richardson, for example, assert that the loss of prime agricultural land due to sprawl is not significant; that attempting to serve low-density areas with public transit is merely wasteful; that claims that compact development is more efficient have not been adequately demonstrated; that decentralization and dispersion continue to be the driving forces behind urban development; and that downtown renewal efforts have failed.[43]

While contending that the costs of sprawl are at least overestimated, sprawl proponents are able to point to few direct benefits. The main benefit noted is that suburbanization, particularly of employment, has allowed commute times to remain relatively constant, despite the increasing size of urban regions and low-density growth on the periphery (as noted above).

Mills captures the sprawl proponents' argument when he claims that

> the benefits of suburbanization are great; tens of millions of people have been able to acquire inexpensive housing in pleasant, low density communities with fine schools, low crime rates, and recreation areas for children. Widespread car ownership provides great flexibility in choice of home and work locations without high commuting costs, and has provided flexibility in travel for shopping and social trips. In addition, suburbanization of both people and jobs has enabled large metropolitan areas to function efficiently, with no more than modest road congestion.[44]

It is true that suburbanization tends to produce lower-cost housing and business premises. Greenfields land on the fringe is typically cheaper to buy and cheaper to develop than is property within already-urbanized areas. Thus, sprawl is seen as a positive factor in promoting homeownership and business competitiveness.

However, it could be argued that this is a false economy, given the public costs of sprawl outlined earlier and taking into account the hidden subsidies to this form of development (see Part 3). When these factors are considered, it appears that sprawl may not provide cheaper housing; rather, its costs are simply spread across a broader group of payers. Even the private costs of suburban development to the homeowner herself are not always well understood, especially the direct travel costs. A study by Miller et al., for example, shows that the costs of travel increase directly with distance of the home from the city centre. Annual travel costs for a household located fifty kilometres away from the city centre were estimated at $5,800 per year in 1996.[45] As Miller et al. conclude:

> The notion that a household should locate at or beyond the urban fringe in order to obtain "cheap" or "affordable" housing is called into serious question. That is, the increased cost of transportation in such areas more than compensates for any savings in housing costs. Indeed, these findings raise the issue of whether there really is such a thing as "cheap" housing, even before one factors in the "cost" of travel time and the environmental costs associated with auto-dominated travel.[46]

Naturally, long-term increases in gas prices make these findings even more relevant and robust, challenging the notion of fringe development being more affordable than development at the centre.

Other benefits are perceived to be related to sprawl, but many of these are either not strictly related to sprawl itself or are not true benefits. The *Costs of Sprawl – 2000* study reviews the alleged benefits of sprawl and finds only a few that could be corroborated by the evidence – that it provides larger average lot sizes as well as a wider range of choice in terms of combinations of services and tax levels and that it reflects consumer preferences for low-density living.[47]

Regarding the last claim, the analysis neglects to account for the critical fact that low-density suburban development is heavily subsidized through a variety of opaque mechanisms. This fact calls into question the results of consumer preference surveys that fail to take this into account. When surveys and polls reveal that consumers prefer a low-density lifestyle, they do not include questions about what consumers would be willing to pay to achieve that lifestyle. As I show in Part 3, consumers do not pay the full direct costs of their low-density choices. If they paid prices that reflected the actual direct costs incurred, their preferences would undoubtedly be vastly different than they are now.

Do the Costs of Sprawl Outweigh the Benefits?

Those concerned about sprawl see the problem as a specific form of urban development that is the source of a broad range of environmental, social, and economic costs. Sprawl brings wider costs, and these costs are too high. Indeed, the preponderance of evidence supports this view: there is little in the way of credible evidence to suggest otherwise.

Comparing the costs of sprawl to the benefits, the case for substantial costs does seem to be much stronger than does the case for substantial benefits. And, based on the evidence available to date, it seems likely that, in general, the costs far outweigh the benefits. However, it is interesting to note that, where growth management policies are being developed for specific urban areas, rarely does the policy development process look comprehensively at the benefits as well as the costs of a sprawl scenario – that is, at *net* social welfare. Inevitably, the focus is solely on the potential costs of sprawl, leaving the picture incomplete. However, it is important to note that, whereas the benefits of sprawl tend to be private in nature (e.g., larger lots and houses, freedom of automobile travel), the costs tend to be public (loss of farmland, higher infrastructure costs, greenhouse gas emissions, etc.).

Planning interventions are legitimized on the basis of these high public costs – indeed, they form the primary rationale behind the considerable efforts to curb sprawl. Probably the most significant benefit of a sprawl scenario, though one that is curiously unmentioned by sprawl advocates, is that, implemented in a pure, laissez-faire form, a sprawl scenario could avoid a significant portion of the costs of planning. These costs are explored below.

PART 2

THE PROBLEM WITH PLANNING

4

The Costs and Benefits of Planning

In the debate on urban sprawl, attention has overwhelmingly focused on costs. Substantial amounts of research have been conducted on this issue, particularly since the 1970s (see Chapter 3). The preponderance of evidence clearly points to significant costs related to a low-density, single-use pattern, with development taking place primarily on greenfields lands at the urban fringe. There is widespread agreement that urban sprawl is an expensive development pattern, to which there are alternatives that bring lower environmental, social, and economic costs.

What is surprising is that the debate around urban sprawl rarely if ever touches upon the costs involved in managing and redirecting urban growth patterns in order to achieve these cost savings and other benefits. There is little consideration of the costs of planning and of whether these are warranted given the outcomes achieved. Because we ignore its costs, we cannot know for sure whether, overall, planning results in positive benefits. Yes, the costs of sprawl are by all accounts significant. But what is the level of magnitude of the costs of planning? Do the costs of sprawl outweigh the costs of planning? Surely, from the perspective of good public policy, this is something we ought to know or at least take into account.

Should we adopt an active planning approach, taking on sprawl and attempting to reshape it into something more efficient? Or would we be better off with a more laissez-faire approach, with minimal planning interventions and cost, while maximizing the "benefits" of sprawl? Which scenario produces the highest net public good – planning or sprawl? Can we determine the net benefit (or loss)? It is only when we compare the net benefit of different policy scenarios that we can arrive at an informed approach.

Of course, the broad alternative to the laissez-faire, sprawl scenario is the managed-growth, planning scenario. That planning produces considerable net benefits is a given and is rarely questioned, explored, or verified. And, by implication, it is assumed that the planning scenario produces superior net benefits to the sprawl scenario. But can this be assumed to be the case? Perhaps we should look more closely at the benefits of planning relative to its costs.

Benefits of Planning

Planning began as a means of avoiding catastrophes within the city, such as the spread of fires or disease. It was also a means of reducing land-use conflicts (e.g., smoke and effluents from factories keeping customers away from nearby shops). As planning evolved, it became charged with ensuring the rational, orderly, and efficient development of the city.

Modern planning has its roots in micro-economic theory, particularly the idea that planning can address, at least in part, various market failures related to the use of land and property. These market failures usually fall into the categories either of externalities or public goods. Externalities refer to the impacts of a market decision whose cost is not accounted for within the price used in the market transaction. Air pollution associated with transportation is one example of this: the costs of air pollution are generally not reflected in the price of transportation and so are external to the transaction. Externalities might include very localized impacts, such as one building's casting a shadow over another and thus affecting property value. At the scale of urban regions, externalities lead to outcomes that are bad for the public as a whole, such as traffic congestion or air pollution that results from the aggregate of individual decisions to drive. The public goods dilemma relates to the fact that, although certain public goods are essential if cities, the economy, and society as a whole are to function, individuals or the private market may not be able or willing to provide them. Road networks and public parks are two examples of public goods.

The presumption is that planning can, at least in part, address these problems, leading to an overall public benefit that surpasses that which would be achieved without planning. These benefits may be seen in the quality of the urban environment, greater mobility, reduced congestion, or other factors related to quality of life. With respect to planning's role in curbing sprawl, the usual rationale is that planning can avoid or reduce those considerable costs of sprawl outlined in Chapter 3 (e.g., infrastructure costs, congestion costs, air pollution and greenhouse gases, health care costs, etc.). This cost avoidance is commonly seen as the central benefit that planning offers in curbing sprawl.

More recently, it has been argued that planning plays a key role in supporting the economic competitiveness of cities. In an economy that is both global and subject to increasingly intense competition, desirable, liveable cities attract investment and talent. In addition, compact, diverse cities offer agglomeration economies that support innovation and make businesses more efficient and competitive. It is argued that, through good planning, cities can deliver heightened productivity. The theory is that large, compact cities with good accessibility and efficient transportation infrastructure will be the most economically productive. These efficiencies can only be achieved through good city management and planning – management and planning that will provide efficient and effective access and mobility between job locations and residences.

Robert Cervero analyzes the relationship between urban form and transportation networks, on the one hand, and labour productivity, on the other:[1] "Experience suggests that such outcomes – compactness and land use/transportation integration – are not products of happenstance, but rather decades upon decades of carefully managed and guided urbanization."[2] Cervero finds that, "all else being equal, bigger areas with large laborsheds, good accessibility between jobs and housing, and well-functioning transportation systems appear to enjoy some economic advantages."[3] Similar findings arise in the case of French cities and in a comparison between London and Paris. The fact that Paris's labour productivity is superior to London's is attributed, in part, to that city's more efficient transport system. Ciccone and Hall find a strong positive link between employment density and average labour productivity. A doubling of density results in a 6 percent improvement in productivity.[4]

Related to this argument is a point that is not usually raised regarding the benefits of compact cities, but it is an important point nonetheless. It is that, to the extent that planning can create more compact and efficient cities, and reduce or avoid the usual costs of sprawl, the savings derived from this can be reinvested in more productive activities. In other words, sprawl presents an opportunity cost. For example, instead of investing in many additional kilometres of arterial road (as we would under a sprawl scenario), with the savings in road costs resulting from a more compact urban form we could invest in schools, or training, or other competitiveness-enhancing activities.

Finally, a major thread in the current discussion of cities is that the global knowledge economy is increasingly driven by human creativity, knowledge, and expertise – or what has come to be referred to as "talent." Cities are competing against each other to attract talented individuals. The ability to do this rests on the attractiveness of cities – the ability to provide high-amenity, good-quality, diverse, and safe urban environments. This, in turn, relies, at least in part, on effective, creative urban planning, including efficient transport, centres for arts and culture, healthy neighbourhoods, and so on.[5]

In other words, historically, planning has been seen to deliver a range of public benefits that support quality of life, environment, and the economy. More recently, planning has taken on a new and more central economic role in the global knowledge economy, as a supporter of the competitiveness and dynamism of local economies. And yet, we know little about the extent of these benefits, their magnitude, and the degree to which they can be linked directly to urban planning and related matters, such as the provision of municipal, transportation, and cultural infrastructure, design of neighbourhoods, or the quality of building.[6]

Costs of Planning

On the other side of the equation, the costs of planning can be thought of as falling into two categories: direct and indirect. The direct costs of planning are those that are directly incurred as a result of the planning system, including both public and private costs. Public direct costs include the staff and operations costs related to the development and implementation of planning policy, such as research, plans development, and development review – essentially, the costs of running planning departments. In Canada, these functions occur within virtually every municipal government as well as at the provincial level (i.e., in provincial planning ministries).

Private direct costs of planning are incurred by businesses and homeowners when they directly engage the planning system. Typically, this occurs when planning approvals are required for a particular project – building an extension on a home, building or expanding an office building or store, for example. Private costs include planning fees that are paid up front in order that a planning application will be processed by the planning department. Increasingly, as municipalities try to recover a larger share of their own costs, these fees are substantial. In addition, companies and private individuals usually have to spend a considerable amount of time and staff resources dealing with planning approvals. They must often also pay for a range of consultants (e.g., professional planners, lawyers, environmental scientists, retail experts, and engineers) to help them through the planning process or to provide required studies. Another form of direct cost of development occurs when public benefits of various types, which may be beyond the scope of the proposed development itself, are required as a condition of planning approval. In Canada, these are known as "public benefits"; in the United Kingdom, they are known as "planning obligations." The improvements may take many forms, from road improvements and affordable housing to provision of daycare facilities or public art.

In North America, there is very little to no research that attempts to measure the direct costs of planning. In the United Kingdom, where the efficiency of the planning system and its broader impacts have become a significant national issue of late, there have been some attempts to quantify costs. A study by the Office of the Deputy Prime Minister estimates the annual costs of planning applications in England at about £100 million, of which £80-90 million is estimated to relate to business applications.[7]

In sum, we know very little about the magnitude of the direct costs of planning. But, given that the costs are essentially represented by the sum total of the budgets of planning agencies at all levels of government, plus the private costs, it is not difficult to imagine them to be significant.[8]

Direct public costs are borne by taxpayers, unless recouped by planning agencies through fees. In this case, they are paid by the applicant (developer, business, or homeowner). For developer applications, it would be expected that these planning costs would be incorporated into rents and land or house prices and, thereby, passed along (in whole, in part, or in increased form) to the final user, depending, in part, on market conditions.[9] Along with the direct costs of planning, several indirect costs have been identified. These, however, are even more difficult to measure than are direct costs, and they are subject to some debate with regard to their existence and their magnitude.

Planning and House Prices
One of the indirect costs most frequently mentioned is the effect of planning and land-use controls on the supply and affordability of housing. In addition to the impact of direct planning costs, several studies suggest a more indirect link between planning and other forms of regulation, on the

one hand, and a restricted housing supply and higher housing costs, on the other.[10] In particular, it is theorized that (where demand exists) policies that in any way restrict the supply of land (or, indeed, are simply perceived to restrict the supply of land in the present or future) will inevitably cause prices to rise. Smart growth and other regulation are seen to be placing upward pressure on land and housing prices. This is an area of lively debate, with some suggesting that markets are being strangled by urban consolidation policies (i.e., smart growth).[11]

Brueckner reviews the impact of planning interventions such as urban growth boundaries, floor area restrictions, and other land-use regulations (such as zoning and/or engineering standards). His own analysis and review of the literature suggest that these instruments increase house prices and shift the makeup of the housing stock.[12] Much research on the effects of UGBs focuses on Portland, Oregon, which, having implemented an urban growth boundary in 1979, is the poster city for smart growth in the United States. As such, it has been the focus of a considerable amount of research. Some claim that the UGB has led to declining housing affordability in the Portland metropolitan area;[13] others conclude that the effect of the UGB is "relatively small in magnitude."[14] Anthony Downs notes no significant long-term impacts of the UGB on housing supply and prices.[15]

In fact, it is difficult to prove an impact in either direction, given the challenge in isolating the effect of the UGB or other planning policies from the many other complex factors that shape local housing markets. Indeed, those who argue in favour of UGBs suggest that it is the higher level of amenity resulting from superior planning (including the UGB) that has led to higher house prices,[16] or, perhaps, that it is the enhanced attractiveness of the area, resulting from good planning, that increases the demand for housing.

In the United Kingdom, urban containment goes back to the 1947 Town and Country Planning Act. It has been noted that, in the years before the Act, there was no increase in the real price of land. In fact, there was an apparent decrease in price (this despite a 61 percent increase in population and a 25 percent increase in real incomes). Post-1947, the real price of residential land increased eleven times, while the real price of houses increased 3.4 times.[17] Today, the supply of houses in the United Kingdom is said to be inelastic – that is, unable to respond to increases in demand resulting from population growth and rising incomes.[18]

It is difficult to draw definitive conclusions based on the research that has thus far been conducted on the implications of planning policy for house prices. Empirical research is limited, in fact, due to the complexity of the issue and to data limitations. However, what is clear is that planning policies in general and UGBs in particular do not inevitably lead to increased house prices. The reality is more subtle and complex, with a range of possible outcomes.

A more nuanced analysis looks not to planning per se but to the particular type of planning associated with restricting housing supply. For example, housing supply has been found to be responsive to demand in Germany and Spain, while very unresponsive in the United Kingdom (as noted above) and the Netherlands. This is attributed not to a lack of planning in the former countries (indeed, these countries have very sophisticated planning systems) but, rather, to the specific ways in which the planning system is structured and operates. The system in Germany and Spain allows development that conforms with plans to proceed with few additional permissions required, while the system in the United Kingdom and the Netherlands requires explicit planning permission for each development and so separates plan from permission.[19] The United Kingdom and the Netherlands also experienced higher housing prices than did Germany and Spain. Thus, the particular approach to planning, the structure of policies, and the approvals process can have an important impact on both direct and indirect costs of planning.

Cheshire and Sheppard's research in both the United States and the United Kingdom finds the impacts of planning regulation and policies on property markets to be even more complex than we thought. They determine, for example, that urban containment policies can depress the price of land while simultaneously increasing the price of housing.[20] In other words, the effects of planning regulation, in general, and urban containment policies, in particular, on land and housing markets are complex and depend on the specific nature of the regulation itself as well as on the specific urban, economic, and institutional context within which it is applied.

Planning's Impact on Businesses

Planning can also have indirect impacts on businesses. House prices that, due to regulation, are higher than they might otherwise be may put upward pressure on wage demands. They may reduce labour mobility and create local labour shortages – at either the intra-regional scale (by preventing workers from living within normal daily commuting distances of jobs) or the inter-regional scale (by preventing workers from moving from low-value housing markets to take up jobs in high-value housing markets).

And, in the same way that regulation may raise the price of land and housing, regulation of industrial, retail, and office development and lands may raise land costs and rents for business.[21] However, there has been much less study of the impacts of planning regulation on commercial land and property prices than on housing, and the existing research is not conclusive. This despite the huge magnitude of the value of commercial rents (estimated in the mid-1990s in England to be on the order of £16 billion).[22] Some research conducted in the United Kingdom uncovered a range of trends, making it difficult to establish a simple link with planning regulation. For example, industrial land prices were shown to be higher in England than in other European countries, but rents showed lower values. Within the United Kingdom, most business rents, except retail, have fallen over a thirty-year period, and the intensity of use of business floorspace has not risen over time, suggesting a lack of physical or economic pressure. It has also been noted that one would expect planning regulation to raise the cost of land and business premises only in cases where land is limited beyond market demand. In other words, planning may or may not increase prices.[23]

Planning and Productivity

Recently, there has been some lively debate on the relationship between planning and economic productivity. This is especially the case in the UK, where lagging productivity is seen as a crucial economic issue at the national level. In Canada as well, productivity levels that consistently and significantly lag behind those of the United States are seen as a major national economic issue, though there has been little to no discussion here of a possible link with planning.

A provocative study in the United Kingdom, conducted by the McKinsey Global Institute, claims that planning regulation is a primary contributor not only to poor labour productivity in the food retailing sector but also to lagging productivity in the hotel and software sectors.[24] In each case, the reason varies. The argument with respect to food retailing is that there are economies of scale and efficiencies related to bigger stores that provide higher levels of labour productivity compared to smaller stores (e.g., the number of managers does not increase with store size). Planning regulations in the United Kingdom place limits on the size of food stores, inhibiting food retailers from developing new sites or expanding existing ones. Planning regulations introduced in the mid-1990s have made the construction of new, out-of-town stores very difficult: "recent tightening of UK planning regulation has essentially frozen the evolution of the industry, locking retailers into their current format and size mix and denying them the flexibility to evolve."[25] Because the structure of the food retailing sector has been prevented from evolving, the United Kingdom has a less productive mix of retail formats than do other countries (in this case, the United States and France were the comparisons). It has a larger number of smaller, more traditional (and less productive) stores and fewer larger (more productive) stores. Moreover, its large stores are smaller than are those in other countries.

This study is often pointed to as providing evidence for the existence of a significant problem – namely, that planning regulation comes at the cost of lost labour productivity. However, according to the same study, the United Kingdom is still the most productive country overall for food retailing because it has by far the highest space productivity – that is, output per square metre of selling space.[26] There are no apparent impacts on overall sales; rather, UK shops are simply more efficient: "Sales per capita are not significantly different between the US, UK and France. However, as there is significantly less space per capita in the UK, the UK achieves much higher space productivity. Essentially, the UK is selling close to the same amount of goods in 50 to 75 percent of the space."[27] On this basis, one could argue that the United Kingdom's tough planning stance on food supermarkets is very successful policy. Not only does it achieve what it set out to do – that is, protect the traditional high street grocer and support efficient use of space and urban containment – but it also fosters "world-leading supply chain management practices."[28]

At this point, it can only be said that the jury is still out on the links between planning and productivity. While some allege that planning hurts productivity, others suggest that planning plays a major role in supporting labour productivity in urban environments.

Do the Benefits of Planning Outweigh the Costs?

Returning to the broader question, do the benefits of planning outweigh the costs? The various costs of planning described above are rarely considered in the development of planning policy. The benefits of planning are more well known and reasoned, but they are rarely measured. Cheshire and Sheppard attempt to estimate the benefits and costs of land-use planning.[29] They quantify the benefits of planning in the form of environmental amenities provided to residents. In this case, three specific amenities, or benefits, of planning are analyzed: (1) provision of accessible open space (e.g., public parks within the existing urban envelope), (2) provision of inaccessible open space (e.g., preservation of agricultural lands at the periphery), and

(3) reduction of land-use conflicts through the control of location and amount of industrial land uses in relation to residential uses. The costs of planning "come in the form of increased land and housing costs from restrictions on the availability of developable land."[30]

The study finds that land-use planning produces benefits of considerable value. However, the cost of producing these benefits is also very high, such that the overall effect is negative – that is, there is a net cost to planning rather than a net benefit. The net cost is estimated at as much as 3.9 percent of annual household incomes.[31] This is just one study that attempts to measure quantitatively the net costs or benefits of planning and, as such, must be interpreted with caution. It only examines a few of the potential benefits of planning (a fact noted by the authors themselves), disregarding many other acknowledged benefits (e.g., reduced infrastructure costs, reduced air pollution and health costs, etc.). Including these benefits may indeed tip the scale towards a positive net outcome.

Brueckner also attempts to weigh planning benefits against its costs. His work suggests that planning may produce net social losses primarily because of the collateral costs associated with UGBs, floor area restrictions, or other regulations, especially higher house prices.[32] However, his calculation of the benefits from planning is also extremely limited – in the case of a UGB, for example, to the social benefits of open space conservation. The motivation behind planning interventions are certainly much broader than this and are aimed at reducing the wide range of social costs associated with sprawl.

Of course, the other important implication to be drawn from this is the need to be more efficient in the pursuit of planning objectives – that is, the need to reduce the cost at which planning benefits are obtained. Clearly, an anti-sprawl policy that minimizes or eliminates distortions in land and property markets would significantly reduce the costs of planning and help to make planning of positive overall benefit. And, of course, reducing the direct costs of planning – both public and private – can further bring down planning costs. In sum, we cannot at this point determine the net cost or benefit of planning. There is little research upon which to rely. And, in any event, as is noted above, the net cost or benefit is likely to be specific to the type of planning policies adopted and to the context within which they are applied.

A More Complete Accounting Is Needed
Generally speaking, there are two approaches to sprawl. The first is an interventionist approach based on regulation and design, which we might broad-

ly call "planning" and which, in practice, could include growth management or its newer forms (e.g., new urbanism or smart growth). This kind of approach has been implemented in many jurisdictions, especially in Canada and, perhaps more unevenly, in the United States. The second approach to sprawl is a minimally interventionist, laissez-faire approach, which resists planning interventions and relies on the market to deliver optimal outcomes. By and large, this approach accepts sprawl as the reasonable result of consumer preference and a functioning marketplace.

At the moment, we have little real evidence to show which approach produces the best overall result – that is, the highest *net* social benefit. We have taken it as an article of faith that planning produces the best overall result and positive social benefits. However, we have little understanding of the costs that planning involves – indeed, this question is rarely if ever asked. And we have only a partial understanding of the potential benefits of planning and how these compare to its costs. There is a need to inform policy development by addressing the costs of planning – acknowledging them, understanding them, weighing them against the planning benefits produced.

Cheshire and Sheppard's conclusion with regard to their analysis of the net benefits of planning is widely applicable: "Without examining the benefits as well as the cost one could not draw conclusions as to whether regulation in a particular community was producing suboptimal outcomes."[33] Very little of this work has been done. Nor do we pay much attention to the costs and benefits of the minimal intervention alternative, which might aim to maximize the benefits of sprawl while minimizing the costs of planning. We also need to better understand the benefits and costs of the alternative scenario.

This is not to say that planning should not be pursued but, rather, that, in order to make effective policy choices, we must be aware of the broader context of the net benefits of a planning scenario compared with other scenarios. Even the researchers who calculated that planning produced a net cost clearly note that this does not mean that no planning would produce a better outcome: "The large net costs associated with the planning regime do not necessarily imply that households would be better off with no land use planning whatsoever." [34] However, when choosing among policy options that will shape the physical evolution of cities, given the magnitude of the potential costs and benefits involved, a complete picture, involving net costs, is needed.

5

How Do Our Cities Grow?
Plans versus Reality

It is by now clear that considerable effort and money have been invested in planning initiatives aimed at curbing sprawl. What exactly are these efforts aimed at achieving on the ground? What is their underlying rationale? What are their mechanics? Below, I begin by examining the physical components of the alternative to sprawl: the basic building blocks of the compact city. Then I look at how these physical components are linked to the broader outcomes that planners are trying to realize. This represents the underlying theory of contra-sprawl, which is that a different urban form will bring about a wide range of socially desirable results. Finally, I look at how successful these efforts, which have been taking place over the last two decades or so, have been.

Ideal City Form: The Vision for the Physical City

There is a remarkable consensus among forward-looking plans across the continent regarding the structure and key urban form elements of a sustainable, "smart" city. A few key urban form elements appear again and again. These elements are the central pillars of the vision for the physical city:

- more compact, denser development, particularly at the urban fringe;
- more close mixing of different land uses;

- a higher proportion of new development that is directed to the already-urbanized envelope, including under-utilized, vacant, or abandoned sites; and
- creation of denser, mixed-use centres, or "nodes," across a region as it expands.

Compact development, for example, has been defined thus:

> The term "compact development" does not imply high-rise or even uniformly high density, but rather higher average "blended" densities. Compact development also features a mix of land uses, development of strong population and employment centers, interconnection of streets, and the design of structures and spaces at a human scale.[1]

But how, exactly, is attaining these urban form components supposed to achieve the broader objectives about which planners are concerned?

The Social, Economic, and Environmental Vision

Of course, urban structure is not particularly important in and of itself. We do not directly enjoy or suffer urban form per se. We rarely hear someone say, "I really enjoy Toronto's polycentric nodal structure, don't you?" When looking to move, homebuyers don't usually claim: "I really prefer to live in a neighbourhood with a density of 25 uph gross." Rather, we care about urban form only insofar as it is closely tied with outcomes that directly affect our quality of life, our daily experience, the quality of the urban and natural environments, a region's economic competitiveness, and so on. So, underlying the physical vision for the city, and more important, is a vision – most often explicit in plans but sometimes implicit – of the qualitative aspects of urban life, a vision of how we would live, work, and play within this alternative urban form. For example, Smart Growth America defines smart growth in terms of its outcomes rather than in terms of its urban form. These are identified as: neighbourhood liveability; better access; less traffic; thriving cities, suburbs, and towns; shared benefits; lower costs and lower taxes; and keeping open space open.

Several key themes pop up in city plans from Portland, Oregon, to Portland, Maine; from Toronto to Vancouver. These key themes attempt to address the major perceived problems associated with sprawl outlined in chapters 2 and 3. A central thrust of plans today is to address and to reduce auto dependency. Rather than having to drive, we would be able to easily and enjoyably walk or cycle to buy a litre of milk, or to take our children to school or daycare, or to enjoy a restaurant meal, or to drop off our dry cleaning, and so on. In other words, walking, cycling, and transit are emphasized as viable alternatives to the car, as alternatives embodying a healthier lifestyle.

Urban form and land-use patterns cannot be looked at apart from transportation. The many individual decisions that collectively determine how our cities grow and develop depend, in large part, on transportation choices and vice versa. Urban form shapes the total amount of travel – how many trips and how long they are. It also determines the mode of travel – whether it is by car, public transit, bicycle, or on foot. In choosing a new house, for example, families tend to consider how they will travel to and from that home, how long their trips will take, and how much they will spend on cars, gas, parking, or public transit. Similarly, businesses must factor in the ease and costs of transporting goods and people to and from a potential new location as well as its accessibility for its workforce. And, of course, urban transportation directly affects the quality of our environment, particularly, as anyone living in a large, smog-prone city will know, the quality of the air we breathe, the noise levels, and, ultimately, our health.

A second planning theme addresses what is seen as costly, inefficient, and uncompetitive urban form. Cities that are more efficient, competitive, and productive spend less on putting infrastructure in the ground and on maintaining it once it is there. Savings can be returned to local homeowners and businesses or reinvested in other, more productive endeavours that tangibly improve quality of life and economic competitiveness (e.g., education programs, cultural facilities, social services, and environmental protection). The plans often envision more mixed, harmonious, and safer neighbourhoods, with different socioeconomic groups living together within individual communities. This notion embraces ideas such as the ability to age in place (i.e., within the same community) and to have alternative housing forms from which to choose as a household's needs change over time.

Finally, the natural world figures prominently in urban plans, particularly in recent decades. Natural areas, habitats and wildlife, agricultural areas, and picturesque rural landscapes are protected, preserved, and, where necessary, restored.

These planning themes are illustrated in the vision statement for the Toronto region's recent plan, *Places to Grow*.

Places to Grow: Vision for 2031

More than anything, the Greater Golden Horseshoe (GGH) will be a great place to live in 2031. Its communities will be supported by the pillars of a strong economy, a clean and healthy environment and social equity.

The GGH will offer a wide variety of choices for living. Thriving, livable and productive urban and rural areas will foster community and individual well-being. The region will be supported by modern, well-maintained infrastructure built in accordance with a broad plan for growth. Residents will have easy access to shelter, food, education and health-care facilities, arts and recreation and information technology. ·

Getting around will be easy. An integrated transportation network will allow people choices for easy travel both within and between urban centres throughout the region. Public transit will be fast, convenient and affordable. Automobiles, while still a significant means of transport, will be only one of a variety of effective and well-used choices for transportation. Walking and cycling will be practical elements of our urban transportation system.

A healthy natural environment with clean air, land and water will characterize the GGH … .

Urban centres will be characterized by vibrant and more compact settlement and development patterns and will provide a diversity of opportunities for living, working, and enjoying culture.[2]

Linking Urban Form and Socioeconomic Outcomes

What are the specific links between urban form and the broader vision for a sustainable, healthy, equitable future? Here I break out the main components of compact urban form, isolating the effect of each main component on costs and the attainment of the other elements of the planning vision. The focus is on the four elements of urban form identified above: reurbanization, density, mix, and centres. I also examine the urban form/transportation nexus.

Why Reurbanize?

Directing development to sites within the built-up urban area is very efficient, making use of infrastructure that is already in place. Often, due to demographic change, this infrastructure has become underutilized over time. For example, average household size typically falls as a community ages, resulting in lower levels of population. Also, economic restructuring due to the deindustrialization of older industrial areas near the centre or, more recently, the impact of information and communication technologies can result in less intensive use of existing urban areas (e.g., the automation of banking processes has reduced the number of bank branches).

Often, there is considerable infrastructure capacity of all kinds within a city's existing urban area. This has been demonstrated for the Toronto area, for example, where sewer and water capacity, school places, and transit and road capacity were found to exist in substantial quantities within the already urbanized area.[3] A suburban Toronto school board in a rapidly urbanizing area proposed to spend $350.1 million to build 24,900 school seats between 2002 and 2005, while it was estimated that the region's two central city school boards had 54,253 vacant places during the 2002-03 school year.[4] In Minneapolis-St. Paul, seventy-eight new schools were built in outer suburbs between 1970 and 1990. During the same period, 162 schools in good condition were closed within the city limits.[5] A study in Rhode Island compares the cost of school facilities under current development patterns to costs under a smart growth scenario. Altering development patterns to place more growth near existing school facilities produced savings of $31 million over twenty years.[6]

Of course, where capacities in already-urbanized areas are exhausted, additional infrastructure costs associated with accommodating further growth will be incurred. And development and redevelopment can be expensive, in part due to higher land costs in central locations and in part due to the physical and logistical difficulties of construction within an existing, functioning urban environment. In addition, lengthy planning approval processes and political obstacles, such as local opposition, can add to costs. It is for these reasons that it is sometimes found that, at very high densities, infrastructure costs can rise. In such instances, the costs must be weighed against both the revenues generated and the broader external costs and benefits, such as impacts on car travel, emissions, air quality, and so on. And, of course, in a growing region, if reurbanization does not occur, development will have to be accommodated elsewhere, and this, too, will incur infrastructure costs. However, except in the world's most dense cities, such as New York or Hong Kong, there is usually a considerable supply of land for redevelopment in urban areas (e.g., former industrial sites, surface parking lots, or low-density strip malls).

Directing new development in a strategic, surgical manner to specific locations with existing capacities can also enhance the physical environment in older parts of the city. It can increase the mix of uses or housing types, introducing jobs to residential areas (or vice versa) or shops and services within walking distances. Or it can improve the quality of public spaces, streetscapes, and parks. In other words, it can play an important role in retrofitting older areas.

Reurbanization can increase transit ridership by adding riders in proximity to existing lines. It can also provide a basis for increasing transit service levels by providing the new riders needed to warrant them. And, of course, to the degree that new development can be directed to the already-urbanized areas of the existing city, agricultural and sensitive environmental areas at the fringe can be saved from urbanization.

Reurbanization can, therefore, present a relatively low-cost way to accommodate new urban growth. Why build expensive new infrastructure to service development in greenfields areas when capacity exists and is languishing in the already-urbanized areas? This is like expanding a factory when it already has excess capacity. No plant manager would do this. So why do we manage our cities this way?

These are some of the reasons that a good deal of planning focuses on trying to direct new development away from greenfields sites and towards under-utilized lots within the existing city. Different approaches have been taken towards this, the most common and oldest being "urban containment." This involves trying to physically limit the outward expansion of urban areas through the creation of an urban boundary. This is not unlike the wall that provided a physical boundary in medieval cities; however, in modern times it is a policy boundary, a line drawn on a map that shows the area beyond which the city will not expand. The most famous North American example of this is Portland, Oregon, metropolitan area, which instituted an urban boundary in 1979.

More recently, reurbanization targets have been introduced in some jurisdictions. In this case, a minimum percentage of new growth (usually only relating to housing units) is intended to be directed to the existing city. Perhaps the most famous example of this is in the United Kingdom, where a target of 60 percent of all new housing units directed towards already-urbanized land has been established (compared to an existing rate of 40 percent). The *Places to Grow* plan for the Toronto region also establishes minimum reurbanization targets. A minimum of 40 percent of all residential (only) growth is to be directed towards the existing built-up area by 2015.[7] Other metropolitan regions adopting reurbanization targets include Sydney, Australia; Vancouver, British Columbia; and Auckland, New Zealand.[8]

Why Densify?

Higher urban density levels are inherent in most of the elements of land use deemed to be desirable in visions for the physical city, such as compact development, reurbanization, and the creation of nodes or urban centres. Density is probably the single most important determinant of the efficiency of the use of land and infrastructure. Increasing the number of houses and businesses that can share a kilometre of sewer or water pipe, roads and sidewalks, electrical wires and poles, or underground cables makes it that much more efficient, lowering the per unit cost of infrastructure.

As many of the studies reviewed in Chapter 3 show, the costs of network infrastructure and services, such as water and roads, vary directly with density. The capital costs associated with network infrastructure vary with density, as do maintenance and operating costs. Network infrastructure can also include services such as postal delivery, courier services, school busing, garbage pickup, recycling, and snow clearance. And, of course, the denser the development, the less land at the fringe needs to be urbanized, reducing pressure for greenfields development and helping to protect farmlands and sensitive environmental areas.

One of the central reasons so much attention is focused on density concerns its relationship with transportation. It plays a central role in shaping urban travel patterns. There is little doubt that the number of vehicle kilometres travelled (VKT) (or its imperial equivalent, vehicle miles travelled [VMT]) has been increasing. These increases have been significantly outstripping population growth rates. In fact, since 1980 the number of miles Americans drive has increased three times faster than population and almost twice as fast as the number of vehicles.[9]

And, while other factors come into play (e.g., demographics), urban development patterns clearly play a role. There is considerable evidence that higher densities generate lower levels of VKT. Even holding levels of transit service and vehicle ownership constant, Holtzclaw found that a doubling of residential densities reduced VMT by 16 percent.[10] And holding household income and size constant, as density increased, car ownership fell.[11]

Reid Ewing and Robert Cervero's rigorous review of over fifty studies that examine the relationship between travel patterns and the built environment finds that regional accessibility plays the dominant role in determining VMT.[12] While not specifically defined, regional accessibility presumably relates to the relative accessibility of destinations at the regional scale. This would have to do with a number of factors, including location, traffic congestion, and regional structure. The authors conclude that density has a lesser effect than does regional accessibility in determining VMT and, further, that "this means that dense, mixed-use developments in the middle of nowhere may offer only modest regional travel benefits."[13] This result is not surprising (though such developments probably still perform better than low-density, single-use developments in the middle of nowhere). However, for developments that are not in the middle of nowhere, there is considerable evidence (including that found in many studies contained in the Ewing and Cervero review) to show that density does play a role in moderating VMT. Ewing and Cervero also note that trip *lengths* are generally shorter at locations that are more accessible and that have higher densities or mixed uses.

The same review also finds that density plays the dominant role in determining the mode of travel: "Transit use depends primarily on local densities."[14] Denser development tends to support transit because it offers large numbers of potential riders in close proximity to transit stops. This relationship has been extremely well documented and makes intuitive sense – a concentration of potential riders is needed to make transit efficient.[15] And, in general, higher densities make higher levels of transit service feasible. A minimum threshold density is needed to support a rudimentary level of transit service (say, a bus every half hour). As densities increase, so, too, does the economic viability of higher levels of transit service – more frequent bus service, streetcars, and subways.

If development is dense, the ability and likelihood of being able to walk or cycle for certain kinds of trips becomes feasible (though this relies on mix too [see below]). This also makes intuitive sense: trip origins (e.g., homes) and destinations (e.g., schools, shopping, offices, community centres) need to be relatively close together in order for walking or cycling to be practical. The densities of employment areas, while often overlooked in the research, are identified as another important determinant of transit use and walking. In the case of transit use, densities at employment destinations may be a more important factor than residential density at the trip origin.[16] It is this close relationship between development patterns and travel patterns that underpins much of the thinking behind the belief that compact development is needed to support viable transportation alternatives to the car as well as to support reduced car travel and increased use of transit, walking, and cycling.

Why Mix?
Density is just one measure of the efficiency and sustainability of the use of land. Another important measure is the degree to which different types of

land uses – employment, shopping, services, and homes – are found togeth-er at the neighbourhood and city scale. When different types of land uses are closely mixed, automobile use is reduced because stores or jobs can be reached on foot or by bicycle. At the very least, trip lengths are reduced if these amenities are close by. For the young, the elderly, or those with lim-ited or no access to a car, having services nearby is a necessity.

In fact, Ewing and Cervero find that, after density, transit use depends on the degree of mixed land uses. Walking depends as much on mixed use as it does on density. For example, areas of high density or mixed land use had higher levels of walking-to-work than did low-density, single-use areas. But high-density, mixed-use areas showed the highest overall levels of walking-to-work.[17]

Why Create Centres?

Another important element of urban form that has direct implications for sustainability is the degree to which the city has well-established centres and subcentres. As urban regions expand, a polycentric urban form can be environmentally beneficial in that the average length and number of auto-mobile trips for work or shopping can be reduced. Concentrating offices, shops, and services in a few key locations across an urban region can also make transit more viable and efficient than can a model in which jobs are dispersed across low-density suburbs (though, for transit, this may not be more efficient than the single-centred model).[18]

Centres also provide a functional focus and a civic heart to an urban area. They can become a central place with which residents can identify and come to consider their "downtown," a place to go for special occasions or simply when one wants to go to a theatre or a restaurant. This function becomes increasingly important as cities expand beyond a size at which suburban residents feel connected to a single central downtown and in which feature-less, unrelenting sprawl repeats its pattern of shops, houses, and business parks over the urban landscape. Ideally, centres are mixed-use, dense, and walkable, offering a concentration of activities and forms of housing (such as apartments) that may not be found elsewhere.

The Reality

By now we have several decades of experience in implementing a wide range of policies to control urban sprawl. Has the reality on the ground responded? If so, we would expect to see the results of these policies in the form of denser, contained, more mixed urban environments. Below, I review the evidence on the major elements of compact growth as well as trends in transportation.

Reurbanization

Despite the important role played by reurbanization in sustainable city-making, very little is known about how much reurbanization is actually taking place. Data on this factor are rarely tracked or available even for individual cities, let alone consistently across the United States or Canada. As more cities adopt intensification targets and need to monitor progress, this situation may improve.

There has been considerable anecdotal evidence about the resurgence of downtowns but little systematic analysis of the levels of growth and development involved. The downtowns of major US cities, the majority of which lost population in the 1970s and stagnated in the 1980s, experienced population growth in the 1990s. Though patterns in individual cities varied, this meant that, overall, the cities had almost regained their lost population by the end of the 1990s.[19] The extent to which this resurgence was aided or thwarted by planning policies was not explored. One study of six Canadian cities finds that reurbanization is occurring to some extent but is very much limited to downtowns and nearby neighbourhoods. Except in municipalities that are already fully built out, urban development is taking place almost exclusively on greenfields lands at the urban fringe.[20]

Monitoring is typically undertaken in those urban regions that have adopted reurbanization targets. Prior to adopting a target of 40 percent reurbanization in the GTA, efforts were made to measure just how much of new growth was taking place on already-urbanized land. One assessment indicates that – disregarding the City of Toronto, which is fully urbanized – in the remaining GTA municipalities, about 15 percent to 20 percent of residential development is occurring within the built-up urban area but that most municipalities did not even track this development pattern.[21] Other data, based on planning applications, suggest that the rate in those suburban municipalities is around 2 percent to 3 percent, though some of this difference may be attributed to variations in definitions.[22] The degree to which non-residential development has been redirected to already-urbanized lands is not investigated with respect to the Toronto regional plan. Indeed, despite the critical role of employment lands (i.e., lands used for non-residential purposes such as retail, offices, manufacturing or warehousing) in generating sprawl, the reurbanization policies apply only to residential development.

In 1996, Vancouver, British Columbia, set a target of achieving 70 percent of regional population in its core municipalities, up from 65 percent in 1991.[23] By 2001, the core's share had remained stable at 65 percent, and the core municipalities had accounted for 65 percent of regional growth in the preceding decade.[24] In other words, there was no improvement; reurbanization levels were simply holding steady.

In the United Kingdom, a target of 60 percent reurbanization by 2008 was established in 1998. The target was met in 2001 because of the huge share of national growth that takes place in the London region and that occurs there overwhelmingly (90 percent) on already-urbanized lands. Only one other region actually achieved the 60 percent target.[25]

Given that reurbanization targets are a relatively new planning tool, and that data on reurbanization patterns and trends are extremely scarce, it is difficult to draw firm conclusions regarding the degree to which reurbanization is actually occurring. Certainly, there is considerable anecdotal evidence about the rebirth of the downtown in North American cities, as elsewhere; however, as yet, there is little in the way of objective measurement.

Density

As noted above, density is an important indicator of the efficiency and sustainability of land use. With compact development planning initiatives that have been in place for two or three decades now, we would expect to see increasing urban density levels in recent years. In Canada, 15,200 square kilometres of land was urbanized (i.e., converted from non-urban uses such as natural areas or farmland to urban uses) between 1971 and 2001.[26] This is an area equivalent to almost three times that of the Province of Prince Edward Island and represents a 96 percent increase over this time period. This compares to urban population growth of about 45 percent, from 16 million to 24 million, during the same period.[27] In other words, the rate at which we are urbanizing land is outstripping the rate of population growth by about two to one. The actual urban density in Canada fell from 1,030 persons per square kilometre in 1971 to 773 persons per square kilometre in 2001, a 33 percent decline.[28] Within metropolitan areas with a population of more than 250,000, the overall density loss was 7.3 percent between 1971 and 1996.[29]

In the United States, about 25 million acres (101,175 square kilometres) of land was urbanized between 1982 and 1997, equivalent to the land areas of Maine and New Hampshire combined. This represents an increase of

47 percent, compared to a population increase of 17 percent during the same period.[30] Here, too, land is being urbanized at a much faster rate than population is growing – in this case, by a factor of almost three times. Kolankiewicz and Beck estimate that only about half of the newly urbanized land can be attributed to population growth, with the other half being directly attributable to urban sprawl.[31] However, comparing the rate of urbanization of land with the rate of population growth is not an entirely satisfactory measure of sprawl as it says nothing about actual densities. It simply says that land use is becoming relatively less (or more) efficient, but it does not say how efficient it is in absolute terms. The rate of urbanization may surpass the population growth rate in one city, but actual density levels may nonetheless be higher than in a city where the rate of urbanization of land is lower than population growth.

Between 1982 and 1997, the metropolitan density of the United States declined from 5.00 persons per urbanized acre in 1982 to 4.22 persons per urbanized acre in 1997, a 15.7 percent drop.[32] In fact, the rate at which densities have been falling has accelerated: densities declined 0.22 persons per acre between 1982 and 1987, 0.26 persons per acre between 1987 and 1992, and 0.31 persons per acre between 1992 and 1997.[33] Most metropolitan areas in the United States experienced sprawl in the 1980s and 1990s. In one study, only seventeen of the 281 metropolitan areas examined increased density or managed to hold it steady.[34]

National density figures, or even those for individual metropolitan areas where density reflects the entire urban region, can be misleading, however. These figures say little about how density of new development is changing over time, especially density at the urban fringe. They may mask dramatic declines in density at the fringe by averaging across an entire urban area (by definition, adding any new growth to already-urbanized areas results in an increase in urban density).

Research by Bunting et al. on suburban density trends in larger Canadian cities finds increases in some of these cities and decreases in others.[35] However, density in suburban areas is still at about only half the levels found in inner cities.[36] In Toronto, for example, it is often argued that density trends have turned around and that density at the urban fringe has been increasing. In fact, there is some evidence to suggest, at least in some of the suburban municipalities of the region, that residential densities increased between the mid-1980s and the late 1990s.[37] However, this increase was, in large part, attributable to a shift in the mix of housing types – a shift towards a higher proportion of town houses and a smaller share of single detached units. This may reflect shifting market demand as much as compact development planning policies.

Many of the touted new forms of community-level planning, such as new urbanism, are seen as heralding a new wave of mixed-use, dense development at the urban fringe. At the moment, the jury is still out on this issue, perhaps because this form of development is still too new and incomplete to evaluate properly. A Gordon and Vipond study suggests that new urbanist development is significantly denser than is conventional development, but this is based on the density as envisioned in the plans, not the actual development on the ground, which may or may not realize some of the denser, less conventional components once built.[38]

The analysis of sprawl focuses on residential development. However, as a user of land, employment is at least as significant as is housing, if not more so. And employment uses may in fact be losing density at a faster rate than housing uses. Yet, there appear to be no systematic analyses of employment densities and how these are changing over time in the North American context. This is a serious and significant gap in our understanding of patterns of urban growth.

Why are densities falling? In some cases, there can be a "hollowing out" of the core – a loss of population, particularly in slow-growth cities. In growing cities with steady or rising core populations, this occurs simply because, as the city grows, new suburban areas are built at progressively lower densities than the existing areas. Bigger houses occupy bigger lots. In Toronto, for example, neighbourhoods built prior to the 1960s are, on average, more than twice as dense as neighbourhoods built since 1980.[39] When looking at national density averages, we see that falling densities can also be the result of low-density cities growing more rapidly than high density cities.

It is sometimes argued that falling gross densities are attributable to the increasing protection of sensitive environmental areas. As the impacts of urban development on the natural environment have become more of an issue, policies have been put in place to protect sensitive environmental areas from development. Wetlands, lakes, river courses, special habitats, and other natural landscape features have come to be off-limits to urban development, often with an added "buffer zone" between the natural and the urban areas. If net development densities remain the same (net densities are measured over the area of lots only), as they typically have, then overall (gross) urban densities will fall if the proportion of protected lands increases. There is little empirical analysis of this issue upon which to draw. In a sample of Toronto region communities, the proportion of land devoted to parks, hazard lands, and protected environmental areas does show a slight increase, from 9 percent of total land area for pre-1960s development, to 12 percent for development built in the 1960s and 1970s, to 14 percent for the 1980s and 1990s.[40] However, there was quite a bit of variation between all communities, regardless of their age.

While some of the decline in gross densities might be attributed to a higher share of land protected from development in newer communities, lower net residential densities still play the more dominant role in the over-all downward trend in residential densities, at least in the case of the To-ronto evidence. If the planning policies aimed at more compact development had been effective, we would have expected to see falling densities turn around and evidence of an increase in residential density levels. However, the evidence shows that residential densities have continued to fall in the vast majority of North American cities and, if anything, that the pace of decline has picked up.

Mix

One of the important dimensions of urban sprawl involves large expanses of land devoted to a single use. Where factories were at one time mixed close-ly with worker housing, for example, now they are housed in expansive in-dustrial areas or business parks. Industrial areas have become progressively larger and larger. Gone are the days when factory workers strolled across the street to work or rode a streetcar or bus. There are some good reasons for this separation of uses, particularly where industrial uses are potentially noxious. But much separation of use these days has little to do with safety or health concerns.

"Innovation" in "retail formats" has meant that shopping has moved from main streets to shopping centres to big boxes to power centres. Each trans-formation has meant larger and larger retail facilities, making it very diffi-cult to integrate shops into a walkable neighbourhood. In just ten to fifteen years, big box stores have emerged from nowhere to dominate the retail and physical landscape. Big boxes are defined as stores that are several times larger than the average store in the same category.[41] They range in size from 20,000 square feet to over 150,000 square feet.[42] By 2003, they accounted for nearly one-third of non-automotive retail sales in Canada.[43]

Big boxes have evolved into "power centres" (defined as three or more big boxes with a shared parking lot, along with smaller ancillary retail outlets such as banks or fast food outlets). The average power centre in Canada has

380,000 square feet of floor space, ranging from around 60,000 square feet to 1.4 million square feet.[44] They each occupy from twenty-five to eighty acres of land.[45]

Recently, "power nodes" – defined as extended clusters of big box stores and/or other power centres located within one kilometre of a power centre or major mall – have materialized.[46] One power node in the Toronto area includes five separate power centres, three shopping centres, fifty-four big box stores, and almost 2.8 million square feet of retail space.[47] Walking between different stores, even within the same power centre, is virtually impossible.

To compete, regional shopping centres have also been growing. Vaughan Mills is the first shopping centre to be built in the Toronto area in almost two decades. It has 200 shops, 1.2 million square feet of retail space, and 6,300 parking spaces on 200 acres of land.

Even the movie house is no longer built on a main street but, rather, within "megaplexes" (typically with more than twenty screens), "entertainment complexes," malls, or entertainment power centres. These complexes are designed as self-sufficient worlds unto themselves. In suburban locations, they tend to be set in a massive parking lot. A typical new entertainment complex has more than forty thousand square feet of space.[48] A recent complex in suburban Toronto, designed to look like a spaceship launching pad, has eight screens and seating for 5,200, along with a cafe, video arcade, party rooms and fast food, and a total of 124,000 square feet of floor space. An evening stroll to a local movie is clearly out of the question under these circumstances. Even traversing the parking lot can be daunting.

In the United States, megaplexes are often integrated into "lifestyle centres" of 150,000 to 500,000 square feet, along with high-end retail and dining and other entertainment uses on ten to forty acres of land.[49] Now new and bigger lifestyle centres are under way, ranging from 1 million to 2.7 million square feet. The scale is such that even industry analysts note that "the size of these projects defies the International Council of Shopping Centers' standard definition."[50]

Studies that measure the degree of mix of land uses are recent and relatively few. There are no national data and no trend data. Snapshots of individual metropolitan areas have been undertaken. Smart Growth America, for example, has measured mix in eighty-three US metropolitan areas, ranking each city according to how well "mixed" it is from a land-use perspective.[51] (Raleigh-Durham, North Carolina, is the least mixed; the most mixed cities were medium-sized northeastern ones, with Jersey City, New Jersey, being the most mixed.)

In Canada, no country-wide analysis of the degree of mix in our cities has been undertaken. A few studies have analyzed the degree of mix for individual urban areas.[52] Typically, it is the older pre- and early postwar urban areas that exhibit the most mix. These areas are characterized by corner stores and main streets with shops at ground level and offices above. More recent suburban areas are more homogenous in use, with the expanse of single-use areas becoming larger and larger as the scale of facilities such as retail centres and distribution facilities increases.

A study comparing the composition of areas of different vintages within the Toronto region found that,

> in contrast to the pre-1960 cases, which feature small-format retail and services on pedestrian-oriented streets, employment in recently developed areas is consolidated into fewer, large-scale parcels such as malls and segregated, single-use employment lands. More recently developed study areas tend to contain fewer jobs, because most jobs are located in large-scale, specialized employment districts such as business and industrial parks.[53]

Some new suburban developments, such as those under the "new urbanism" banner, have made a deliberate attempt to redress the lack of mix. They have attempted to integrate shopping within new subdivisions, allowing residents the opportunity to walk or cycle to stores and services. However, while they may make local shopping somewhat more accessible, these initiatives have not dealt with the larger regional issues of the patterns of distribution of employment that are typical today – namely, large, single-use business parks, distribution centres, big boxes, and industrial parks. While there is general agreement that land uses have been becoming less mixed over time, this is one area that could benefit from more systematic research.

Centres

There is no doubt that North American cities have been evolving from the traditional single dominant "downtown" to a city of many centres – the so-called "polycentric" city. This phenomenon is related to the decentralization and suburbanization of employment that has characterized the growth of North American cities for the last several decades.

Centres can and do take many forms. "Edge cities," for example, are defined as areas with significant amounts of office, retail, and entertainment space (but little residential development). Joel Garreau, who coined the term, identifies more than two hundred edge cities in the United States, such as "the area around Route 128 and the Massachusetts Turnpike" near Boston (the lack of coherent urban structure in edge cities is apparently reflected in their lack of coherent names!).[54] Most "centres," however, are really just areas where jobs are sequestered. Few new suburban centres have the other characteristics of older downtowns – especially being walkable and denser than their surrounding areas. Nor do they typically provide a true mix of activities, including housing, restaurants, cultural facilities, shopping, and other services that would allow them to be venues for twenty-four-hour activity.

Smart Growth America ranks US cities according to the degree to which they have strong centres.[55] Urban areas with the weakest centres include Riverside and Anaheim in California; and the Tampa-St. Petersburg-Clearwater area and the West Palm Beach-Boca Raton-Delray Beach area in Florida. The most "centred" region is, perhaps not surprisingly, New York. The other centred urban areas tend to be medium-sized cities with a single strong downtown, such as Springfield, Massachusetts.

The Brookings Institution studied the degree to which jobs were located in the main downtown or were decentralized in the one hundred largest US metropolitan areas.[56] Findings were similar to SGA's: the cities with the most significant centres included New York, Boston, San Francisco, Pittsburgh, and Portland-Vancouver; the cities with the most dispersed employment included Los Angeles, Detroit, Tampa-St. Petersburg-Clearwater, and Riverside (California). It was found that, on average, across the one hundred cities, only 22 percent of people worked within a three-mile radius of the city centre – the remaining 78 percent of jobs were located elsewhere in the urban region.

In Canada, there is scant comparable nation-wide research that assesses the degree to which our cities have viable centres. However, census data show that employment has been growing in suburban areas much more rapidly than in central municipalities. Between 1981 and 2001, the number of jobs in Canadian central municipalities increased by 300,000, or 7 percent. In the same period, suburban employment increased by 1.2 million, or 63 percent. In 2001, 3 million people worked in suburban municipalities, and 4.9 million worked in central cities.[57]

This information does not tell us about the pattern of development, particularly the degree to which new employment growth is either concentrated in centres or scattered across an urban region. This has been assessed for some individual cities, however. In the Toronto urban area, strong centres exist in the older urban fabric. In the 1950s and 1960s, high-density, mixed-use centres on subway lines were the result of a deliberate planning policy. These centres continue to evolve and develop today.

More recently, a key element of planning policy has been the creation of mixed-use, denser centres across the Toronto urban region and, particularly, in the newer, post-1980s suburban areas. Most of these new centres have not materialized, despite having been entrenched in planning policy for many years.[58] Much development has been occurring in the municipalities where these centres have been identified, but it does not take hold within the centres themselves: "Of the numerous nodes that have been designated by various planning agencies, only a few have taken shape and only four have achieved substantial levels of development."[59] A study of six major Canadian cities finds that, despite the fact that each region had in place plans to promote the concentration of activity in centres, none of the designated centres had seen significant levels of employment growth, with the exception of two in the Toronto region.[60] In fact, it often seems that development takes place everywhere but in the designated centres. Upon closer inspection, one can see why this might be the unintended result of policy, as discussed in subsequent chapters.

Urban Transportation

As noted above, a central component of the rationale for compact, mixed urban form lies in its potential to change urban transportation patterns and to reduce environmental impacts. Particularly, one goal is to decrease auto dependence and to increase the use of other modes of travel, such as walking, cycling, and transit. If planning policy has been successful in moving urban form towards more compact forms, we would expect to see related improvements in transportation and travel patterns within cities.

In Canada, between 1989 and 1999, the total amount of transit travel has remained virtually constant (at 23 billion passenger-kilometres per year). At the same time, urban auto travel increased by 7 percent and, in 1999, stood at 266 billion passenger-kilometres per year. Transit is therefore declining as a share of total urban travel, accounting for about 8 percent of urban passenger-kilometres in 1999.[61]

In six major urban areas, the share of trips taken on transit has been steady or declining in all but one – Vancouver – which showed a modest increase between 1994 and 2004.[62] In the Toronto region, travel by transit for the morning peak period fell from 22 percent of all trips in 1986 to 16 percent in 2001.[63] Particularly in fast-growing regions, investment in transit systems has lagged behind investment in roads. Combined with the vast majority of growth taking place in low-density, auto-oriented suburbs, the falling modal shares for transit are not surprising. In addition, the total number of vehicles on the road has been going up. In 1975, there were 11 million vehicles on the road in Canada, compared to 19 million in 2004.[64] In the Toronto area alone, it is projected that the number of vehicles will increase from 3.7 million to 5.6 million by 2031 – almost 2 million more cars.[65]

In the United States, the pattern is similar. The number of vehicles increased from 127 million in 1975 to 231 million in 2005.[66] Car passenger-kilometres travelled increased from 4 trillion in 1980 to 7.2 trillion in 2005.[67] Vehicle-kilometres travelled increased from 2.25 trillion in 1980 to 4.4 trillion in 2005.[68] Since 1980, distances driven have grown three times faster than the US population and almost twice as fast as the number of vehicles.[69] Between 1980 and 2000, travel within cities has increased 95 percent, compared to 61 percent for rural travel.[70] In 2000, 61 percent of all roadway travel was urban and 39 percent rural.[71] While auto travel has been rising steadily, travel by transit has shown a more variable trend. Transit ridership declined in absolute terms in the first half of the 1990s, then rebounded in the latter half to level off in the first years of this decade.[72] By 2003, about 9 billion trips per year were taken by transit.[73] The US trend in transit ridership is compared with urban roadway travel in Figure 5.1.[74]

Given steady increases in auto travel and fluctuating or stable levels in transit ridership, the not surprising outcome is that transit's share of total travel has been falling – from 1.2 percent of all person-miles travelled to just about 1 percent in 2004 – "one of the lowest historical levels."[75] When only urban person-miles travelled is used as the base for calculating transit modal share (as opposed to national figures, which include rural travel), the current US transit modal share estimate rises to about 1.75 percent.[76]

Using either measure, it is clear that transit is currently playing only a small role in urban transportation at the national level. Furthermore, it has failed to make substantial gains in modal share since 1990. There are many factors that could account for these trends, including general economic conditions, investment levels in transit versus roads, as well as whether urban form has adapted to better support transit ridership and investment.

Figure 5.1

Rates of change in transit ridership and vehicle miles travelled, United States

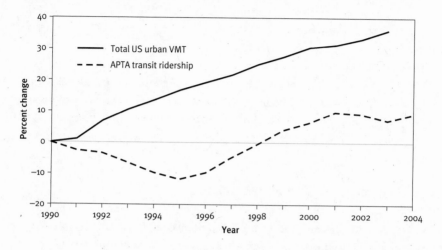

Source: Polzin and Chu, "A Closer Look at Public Transportation Mode Share Trends," 2.

Whatever the causes of the lack of progress, this aspect of the planning vision has failed to materialize in any significant way in recent decades.

Plans and Reality: Are We There Yet?

In municipalities and city-regions across North America, there has been a sustained, decades-old campaign to put an end to urban sprawl. It has been largely based on defining sprawl as costly and on policy responses that rely heavily on various kinds of regulation as well as on an alternative urban design vision. In other words, sprawl is seen and addressed as a planning problem with planning solutions. Regardless of the specific approach – new urbanist or smart growth or others – the ultimate objective has been to alter the pattern of physical evolution of cities to one that is more sustainable – economically, socially, and environmentally. Yet, as the preceding review of development patterns and trends shows, there is little evidence that this campaign has actually led to concrete changes to urban form of the magnitude necessary to reap the benefits of compact development.

With the exception of some minor changes to development trends, and in the vast majority of cities, development continues along the trajectory established decades ago. Patterns and trends in urban growth have been remarkably similar across North American cities. The vast majority of new housing, offices, manufacturing and distribution centres, and shops have been built on greenfields lands at or beyond the urban fringe. Some redevelopment within the already built-up area has occurred in many cities, but, typically, this is a small proportion of overall urban growth. Most new urban development has proceeded and will, under current trends and circumstances, continue to proceed at the urban fringe, on previously undeveloped land, at low densities, with little mixing of different land uses, and with a traditional postwar suburban-style street system. In short, while the planning vision may have evolved in recent decades, the way in which our cities continue to grow has not. Planning has not been achieving its vision – physical or otherwise.

Double Whammy: Paying for Sprawl and Planning

At this time in Canada, because we have an elaborate, multi-tiered planning superstructure, we are incurring substantial planning costs – both direct and indirect – in the name of curbing sprawl. But because this campaign has not proven very effective, we are at the same time incurring the not insignificant costs of sprawl. In other words, the benefits of planning are largely unrealized because it has failed to significantly alter land use, urban development, and transportation patterns. Meanwhile, we continue to incur the costs of planning. We are in the unenviable position of paying both for planning and for sprawl – a double whammy.

What is also implied is the need for a more sophisticated approach, one that might actually achieve the long-touted benefits of curbing sprawl but produce them more efficiently than has so far been the case. This means not only reducing the direct costs of planning through more efficient planning but also addressing the potential costs of market distortion, such as higher housing prices. It means actually achieving changes to urban development patterns and finally realizing the cost savings and other benefits that accompany that altered pattern. In order to have any hope of altering urban development patterns, it is necessary to address a fundamental problem: both the anti-sprawl planning approach and the pro-sprawl laissez-faire approach have thus far ignored the hidden subsidies and market distortions that drive urban sprawl.

6

Prices Drive Sprawl

The planning approach holds that sprawl is an undesirable and costly urban form. The solution to this problem is to change the urban form to a less costly and more desirable one by mandating an alternative set of regulations, sometimes along with more strategic infrastructure investment. While the conventional approach to sprawl focuses considerably on its economic costs, it looks surprisingly little towards the possible role of economic factors in driving sprawl or towards potential economic solutions. Meanwhile, the sprawl promoters tout a laissez-faire approach to the market, maintaining that the market is already doing a good job of responding to consumer demand for housing and that little intervention is required.

First, it should be said that, by and large, economists have not focused much on the issue of sprawl.[1] The arguments of those who have done so suggest that the planning approach frames the problem incorrectly and misidentifies causes and solutions.

Suburbanization as a Market Process

Not surprisingly, economists see urban growth in its many forms, including suburbanization, primarily as a market process. The spatial expansion of cities occurs when, at the urban fringe, urban uses pay more for land than do agricultural uses. Economists would say that this is not only appropriate but also efficient. The reason urban uses outbid agriculture is that they are the more productive, and the market is simply doing its job of ensuring that resources are put to their most productive uses, guaranteeing efficient allocation. This is the "highest-and-best-use" rationale that we hear so often in land development.

In this view, suburbanization is the necessary and appropriate response of the market to a set of demand conditions. Economists often attribute the spatial growth of cities to three underlying forces: (1) population growth, (2) rising household incomes, and (3) falling commuting costs.[2] Population growth necessitates the spatial expansion of urban boundaries, and rising incomes lead to demands for more space – both land and building. Spatial expansion is further reinforced by the "rent gradient," that is, the fact that land at the urban edge is generally cheaper than more centrally located land. Investments in transportation infrastructure make travel faster and cheaper, reducing the cost of commuting.[3] Jobs then follow the labour force to the suburbs, initiating further cycles of decentralization.

The confluence of these factors is viewed as the "natural evolution" theory of suburbanization: driven by these factors, suburbanization represents the natural evolution of cities.[4] Another theory suggests that suburbanization and decentralization result from forces that push people, jobs, and development away from the central city. These are primarily social and fiscal forces, such as high taxes, low-quality public schools, racial tensions, crime, and low environmental quality.[5] These forces push those who can afford to leave to the suburbs, where they establish socioeconomically homogeneous neighbourhoods, further debilitating the centre and perpetuating a cycle of inner-city decline and suburban expansion. This is often called the "flight-from-blight" theory of suburbanization, or its more racially oriented version, "white flight."

Mieszkowski and Mills note that these theories are not mutually exclusive but, rather, can interact in complex ways. For example, an initial suburbanization of wealthy households precipitates the beginning of the push factors, setting up a downward cycle for the inner city in conjunction with suburbanization at the edge. They conclude that the factors involved in both the natural evolution and flight-from-blight theories play a role in suburbanization. Mieszkowski and Mills describe the forces that drive the process of suburbanization. If a more narrow view is taken, with sprawl defined as a particular subset of forms of suburbanization, then these factors would not be considered drivers. They may form the backdrop to urban growth, the demand for new development, and the expansion of the urbanized area, but there is no *necessary* linkage between these factors and the specific form of urban sprawl.

Sprawl as Excessive Suburbanization

To economists, the spatial expansion of cities is a logical response to increasing demand, technological advancement, and increasing wealth, with no particular inherent cause for concern. However, they also argue that it is possible that too much suburbanization can take place. Brueckner defines sprawl as the "excessive spatial growth of cities": "The key word in this definition is excessive. Although cities must grow spatially to accommodate an expanding population, the claim is that too much spatial growth occurs. If this allegation is correct, current public policies should be altered to restrict the spatial expansion of cities."[6]

In other words, it is possible to have suburbanization and decentralization without sprawl – that is, it is possible to have a right amount of suburbanization. This differs with some planning definitions of sprawl, which assert that all suburbanization is sprawl. Perceived causes of sprawl are of course related to how sprawl is defined. If sprawl and suburbanization or decentralization are taken as synonymous, then all causes of suburbanization are causes of sprawl. If sprawl is seen as only a particular subset of suburbanization and decentralization, in those cases when suburbanization is excessive, then the potential causes are more limited or different.

Sprawl as the Result of Market Failure

Given that economists view the physical evolution of cities primarily as a market process, it is not surprising that they look to the market for explanations when urban growth goes wrong. Whereas suburbanization and decentralization are the result of the market simply responding effectively to demands shaped by natural evolution forces, sprawl is seen as the result of market failure: "Economists use the term market failure to describe a situation in which the invisible hand fails to allocate resources in a socially desirable manner, so as to maximize aggregate economic well-being. Market failure arises when economic agents face incentives that are distorted because of institutional failings or some other reason, leading to economic outcomes that are bad from society's point of view."[7]

Market distortions and market failure are thus seen as the key explanations for sprawl. Market distortions can arise from a variety of sources, such as subsidies, regulations, or specific financial instruments. Brueckner, for example, mentions the effect of property tax in reducing the intensity of land development.[8] Mills emphasizes the fact that motor vehicle use in urban areas is "vastly underpriced."[9]

Planning explanations of sprawl note the direct impact that land-use regulations have in promoting sprawl. In other words, minimum setback, maximum density, and other regulations are a direct cause of more land being consumed than would otherwise be the case. Economic explanations of sprawl see zoning and other forms of land-use regulation playing an important role, too, as they distort the property market. For example, overly rigorous zoning requirements distort the market by limiting supply in urbanized areas, causing property prices to increase and pushing development further outward.[10]

Moreover, the combination of the use of local taxes and land-use regulation can add further stimulus to sprawl. For example, relying on the property tax for revenue, municipalities begin to create a land-use regulation framework that excludes uses that are perceived to place a burden on municipal resources, while encouraging those that are perceived to be lucrative. This "fiscalization of land use" means that certain types of uses that are perceived to place high demand on services are excluded (e.g., lower-income housing) and that other high-revenue uses are sought (e.g., industrial, commercial). This effect is often transparent and is evident in municipalities that require the submission of a fiscal impact statement in conjunction with development proposals. Excluded or pre-empted uses are displaced, forced to other, usually more suburban, locations.

Brueckner identifies three market failures in particular that are critical to promoting sprawl, each one a form of negative externality. The first is the failure to account for the social value of open space. Suburbanization, by definition, involves the conversion of former agricultural or natural lands to urban uses. This open space had social value that was lost in that process, and this cost to society is not reflected in the price of land. The second is that the market fails to account for the social costs of congestion (i.e., the cost that my trip imposes on everyone else by slowing them down). The third is that developers do not pay the full infrastructure costs that their development induces. The failure to pay for these costs means that the development "appears artificially cheap from the developer's point of view, encouraging excessive urban growth."[11] In other words, it is these unpaid-for externalities that are the source of market failure and that lead to excessive use of land.

Sprawl as Urban Development That Generates Net Costs

Another way of saying this is to say that negative externalities associated with urban development generate net social costs. In other words, because of negative externalities, the costs to society of urban expansion are greater than the benefits. For example, Mills maintains that "suburban growth would be excessive if it imposed higher costs on society than would corresponding central city growth – that is, if the growth were occurring in the wrong places."[12] Wassmer attempts a greater level of specificity when he suggests that the economists' view is that excessive decentralization occurs "when further decentralization imposes greater net marginal costs on everyone in the metropolitan area than if the development had remained more centralized."[13]

Note that the above definitions are relative in nature. Sprawl is defined as a development pattern that causes a higher level of net costs than do alternatives (such as, say, the status quo or compact development). This is because, at present, virtually all typical forms of urban development will, to some degree, generate net social costs. Even compact development will cause net costs because it will also incur negative externalities: it, too, could add to congestion, air pollution, or infrastructure costs (though it would not diminish the social value of open space if it took the form of reurbanization). Still, as the costs-of-sprawl research has shown, compact development would be expected to have lower costs than would sprawling alternatives.

Defining sprawl in terms of its *relative* costs presents some problems at a practical level. In particular, how are we to readily differentiate sprawl from other forms of urban development? With planning definitions, based as they are on urban form, we can identify sprawl easily enough by its physical features – a certain measurable density level or land-use pattern, for example. But with economic definitions, we attempt to identify sprawl by its cost characteristics. This is a bit like using a spreadsheet to identify an elephant. How will we know if a particular urban development pattern is sprawl or not? Where is the cut-off point? When does sprawl stop and not-sprawl start?

The most obvious thing to do, of course, is to undertake a comprehensive analysis of the costs and benefits of a development option or options. A comprehensive analysis does pose some challenges, particularly with regard to evaluating the external costs, for which clear monetary values do not currently exist and must be estimated. However, the costs of some externalities are becoming more apparent with, for example, the introduction of carbon taxes and emissions trading schemes or congestion tolls. At present, analyses that include direct infrastructure revenues are rare. This is not to say that they cannot be done or should not be attempted. There are many instances in which a comprehensive cost-benefit analysis is workable and, indeed, necessary, and in many cases they are undertaken as part of the planning process: large-scale planning; urban, metropolitan, or regional plans; annexations; new subdivisions; expansions of urban areas. At this scale, the costs of servicing and externalities are so substantial that the expense of conducting a cost-benefit study would be insignificant in comparison and would more than likely pay for itself several times over in resulting savings (assuming, of course, that the lower-cost development option is the one that is implemented).

It has been suggested that, in the absence of a cost-benefit analysis, one might be able to definitively link certain development patterns or urban form characteristics with certain predictable cost characteristics. For example, Wassmer suggests that "everyone knows there are types of metropolitan decentralization in which the private and social costs ... are greater than the private and social benefits it generates."[14] Indeed, it would be a useful shorthand if we could create "a specific canon that identifies a type of suburbanization that fails such a benefit/cost test."[15]

The problem is, as already noted, due to unpriced negative externalities such as those mentioned by Brueckner, virtually all forms of development can be expected to impose some level of net costs. So, in order to identify sprawl, one would need to know not only that net costs are incurred but also the relative level of those costs. And this is not really possible where net costs are concerned. A cost-benefit analysis would typically include any revenues generated from development (impact fees or property taxes, for example). But, while some costs and benefits do exhibit predictable causal relationships with urban form, revenues have no *necessary* relationship with it. Prices are policy-driven and depend simply on how (or whether) they are set by the price-setters. They may bear a relationship to cost or benefits, or they may not.

At a practical level, about the best one could do is to rely only on the fairly predictable linkages between urban form and cost levels – particularly with infrastructure costs and externalities. Some benefits also have clear linkages with urban form, though they can be difficult to evaluate (e.g., perceived access to the countryside). This is the kind of work that planners and others have been undertaking in relation to the costs of sprawl (though, as is shown in Chapter 3, with less emphasis on the benefits side). However, this does not alleviate the problem of the relative nature of the economic definition based on net social costs: one town's sprawl is another town's compact development. These economic definitions make it difficult to identify sprawl in a practical way.

Economic Solutions to Sprawl

Economists see land-use regulation, whether intentionally or unintentionally, as contributing to sprawl by limiting supply and density and, in so doing, distorting property markets and generating additional costs. Similarly, they are not fond of urban growth boundaries as a solution to sprawl, claiming that they inflict further distortionary effects upon the market, such as increased house prices (some of which are discussed in Chapter 4).[16] The problem with UGBs lies in the inability to set exactly the right size of boundary: a too-tight boundary would lead to house price rises and excessive densification, while a too-loose boundary would not have the intended effect at all.[17]

It is not surprising, then, that economists' proposals to curb sprawl focus on economic instruments and, in particular, on better pricing. Mills, for example, suggests that the most effective approach to curbing sprawl would be to correct the underpricing of urban transportation. He estimates that, if actual transportation costs were covered (including opportunity cost of the land, road operating costs, and depreciation), an appropriate charge would be a fuel tax of $2.50 per US gallon (about five times the existing level).[18]

Wassmer, Brueckner, and other urban economists think that negative externalities are at the heart of the sprawl problem. They think that the household or business operator only considers private costs and benefits when making decisions about development, not the public costs they might incur. The economists' solution to sprawl is, therefore, to correct this market failure, removing the distortion in order to bring the market back to operating efficiently. This is accomplished by charging a price that represents the cost of the externalities, thereby "internalizing" the costs within the price and making them part of the development decision. Brueckner, for example, recommends charging a development tax on land converted from agricultural to urban use in order to compensate for the lost social value of open space, charging congestion tolls, as well as charging impact or development fees in order to ensure that new development pays for all its infrastructure costs. The expectation is that, when prices reflect the external costs of development decisions, different decisions will be made and the "excessive" nature of urban development will be curbed.

Not surprisingly, economists favour market solutions to sprawl. Of course, planners, environmentalists, and others also recognize the need to charge for negative externalities, and they often suggest this as an antidote to sprawl, along with other regulatory measures.

Sprawl Is Inefficient

Economic definitions of sprawl have merits and, perhaps, are less value-laden and subjective than are planning definitions. However, relying as they do on an assessment of development-related costs, even in a best case scenario in which a comprehensive cost-benefit analysis is undertaken, their relative nature allows us only to say which development pattern is less costly (i.e., most benign or least harmful) overall. But is the best option actually efficient? We still don't know. At best, these definitions allow us to say that, from a social welfare perspective, one development pattern is better than another. However, even the best option can still be inefficient, representing a misallocation of resources.

By aggregating public and private costs and benefits at the metropolitan level, these definitions obscure some important details. For example, home-buyers will make a particular purchasing decision based on private costs and benefits. If their private benefits are greater than their private costs, then they will go ahead and purchase a house. Ultimately, it is these individual decisions, replicated over and over and over, that determine urban development patterns.

The problem is that, inevitably, the householders' own cost-benefit analyses are skewed by the fact that they are able to successfully deflect a portion of the costs they incur elsewhere. This deflection takes place primarily through two mechanisms.

First, as already noted by economists and others, their decision creates external costs – congestion, GHG emissions, and the like – for which they do not pay. In the absence of pricing mechanisms that internalize these costs, they are deflected from the individual and paid by society as a whole. Second, cross-subsidies can occur in relation to payment for land and buildings, infrastructure and services (what we have called "urban goods and services"), as well as externalities. Though unlike most externalities, these services (such as water, sewers, roads, electricity, etc.) are currently priced and paid for and do have revenues attached to them. For these urban goods and services, the fact that households can transfer a part of the private financial cost their development decisions precipitates to other households, where it becomes part of their private costs, is not revealed in these definitions. They focus on the aggregate of private costs versus aggregate private benefits, which may balance out. But this overall outcome can pertain even though each household does not pay its own real costs: some households pay more than the costs they incur, while others pay less. In other words, cross-subsidies can occur within the metropolitan region, and the economic definitions of sprawl offered so far do not adequately recognize their critical role.

So even if, for the metropolitan area as a whole, infrastructure revenues covered infrastructure costs, private benefits exceeded private costs, and externalities were paid for to bring net costs to zero, even then an individual household or business may not pay at a level that reflects the costs it incurs, thus creating cross-subsidies. Property taxes, for example, rarely correspond to the actual level of municipal costs a household or business incurs. There are infinite cross-subsidies, with some paying taxes that exceed the costs they incur and with others paying less.

When households and businesses do not pay for the costs they incur, when they pay either too much or too little – that is, when cross-subsidies occur – the result is an inefficient allocation of resources and inefficient urban development patterns. This can be true even if, as a whole, externalities are charged for. It is not enough for the total costs of externalities to be charged, each actor must also be charged in proportion to the costs he or she incurs. This is what is needed in order to achieve the efficient allocation of resources, such as land, building, infrastructure, or services.

Urban Form, Costs, and Prices

What does it mean to say that each actor must be charged in proportion to the costs she or he incurs? An accepted economic principle is that prices should reflect marginal costs. Marginal cost is the cost of providing one additional unit, such as the additional servicing costs associated with building one more housing unit. Setting prices at marginal costs is a precondition to achieving the efficient use of scarce resources, what economists would call "allocative efficiency."[19]

Setting prices at marginal costs means, in general, that prices should reflect actual costs incurred as these costs may vary. Economists often focus on the fact that costs may vary with the quantity of an item produced. In the context of pricing as it relates to urban development – for example, the pricing of housing, municipal services, utilities, or transportation – costs also vary with urban form factors such as density or location. In order to ensure the efficient use of resources, these urban-form-related cost variations must be accurately reflected in prices. This means that prices should accurately reflect not only the usage of a particular service but also the infrastructure costs precipitated by any given user, including amortized capital costs as well as operating and maintenance costs. Using water as an example, the price should reflect both the amount of water used as well as the marginal capital, maintenance, and operating costs of treatment facilities, pumping stations, and pipes needed to deliver the water to the customer. The infrastructure costs precipitated by any single customer will depend, in part, on factors such as the location of the customer vis-à-vis central facilities as well as her/his type of housing unit and size of lot.

When prices do not reflect marginal costs, price signals misfire, demand is skewed, and misallocation of resources can result. Too little or too much spending can take place, as can over- or under-investment in infrastructure. When prices are artificially low, demand and consumption are inflated, resulting in pressure to overbuild infrastructure. Prices can be set below marginal costs, with the shortfall being picked up through other means. Water rates, for example, are frequently set below marginal costs,[20] with general property taxes or other financial means making up the difference. Or prices are commonly set at average costs. While marginal cost refers to the cost of that last unit at the margin, average cost refers to the cost of all the units divided by the total number of units. When prices are based on average cost, but costs actually vary, some consumers will overpay and some will underpay, creating cross-subsidies between the groups. These cross-subsidies are inherent in the price, and, generally, the consumer is unaware that they exist.

> Costs vary with urban form, especially the location of development, density, local context, and type of land use. If prices do not reflect costs as they vary with these elements of urban form, then market distortions and inefficiencies occur. The result is overspending on infrastructure, land, and buildings and, of particular interest in the current context, inefficient urban development patterns, or sprawl.

So costs vary with urban form, especially the location of development, local context, density, and type of land use. If prices do not reflect actual costs *as they vary with these elements of urban form*, then market distortions and inefficiencies occur. The result is overspending on infrastructure, land, and buildings as well as – and this is of particular interest in the current context – inefficient urban development patterns or sprawl. Indeed, we have seen in Chapter 3 considerable evidence that over-expensive infrastructure is one of the major costs of sprawl.

Oates notes the role of accurate prices (in this case regarding property "tax-prices") in promoting effective decision making:

> a critical function of a tax system is to provide an accurate set of signals, or "tax-prices," that make clear to local taxpayer-voters the costs of public programs on which they must make decisions. In a local context, this implies

that the local tax system should generate tax bills that are highly visible and that provide a reasonable indication of costs so that individuals have a clear sense of the financial commitment implied by proposed programs of public expenditure. If taxes are largely hidden or don't reflect the cost of local services, they are unlikely to provide the information needed for good fiscal decisions.[21]

This argument applies not only to the prices charged through property taxes but also to the prices attached to all other elements that affect urban development patterns, such as development charges, utility prices, user fees, parking charges, and so on. When services related to urban development are mis-priced and the actual cost variations between development types and locations are not captured, the real cost implications of choosing between development alternatives are not apparent to either the consumer or the developer. When property taxes, development charges, water rates, hydro rates, parking charges, auto insurance charges, and so on do not reflect levels of cost incurred as these vary with consumption, location, density, local context, or land use, then they can skew decision making on both the demand and supply sides of the equation. This causes homebuyers to demand more inefficient forms of development than they otherwise might and causes developers to supply them more often than they otherwise might (i.e., if accurate pricing prevailed).

The City as a Distorted Price System

Mis-pricing of urban goods and services is a second type of market failure. While economists emphasize the role of externalities in contributing to sprawl, the mis-pricing of urban goods and services is rarely mentioned, nor is its critical role recognized. One early writer who did see the importance of prices in shaping how cities evolve and grow was Wilbur Thompson. In 1968, he urged us to consider "the city as a distorted price system."[22] He noted that the failure to use price – as an *explicit* system – was at the root of many urban problems, including urban sprawl. Thompson rightly identified the role of a number of distorted prices in shaping city form, such as the use of flat prices to pay for sewer and water infrastructure and the lack of congestion pricing. There are many more examples, not only relating to externalities but also with respect to urban goods and services that households and businesses pay for every day. Thompson's ideas are echoed by Mills, who remarks that it is all about pricing: "Every market failure reflects a failure of governments to get prices right."[23]

Sprawl as an Inefficient Land-Use Pattern

For our purposes, sprawl can be defined as an inefficient land-use pattern. It embodies a misallocation of resources that is wasteful, using resources that could have been put to more productive uses. It occurs when prices for urban goods, infrastructure, and services do not reflect marginal costs as they vary with urban form.

Note that, with this definition, it is possible to have suburbanization without sprawl, or urban decentralization without sprawl: these terms are not synonymous. Whether a particular land-use pattern is efficient or inefficient depends on the actual costs of development and on whether those who generate the costs pay for them. If they do pay the true costs as they vary with urban form, then no misallocation occurs.

> Sprawl can be defined as an inefficient land-use pattern. It embodies a misallocation of resources that is wasteful, consuming resources that could have been put to more productive uses. It occurs when prices for urban goods, infrastructure, and services do not reflect marginal costs, as they vary with urban form.

How will we know, in practice, whether this condition is met? How will we know when any given urban development pattern can accurately be called sprawl? We need to look both at the costs for the urban goods and services that comprise development and location decisions, as they vary with urban form, and compare the prices charged for those urban goods and services.

On the costs side, we know from research to date on the costs of sprawl that certain urban form factors are known to be determinants of cost. Additional evidence of the influence of urban form factors on the cost of different types of urban infrastructure and services is presented in Part 3. Chief among these are density, location, local context, type of land use, and contiguity of development pattern. Other factors that likely influence costs but whose impact has been less studied to date include mix of uses and the presence of nodes or centres.

On the pricing side, we need to check that the prices charged for those urban goods and services accurately reflect cost variations associated with urban form. When costs vary with density, prices should vary with density. When costs vary with the type of urban use, prices should vary with the type of urban use. When costs vary with location, prices should vary with location. Where prices do not reflect costs, inefficient development occurs.

There are a few common pricing flaws that tend to be repeated over and over, leading to inefficient urban development patterns (see Part 3). These common pricing flaws provide tangible clues regarding whether or not efficient prices are being charged.

A critical question then, in looking for explanations of the persistence of urban sprawl, involves determining whether prices of urban goods and services reflect marginal costs (including capital, operating, and maintenance), as they vary with urban form, for the full range of urban goods and services that forms part of decision making about land use. To this end, chapters 7, 8, and 9 review the relationship between costs and "prices" in their many forms in order to assess the degree to which prices for the many urban goods and services that shape development decisions and patterns accurately reflect their costs. Other government policies and programs that affect decision making and urban development patterns are also reviewed. Chapter 7 begins with a review of costs and prices for municipal services, particularly development charges and property taxes.

> In looking for explanations of the persistence of urban sprawl, a critical question involves determining whether – for the range of urban goods and services that forms part of decision making about land use – prices reflect marginal costs as they vary with urban form.

The examples explored below are mostly drawn from Toronto, Ontario, and other Canadian contexts. However, they represent financing tools and other programs that are common across North American jurisdictions as well as in Australasia and Europe. While the specifics of individual policies may vary from place to place, the analysis is broadly applicable.

PART 3

SUBSIDIES, CROSS-SUBSIDIES, AND MIS-INCENTIVES
How Public Policy Finances Sprawl

7 Municipal Services Costs and Prices

In North America, property tax and development charges (often called impact fees in the United States) are important financial tools used by municipalities to finance urban growth, maintain and operate infrastructure, and provide services. Do the "prices" charged under the property tax and development charges for these services meet the efficiency test, supporting efficient development patterns? That is, do they reflect marginal costs as they vary with location, local context, density, and land use?

Development Charges

Development charges (DCs) are charges imposed by a municipality to cover the one-time costs associated with new development – the capital costs of hard infrastructure, such as roads, water and sewer networks, transit networks, and vehicles. In addition, they can be applied against "soft" service costs, such as ambulance stations, fire stations, schools, or community facilities. DCs usually only cover the costs of network infrastructure outside the subdivision – so-called "off-site" costs, such as arterial or collector roads. Infrastructure within the subdivision, such as local roads, is typically installed directly by the developer and ownership is assumed by the municipality upon completion of construction.

The way DCs work is that the capital costs associated with anticipated growth within a municipality are estimated. These costs are then apportioned among the anticipated development. In Ontario, this typically means that there is a charge per dwelling unit. This varies by the kind of residence, with highest charges for single detached homes to lesser charges for apartments. Commercial space is charged on a per-square-metre basis – so many dollars for every square metre of building constructed.

The charges can be substantial. For example, in the City of Mississauga (a suburban Toronto community of 680,000), total charges for a small apartment are $8,177.43, for larger apartments they are $14,167.59, and for houses they are $19,159.09.[1] For industrial buildings, a total charge of $68.72 per square metre is applied, and $88.53 per square metre is levied for other non-residential buildings, such as stores or offices.[2] These high amounts are not surprising as infrastructure is expensive.

The adoption of DCs was intended, in part, to be an improvement upon the old way of doing things, when growth-related infrastructure was paid for out of general municipal taxation revenues. They are thus heralded as making "growth pay for growth," and, to some extent, this is true, though some costs are excluded by law.[3] In this sense, the fact that they are in place in many cities and towns is good news. Many other jurisdictions, particularly in the United States, do not use impact fees. Unfortunately, where they exist they are usually poorly structured, so they act as a source of hidden subsidy to sprawl. There are several ways in which this occurs, and these are detailed below.

Low-Cost Areas Subsidize High-Cost Areas

Residential DCs are typically levied according to the type of unit, irrespective of its location within the city. They do not take into account how infrastructure costs may vary from neighbourhood to neighbourhood. There are many reasons why variations may occur, such as soil conditions, geology or topography, distance to central facilities such as treatment plants, or existing capacity. Not only are costs likely to vary between older urban areas and greenfields sites but they can also vary substantially even between different greenfields expansion areas within a municipality.

Compare the case of a new townhouse to be built in an older urban area with a new townhouse of the same size to be built on a greenfields site, bearing in mind that DCs are most often the same regardless of location. In the former case, the townhouse can use existing roads, sewer and water networks, possibly schools, and add riders to existing transit routes, potentially allowing service improvements over time; in the latter case, all necessary infrastructure must be constructed from scratch, including roads, sewer and water networks, electrical utilities, community centres, and schools.

The costs are very likely to be significantly lower in the older urban area and substantially higher in the greenfields area. But the DC is the same.

What this does is overcharge the new townhouse built within the older neighbourhood and undercharge the townhouse built on greenfields land. A cross-subsidy occurs through the DC, with the townhouse in the mature neighbourhood subsidizing the townhouse on greenfields land. The cost differentials can be substantial. In the City of Ottawa, DCs are based on house type but also vary by zone within the city. There is one charge for development "within the greenbelt" (essentially the already-urbanized part of the city) and another for development "outside the greenbelt" (essentially on greenfields). In Ottawa, the charges more closely reflect the actual servicing cost variations between already-urbanized land and greenfields. The DC in the former case is about $11,200 per single or semi-detached unit compared to about $20,000 for each unit outside the greenbelt.[4] In other words, the actual costs to develop on greenfields lands are about 80 percent higher than are those to develop on already-urbanized land, a difference of about $8,800 per house in this case. To its credit, the City of Ottawa approach recognizes these significant cost variations, but those of most municipalities do not. The norm is to have a standard charge for each unit type, regardless of where within the city development occurs and regardless of significant cost variations.

Small Lots Subsidize Large Lots

As noted above, the DC is usually based on the type of house. But the cost of hard services – water, sewer, roads, transit – is more directly related to the size of the lot (i.e., density). A detached house on a lot that is twenty feet wide pays the same charge as a house on a sixty-foot-wide lot. Yet, the actual costs associated with the sixty-foot lot are significantly higher than those for the twenty footer. The difference in lot size may seem insignificant, and if we were talking about one house or even a few it might indeed be. However, about 100,000 new single detached houses are constructed every year in Canadian urban centres – over thirty years this will mean 3 million new homes.[5] When one considers the cumulative impact of larger lots, multiplied over hundreds of thousands of new units as cities grow, the implications are clear for regional capital costs – more kilometres of regional roads, water, and sewer pipes than would otherwise be needed.

Even though the DC is applied against the costs of infrastructure that are outside the subdivision itself, there is a clear relationship between the lot size and the local pattern of development, on the one hand, and the costs of off-site infrastructure (i.e., the municipal infrastructure that links individual subdivisions and forms the framework for the city, such as arterial roads and the underlying sewer and water networks), on the other. Many studies looking at how the costs of infrastructure vary with urban form focus only on the infrastructure costs internal to a new development or subdivision and so end up significantly underestimating the impact of urban form on development costs. But larger lot sizes mean lower local development densities, which increases the overall area of the city, requiring longer pipe lengths for off-site as well as for on-site infrastructure. Using the average-cost-per-housing-type approach to DCs creates a situation in which smaller lot properties, which contribute less to demand for off-site infrastructure, are cross-subsidizing larger, higher-than-average-cost lots. Perversely, the more efficient house ends up subsidizing the inefficient house – akin to a Smart car subsidizing a Hummer.

Smaller Residential Units Subsidize Larger Units

DCs are often arrived at by allocating costs on the basis of the average number of persons per unit, as this varies between different house types. However, this methodology ignores the fact that, for network infrastructure, the density of development itself has as significant an impact on infrastructure costs as does occupancy levels. For example, a one-hundred-unit apartment building will account for much lower demand for linear infrastructure on a per unit basis than will one hundred single detached units. Yet, the charge only considers how the variations in average occupancy levels affect infrastructure needs, not the impact of the development pattern itself – specifically, net density. So, even though charges tend to be lower for smaller unit types than for larger types, they would be lower still if a better methodology for setting the charge levels were used – one that took into account how cost causation is influenced by urban form itself.

A separate issue relates to education levies. A DC is often imposed to fund the construction of new schools needed to support new urban growth. But here the charge is often set at the same amount for all units in all areas. However, smaller units, such as apartments, are less likely to contain children than are larger apartments and, especially, houses. For example, in York Region, a charge of $1,670 per unit is imposed by the York Region School Board, regardless of the type of unit – single detached or apartment. However, in York Region, single and semi-detached houses have, on average, 3.6 persons per unit, compared to 2.9 for row houses, 2.1 for larger apartments, and 1.5 for smaller apartments.[6] Larger units are likely being undercharged for new schools, while smaller apartment units are over-charged. These are other perverse instances in which a cross-subsidy occurs, with smaller units subsidizing larger homes.

More Intensive Use of Employment Land Is Discouraged

DCs for new commercial structures are charged on the basis of the building's floor area. While the amount of floorspace in a development may have some impact on infrastructure costs (e.g., affecting the sizing of pipes or traffic generated), the DC does not reflect how the size of the lot itself influences network infrastructure costs. Larger lots require more linear metres of road, pipes, and wires, for example – a factor that is not captured by a DC based on floorspace. Floorspace only partly accounts for levels of infrastructure costs generated.

Moreover, by charging for every square metre of floorspace, denser development is discouraged: the more you build on a given site, the more you are charged. Charging according to a per-square-metre-of-floor-area-built basis is a distinct disincentive to using land more intensively and efficiently. Again, this policy has exactly the opposite effect of planning policies that call for denser, more compact and efficient land-use patterns.

Uses That Generate Lower Levels of Car Trips Subsidize Uses That Generate Higher Levels of Car Trips

Another example of how DCs provide hidden subsidies to sprawl involves retail and fast food uses. These uses tend to generate high levels of traffic, particularly auto trips. Yet, the non-residential DC is typically set at the same level for all commercial development and is based on the amount of floor area. It does not reflect the significant variations in auto trip generation between different types of employment uses. For example, retail and fast food outlets generate many more trips and, therefore, place much higher demand on roads than does office development. The Institute of Transportation Engineers (ITE) estimates afternoon peak hour trip rates for office buildings at roughly 1 to 3 vehicle trips per 1,000 square feet of floorspace, compared to 3 to 14 vehicle trips for every 1,000 square feet of shopping centre, and 26 vehicle trips per 1,000 square feet of fast food restaurant. By ignoring these significant variations in trip generation, the DC creates a situation in which uses that generate relatively low numbers of trips subsidize those that generate high numbers of trips. It is this disparity that has led some municipalities to implement a different DC for retail uses,[7] but this is the exception rather than the norm.

DCs: Efficient Development Subsidizing Inefficient Development

The essence of the problem with DCs, as typically structured, is that the charge levied does not reflect the actual servicing costs of different types of development in different locations; instead, it is based on the average cost – across a given type of residential unit say, or across all non-residential development. This approach ignores some very significant cost variations. Some types of development will have substantially lower than average costs, and some will have substantially higher; and, in these instances, the lower-cost uses, in effect, end up subsidizing the higher-cost uses.

As illustrated schematically in Figure 7.1, the typical DC systematically overcharges efficient development and undercharges less efficient development. The left arrow shows the amount of overcharging for efficient development, and the right arrow shows the amount of undercharging for inefficient development, given a typical DC. Ironically, especially penalized and most overcharged are the absolutely most efficient uses, such as the small units on small lots on already-urbanized land. Conversely, the most subsidized are the least efficient uses, such as the largest lots on greenfields lands. Moreover, overall infrastructure costs are higher because an inefficient development pattern is encouraged.

If passed through to the consumer, inaccurate DCs can distort the market prices of new homes, offices, stores, and other business premises. Naturally,

Figure 7.1

Actual costs vs. typical development charge

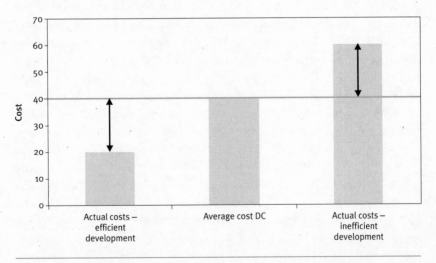

these market prices are key in influencing the choices of home buyers and businesses, and in shaping the nature and level of demand regarding lot sizes, building sizes, and locations of development.

Incidence of Development Charges
The DC is typically paid by the developer or builder at the time the building permit is issued. But is the charge passed along to the final user – in the form of higher house prices or commercial rents, for example – or is it absorbed by the developer or landowner? In other words, what is the "incidence" of the DC? Conventional economic theory assumes that the DC acts in a manner similar to an excise tax. A range of possible outcomes is theoretically possible: the cost of DCs could be passed along to the final consumer in whole, shared by the developer and the consumer, reflected in prices that are greater than the charge itself, or passed backward to the land seller (in whole or in part). The specific outcome depends on the supply and demand conditions prevailing in any given housing market.

Huffman et al. contend that, at least in the short term, when a DC is first introduced, the cost will be shared by the developer and the homebuyer.[8] Yet, they note that the burden can shift back and forth depending on market characteristics. For example, in cases where buyers are insensitive to modest changes in house prices (e.g., in small, isolated markets), the developer can pass the fee along to home buyers. However, in most cases, particularly on the more affordable end of the spectrum, price sensitivity is a reality. Under this condition, Huffman et al. predict that, in the long term, developers will leave the market if DC costs cannot be passed forward. This will reduce supply, which in turn will raise prices, at which point developers will re-enter the market and the DC cost will be passed along to the homebuyer.

Huffman et al. conclude that, in the long term, developers will not absorb the fee cost and will instead seek to shift it backward to landowners or forward to homebuyers. They argue that backwards shifting is not usually possible (though others, such as Ihlanfeldt and Shaughnessy, argue that this may be possible in the long run). They conclude that, "on the whole, the occupants – residents and users – pay the majority of the fees. Landowners may pay a portion, but developers are unlikely to pay any of the fees in the long term."[9] Occupants pay in the form of higher purchase prices or rents, or lower housing quality.

Skaburskis notes, however, that under certain market conditions – especially a hot market in which demand is increasing but supply is limited in the short term and prices are therefore rising – developers absorb the cost of the DC. It comes out of the excess profits that they realize in this market context.[10] However, he also notes that, in the long term, supply will expand, and once again the cost of the DC will be shifted forward to the homebuyer.

A realistic scenario, at least in the Canadian context (where DCs are widespread and have been in place for decades), especially in growing urban areas, is that consumers are price sensitive but that developers are unlikely to abandon growing markets. This is because there are few alternative markets without DCs, and the long lead times characteristic of the land development process present effective barriers to re-entry. Huffman et al. do not explore this scenario. In the long term, however, developer profits would be maintained, so DC costs would either be passed forward in house price increases or quality reductions. It is unlikely that, in a growing market, DC costs could be passed backward to landowners (given fierce competition for developable land).

Recently, another view of the incidence of DCs has emerged, as proposed by Yinger, Ihlanfeldt and Shaughnessy, and others. Rather than treating the DC essentially as an excise tax, this "new view" sees it as a fee for the provision of facilities and amenities that are valued by homebuyers. This view predicts an increase in house prices associated with the DC. Technically, the impact fee is not shifted forward because homebuyers are mobile and could move to non-fee jurisdictions; rather, homebuyers value the amenities that the DC provides, and these benefits are capitalized into the price of the home. The DC is also seen to divert costs from the property tax, lowering taxes from what they would be if the charge was not in place and improvements were, instead, paid for through the property tax. The new view argues that these "savings" in future property taxes can also be capitalized. If the house price increase equals the fee, then neither the developer nor the landowner bears any burden of the fee since developers' profits remain at the normal level. However, if the capitalization of benefits is less than the amount of the fee, then normal developer profit levels require that the price of land declines.[11] Thus, land values can increase, remain stable, or decrease, depending upon whether the house price capitalization is greater or smaller than the amount of the fee.

Ihlanfeldt and Shaughnessy further posit that, if the benefits derived from the DC are valued highly enough by the homebuyer, then the house price could increase by an amount greater than the charge – a phenomenon that has been dubbed "over-shifting." In practice, the range of possible outcomes appears much more limited than it does in theory. Empirical evidence overwhelmingly suggests not only that the charges are passed forward to the homebuyer but also that over-shifting is common.[12] Overall, Burge et al. conclude that $1.00 of DC will result in a house price increase in the range of $1.50 to $1.70.

Very little research has been undertaken on the impacts of DCs on pre-development land prices. In one study of three Toronto-area municipalities, Skaburskis and Qadeer found that $1.00 of DC increased lot prices by about $1.20 – another instance of over-shifting.[13] The new view would suggest that increases in land prices are only possible if house price increases exceed the amount of the fee; however, in this case, evidence on house prices is not presented. Skaburskis and Qadeer suggest that the DC delays development, reducing supply and increasing lot prices (at least in the short term). Another explanation is that the developer in effect pays the DC to front-end needed infrastructure to service his or her project, and the over-shifting is due to the added costs associated with the charge, such as the costs of financing the DC and additional profit charged on this portion of costs. These expanded costs are then passed along to the builder, who recoups them in house prices.[14]

Overall, under most typical market conditions, and in the long term, DCs will almost always be passed forward to the final consumer, and this will be reflected in house prices. Indeed, the potential of the DC to act as a price signalling the actual costs of development will depend upon whether it is reflected in the final price of houses (and prices of non-residential development subject to DCs). In order to influence decision making, the actual costs of development (including those covered by the DC) should be reflected in market prices.

However, when the costs of inaccurate DCs are reflected in house prices, the results can work against planning objectives for compact urban form. With a city-wide charge, for example, an infill townhouse ends up being more expensive than it should be, and the price of a greenfields townhouse is lower than it ought to be if actual costs were reflected in DCs. A differential of several thousand dollars, which should exist between the prices of these two types of home, is eliminated by the average cost-based DC. An incentive is created to purchase the underpriced greenfields townhouse rather than the relatively overpriced infill townhouse. In complete contradiction to what planning policies mandate, this policy actively discourages reurbanization and encourages suburbanization of greenfields land. These inaccurate price signals encourage the building and buying of greenfields homes over infill; of larger lots over smaller lots, and larger units over smaller units; of high trip-generating uses over low trip-generating uses, thus undermining planning and transit objectives for denser, more compact neighbourhoods.

As currently structured, the DC is a deeply flawed tool with respect to development patterns, one that encourages wasteful and expensive development patterns, thus raising the total cost of servicing. Instead of supporting planning objectives, the DC functions to undermine them. It subverts market rationality, eliminating or reducing natural market incentives for smaller lots or for development on cheaper-to-service land first. The DC effectively renders developers, and subsequently consumers, indifferent to cost variations. In ignoring the DC, we are, at best, ignoring a powerful force driving growth patterns and, at worst, missing an important opportunity to harness a potentially very powerful tool for shaping urban growth patterns.

More accurate DCs would encourage efficient development patterns, which, in turn, would bring down the total cost of infrastructure, contributing to lower housing prices and business costs. Fortunately, there is an easy and elegant fix for DCs – one that structures them so that they can become a powerful instrument in support of planning policy (see Chapter 12).

Property Tax

In Canada, the United States, and elsewhere, the property tax is an important tool used by municipalities to raise revenue. Indeed, in Canada, property tax accounts for over half of all municipal revenues.[15] The revenues raised are used to cover a wide variety of municipal programs and services. These include construction, maintenance and servicing of municipal roads, sewer and water systems, urban transit, snow removal, garbage pickup, and police and ambulance services, among others. Of the many services provided, transportation (roads, public transit), protection (police, firefighting), and environmental services (sewer, water, recycling, garbage) account for over half of all municipal spending in every province except Ontario. Among Canadian provinces, Ontario stands alone in that its municipalities are also responsible for a range of social services, which accounts for roughly one-quarter of all municipal spending in that province (bringing down the share of spending otherwise attributable to the three categories mentioned above). These services include welfare and employment services, disability benefits, drug benefits, social housing, child care, and ambulance services.[16] In Toronto, it is estimated that provincially mandated expenditures account for 36 percent of that city's spending.[17] Elsewhere in Canada, the provinces are responsible for these social services.

In most provinces, property tax raised also goes to finance public elementary and secondary education, either through direct taxation by school boards or through sharing property tax revenues with provincial governments for education purposes. In Ontario, one-third of all property tax goes to education, and this portion of the property tax is controlled by the province – essentially, it is a provincial property tax.[18]

The property tax in Canada is levied on the basis of the assessed value of real property. In each province, a property's market value is determined. Then a tax rate is applied to the assessed value to determine the actual dollar amount of taxes to be paid. Municipalities set the tax rates applied to the assessed value to fund municipal services, while, in Ontario, the Ministry of Finance sets the education property tax rate across the province. Property taxes are not insignificant. On average, in Canada, property taxes amounted to $790 per capita in 2001, excluding education-related taxes.[19] For an average home in Toronto, the owner would pay almost $1,900 in municipal taxes, again excluding the education tax portion.[20]

A good portion of property tax pays for linear services – in particular, for roads, streets, snow removal and cleaning, public transit, water and sewer, and garbage collection and recycling. The costs of these services are known to vary with urban form factors such as location and density. In Canada (outside Ontario), these services account for 38 percent of municipal expenditures; in Ontario they account for 30 percent.[21]

Given that property tax is levied on the basis of the market value of the property, taxes cannot adequately reflect the degree to which different types of property contribute to costs. For example, due to their central location, it is common for properties located in and near a city's core to be smaller in size but of higher market value than comparable properties in suburban locations. The smaller, centrally located properties would incur much lower per-unit network infrastructure costs, though they would pay higher taxes overall when compared to their suburban counterparts.

For that 38 percent of the property tax that is spent on network infrastructure and services, the current market value system does not send accurate price signals that reflect variations in costs incurred. Property tax is a major source of funding for the construction, maintenance, and snow clearing of roads, but taxes imposed bear little if any relation to cost causation or road use. When charges do not reflect costs incurred, the result is a misallocation of resources, overspending on infrastructure and services, cross-subsidization, and inefficient urban development patterns.

Aside from the lack of alignment between charges levied and costs incurred, there are several specific flaws associated with market value property taxes that cause price signal distortions and affect urban development patterns in ways that are contrary to planning goals of compact urban form. Perhaps the most significant of these stems from the very nature of a market value-based property tax. Improvements to a property, such as building renovation or expansion, will add to the assessed value and will cause property taxes to increase. In other words, the property tax acts as a disincentive to intensify the use of land and as an incentive to sprawl. By raising the cost of building relative to land, the tax on improvements can lead an owner to reduce his or her tax burden by choosing development options that use more land and fewer improvements.[22] This creates a substitution effect, where land is substituted for building, and it leads to lower densities than would otherwise exist without the influence of the property tax. For example, in the absence of such a tax, a developer owner may opt to provide a smaller office building on a given lot than he/she otherwise might.

Several analyses support this outcome, concluding that the property tax acts as a disincentive to density. Donald Shoup shows that a 2 percent annual property tax rate would reduce the size of a building by 14 percent compared to what would be built with no property tax.[23] Ronald Grieson suggests that, if a 3 percent property tax were replaced with a non-property related tax, housing density would increase by 23 percent.[24] An economic analysis by Brueckner and Kim also concludes that the property tax would contribute to the inefficient spatial expansion of cities.[25]

Of course, it is important to remember that the property tax doesn't simply influence developer and owner decisions about how and where to develop property. As a significant ongoing expense, it also affects the property selection decisions of homebuyers, renters, and business owners seeking new premises. The amount of property tax to be paid annually is a significant part of the carrying cost of a home and will form part of a buyer's decision regarding the type of residential unit she or he wants and in what location. The influence of the property tax on locational decisions is made stronger by the fact that residential property tax rates are determined by individual municipalities. Though the method for determining the assessed value is consistent across the province, tax rates vary from one municipality to another, even within a single urban region. This variation, in effect, makes homes that are otherwise similar but are located in different municipalities bear different costs. This, in turn, influences buyers' housing location choices.

For example, the municipal residential tax rate in the City of Toronto was 0.61 percent in 2005, while in the neighbouring cities of Mississauga, Brampton, and Pickering it was 0.76 percent, 0.94 percent, and 1.08 percent, respectively.[26] In dollar terms, this means a homeowner in Pickering would pay $1,645 more property tax every year for a house of the same assessed value as would a homeowner in the City of Toronto.[27] In this instance, the distortions caused by the property tax act to encourage demand for housing in the City of Toronto relative to surrounding municipalities, all other things being equal.

But the issue is further complicated by the fact that the relative tax rates charged to non-residential (commercial and industrial) and residential development also vary between municipalities. The City of Toronto, along with many other municipalities, undertaxes its residential development and overtaxes its commercial development. For example, some municipalities apply a higher tax rate to commercial development than to residential development. In Ontario, this includes not only the City of Toronto but places like Ottawa, Belleville, and Kitchener.[28] This might not be unfair if business properties exerted a higher burden on municipal services than residential properties. But commercial and industrial buildings contribute a larger share of revenues than they consume in municipal services. Kitchen and Slack show that, within a sample of Ontario municipalities, non-residential property taxes accounted for 28 percent to 51 percent of municipal revenues but only 31 percent to 40 percent of expenditures.[29] A similar study for the City of Vancouver shows that residential properties paid 40 percent of all property taxes and consumed 71 percent of the services, while non-residential properties paid 60 percent of taxes and accounted for 29 percent of municipal services.[30] It should be noted that the City of Toronto is developing a strategy to address the disparity between residential and non-residential property taxes.[31]

In Ontario, a further distortion occurs with the education tax that the province levies on property. For residential development, the tax rate established by the province is constant across all Ontario municipalities (at 0.264 percent in 2006). For non-residential development, however, the province's rates vary from municipality to municipality, based on their historical evolution.[32] As one commentator states: "There is no rationale (other than history) for the rate variation."[33]

The variation in business education tax rates is important in that, all other factors being equal, it can influence the locational decisions of firms.

The evidence shows that, while local taxes are not too important to firms when it comes to choosing which urban region in which to invest, they do come into play once the decision to locate in a particular region has been made and the company must decide between the municipalities that make up that region.[34]

This is of particular concern for the City of Toronto because – at 2.22 percent in Toronto versus 1.74 percent in Peel region, 1.68 percent in York, 1.65 percent in Durham, and 1.53 percent in Halton[35] – the provincially mandated education tax rate for that city is much higher than is that imposed on the surrounding municipalities with which it competes for investment. In combination with municipally imposed overtaxation of non-residential properties, the tax differential for businesses between Toronto and surrounding suburban regions has become significant, in total a rate of about 4.5 percent in Toronto compared to rates of 2.6 percent to 2.8 percent in surrounding municipalities. On a $10 million property, this translates into a difference of around $200,000 per year in property taxes. This tax differential is seen as playing a critical role in what has been a dearth of new office construction and employment losses in the City of Toronto compared to continued office and employment growth in surrounding suburban municipalities.[36] The 2007 Ontario budget recognized the importance of this issue and introduced a plan to lower business education taxes across the province over seven years to a maximum rate of 1.60 percent. This cut is predicted to save Toronto businesses about $250 million in taxes for the year 2014.

One additional idiosyncrasy in the design of the property tax has particular implications for urban form and development patterns: municipalities often charge multiple unit residential buildings a substantially higher tax rate than single-detached, semi-detached, and row houses. This is at best ironic, given that, in general, multiple-unit residential buildings contribute significantly less to municipal expenditures on a per unit basis than do low-rise residential buildings, yet, they are charged more. The City of Toronto, for example, charges a tax rate for multiple residential buildings that is 3.7 times higher than that for low-rise housing. In some other GTA municipalities, multiple unit buildings are levied rates ranging from 1.5 to 2.3 times that of single-family housing.[37] For new multiple residential buildings, municipalities have the option of charging the same tax rate as applies to low-rise residential development, yet, in many instances, this option has not been taken up. This overcharging of multi-unit buildings and undercharging of houses discourages investment in apartment buildings and condominiums, and reduces the density of development.[38]

Last, the province also provides for property tax rebates for vacant commercial and industrial buildings. In addition, vacant or excess industrial and commercial properties are eligible for tax reductions. The former was estimated to cost the province $50 million in 2006, and the latter $30 million.[39] One can understand the desire to provide tax relief to commercial buildings that are not occupied and are therefore not generating income. However, in the long run, this can also remove an incentive to the use of these buildings and to the development of vacant lands, with adverse effects on patterns of urban development.

On the other hand, some property tax incentives are designed to encourage compact development. The Province of Ontario's Brownfields Financial Tax Incentive Program allows municipalities to provide tax assistance to developers who clean up brownfields sites, and it provides matching education property tax assistance.[40] This kind of brownfields tax assistance is quite common across North America and elsewhere. Nonetheless, brownfields development is waging an uphill battle, given the other distortions inherent in the property tax system that militate against compact development.

In conclusion, a market-value-based property tax thus influences the types of development built and the location, density, and timing of development. As a significant cost, property taxes influence developer and building owner decisions on the supply side as well as the nature of demand and the property decisions of homebuyers and businesses.

The influence of the property tax is not neutral across development types and locations; rather, it acts to encourage inefficient development patterns and to discourage densification. Unlike DCs, where the essential problem from an urban form point of view is the use of average costs as the basis for structuring the charge, the underlying problem with the property tax is that, based on the market value of property, taxes are *unrelated* to municipal service costs as these vary with urban form. Particularly for municipal network services, whose cost varies with urban form factors, the "prices" charged (in the form of property taxes) do not reflect costs incurred. This is perhaps not surprising given that the market-value-based property tax was not designed to do so, being instead based on ideas such as the ability to pay or that the property tax reflects benefits received from the municipal government. But the fact that taxes do not send a price signal that links the amount of taxes paid to the cost of supplying services consumed is extremely problematic in terms of its impact on urban form. It fails to signal to potential homebuyers and business operators the *real* cost of choosing a particular development type or location.

While with market value assessment there is no intentional relationship between taxes paid and costs incurred, patterns nonetheless can emerge. In cities where property values are higher (e.g., in the older, central areas), it is the most efficient properties that tend to pay higher taxes, while the less efficient pay lower taxes. When this price/cost disconnect occurs, there is a disincentive for residents and businesses to choose more efficient development forms as more efficient development will tend to result in relatively higher taxes while incurring relatively lower costs for linear services. Moreover, as a tax applied to building and improvements, the property tax discourages densification, thus encouraging the substitution of land for building and lower densities than would be the case with other tax structures or pricing strategies.

In short, a market-value-based property tax violates the fundamental economic principle for efficient allocation of resources – that is, that price should reflect marginal cost. It harbours an extremely complex web of cross-subsidies, incentives, disincentives, and mis-incentives that tend to support the overconsumption of land and oversupply of infrastructure. These systemic biases inherent in a market value approach to property tax are compounded by the multiple idiosyncrasies embedded in many municipal tax systems, such as applying higher tax rates to multi-unit residential buildings. In these ways, a market-value-based tax system encourages inefficient development patterns and urban sprawl, contrary to central tenets of compact development as well as provincial and municipal planning policies.

It is no wonder that there are many calls to simplify and rationalize the property tax system, and to bring it into line with planning objectives. In Part 4, I discuss options for doing this; however, I now turn to problems related to the costs and prices of other types of infrastructure and services related to development decisions.

8

Network Services
Costs and Prices

Studies analyzing the costs of sprawl tend to focus on public infrastructure, such as roads, sewer and water networks, and public transit. However, there is a whole range of other services provided to residential and commercial development whose infrastructure costs are also very sensitive to development patterns and location. But these services are rarely given any attention in discussions of the costs of sprawl. Often provided in the context of a publicly regulated or partially regulated marketplace, they include:

- water and sewer
- electricity
- gas
- telephone
- cable television
- internet connectivity
- postal service.

The way in which these services are priced and, in particular, whether prices reflect variations in cost associated with urban form, land use, and location, is a critical but widely unrecognized issue in the generation of urban sprawl. Here is a whole other set of expenses that influence consumers' decisions about where and how to live as well as business decisions regarding where and how to invest in facilities. Whether the charges for these services are sending accurate price signals, and whether the role of these prices in influencing urban development patterns is positive, negative, or neutral, is reviewed below.

Water and Sewer Rates

For new urban development in Ontario, the first-time installation costs of water and sewer systems are typically covered by DCs, as noted above. However, municipalities or their public utility commissions can also charge a specific water rate to cover the costs of water usage, delivery, and infrastructure maintenance. In some cases, a sewer charge is also levied in conjunction with water rates as the use of water and demand on the sewer system are, of course, closely related. In other cases, sewer-related costs are simply included within the water rate.

Numerous studies in Canada and elsewhere document how the cost of providing water and sewer infrastructure is closely related to urban form.[1] Generally, the per unit cost of constructing and maintaining water and sewer infrastructure falls as density increases. A contiguous built-up urban fabric also minimizes infrastructure costs, as does redevelopment of already-urbanized areas, where water and sewer capacity already exists. In one analysis, Speir and Stephenson find that lot size (an indicator of density) is by far the most significant urban form factor affecting water and sewer costs.[2] A doubling of lot sizes increases infrastructure costs by 30 percent.[3] Higher costs are due to the fact that the water distribution and sewer collection mains are the most significant cost components – representing a much larger share of total costs than transmission mains, pump capital costs, or pump energy costs. In short, larger lots require longer distribution and collector mains, the most significant cost component. Also, pressure losses are higher for longer lengths of pipe, which increases pumping costs. Moreover, homeowners on larger lots tend to use considerably more water, principally for watering their expansive lawns in summer. This additional usage generates higher infrastructure costs – for larger pipes, higher pumping costs, and higher water treatment costs.[4]

And density can vary considerably within a given service area. Communities within the Cleveland Division of Water's (CDOW) service area, for example, have a wide range of densities. The thirteen most dense communities in the service area have a density of 607 service units per estimated mile of pipe, compared to 120 service units per mile in the thirteen least dense communities. (The City of Cleveland proper has a density of 546 service units per mile of pipe.)[5] Within a service area, where density varies, per unit service costs can also be expected to vary. Efficiencies would be achieved by having a greater number of service units per mile of pipe, thus lowering per unit servicing costs. On the other hand, pricing rarely reflects these density-related cost variations.

Water pricing in Canada is generally based on either a flat rate or the amount of water used. A surprisingly large share of users pay only a flat rate regardless of the amount of water consumed, estimated at 50 percent of Canadian households by Environment Canada, though this percentage is falling slowly over time as metered consumption widens.[6] Flat rates are most prevalent in Quebec, British Columbia, Prince Edward Island, and Newfoundland. This despite the fact that a clear relationship has been shown between the pricing mechanism for water and the levels of consumption. Canadians who paid volume-based rates consumed an average of 269 litres per day. Those who were charged flat rates consumed 457 litres per day, fully 70 percent more water.[7] The average monthly flat rate was $22.40 per month in 1999.[8]

This is a clear example of how prices based on average costs induce cross-subsidies and overconsumption. As noted above, prices based on marginal costs are widely recognized as necessary to achieving the efficient allocation of resources. And yet, research by Renzetti, which examines seventy-seven Ontario municipalities, shows that, in every city and town studied, the marginal cost of water and sewer service is higher than the price charged. In fact, the marginal cost was over twice that of the price charged for both residential and non-residential customers.[9] In the Cleveland area, it was concluded that, "since it appears that CDOW's current rate differentials do not consider density-related service cost differentials, customers in CDOW's higher density communities are likely subsidizing distribution costs for customers in its lower density communities."[10]

Neither flat rates nor volume-based rates, as currently structured, adequately reflect the actual costs of delivering water to different locations and different types of urban development. They ignore the substantial variations in infrastructure construction, maintenance, and servicing costs associated with location, density, building type, and other urban form factors. For example, even with volume-based charges, consumers on large lots pay the same rates as do those on smaller lots or in multiple unit buildings, though servicing costs in the latter cases are demonstrably lower. Consumers in more distant areas pay the same rates as do those in central locations. Thus, a set of cross-subsidies is established through the water rate, with those incurring the lower costs subsidizing those incurring above-average costs. In other words, efficient development subsidizes inefficient development through the water rate, as currently structured.[11]

Electricity

Aside from using electricity to run appliances and light houses, many Canadian households also use it to heat their water (45 percent) and homes (34 percent) as well as for cooking (92 percent).[12] So for most households, electric power is a major and necessary expense. Given the extensive linear infrastructure associated with the electricity grid, it would be expected that the per unit costs of electricity would vary substantially with urban form. This is especially true of the electricity distribution system, including the wires, poles, transformers, and other equipment that delivers the electricity locally to final consumers, be they homes or businesses.

Indeed, there is considerable evidence of a strong relationship between electricity delivery costs and urban form, especially density. The density of the customer base, along with its spatial distribution, is widely acknowledged as one of the major factors affecting the cost of distributing electricity.[13] In particular, in areas of low customer density, capital and maintenance costs are significantly higher, while in compact areas with high customer density, lower per unit costs can be expected. This has been demonstrated empirically for Ontario, where it was found that the density of the customer base has a strong statistically significant impact on costs. Yatchew concludes: "Utilities with lower density and hence greater distances between customers have significantly higher costs."[14]

Studies in other jurisdictions, including Switzerland and Norway, that examine the impacts of various factors on electricity costs also find a strong correlation between density and cost.[15] Even in these already fairly dense nations, additional efficiencies from density are not exhausted – that is, increasing density beyond existing levels would bring further cost efficiencies.

The electricity sector in Ontario has been going through a deregulation process over the last several years. The former Ontario Hydro monopoly was disassembled, with electricity generation separated from transmission and distribution, resulting in two distinct entities (Ontario Power Generation and Hydro One Networks, respectively). In Ontario, most prices charged for electricity are regulated by the Ontario Energy Board (OEB). As mandated by the OEB, electricity prices are disaggregated into various components, each regulated separately. Four main components appear on most bills in Ontario. These are:

- a charge for the electricity itself, based on usage;
- a delivery charge, comprised of two main subcomponents – (1) transmission (i.e., the cost of delivering the electricity from the generation source to the local utility along high voltage lines that are owned by Hydro One) and (2) distribution (i.e., the cost of local delivery within the utility's service area to final users such as homes and businesses);
- regulatory charges, which include a charge of 0.10¢ per kWh, which goes towards Rural and Remote Rate Protection, a subsidy program whose purpose is to offset higher costs of electricity distribution in rural and remote areas of Ontario; and
- a debt retirement charge, set by the Ontario Ministry of Finance to pay down the residual stranded debt of the former Ontario Hydro.

From the perspective of the potential impacts of electricity pricing on urban development patterns, two charges are of interest: the electricity charge and the distribution charge.

In Ontario, except for those who opt to purchase electricity from a reseller, under the Regulated Price Plan (RPP) the rate charged for the electricity itself is regulated and is standard across the province. The plan was intended to smooth over volatility in electricity prices in a deregulated market, providing more stable and predictable prices to the consumer. RPP prices are based on a number of cost components, such as hourly market prices as well as the cost of electricity provided by non-utility generators.[16] The costs of baseload nuclear and hydroelectric are also key inputs, and the prices charged for these sources are, in turn, regulated by the OEB. In theory, if the RPP prices did not cover costs during one period, they would be adjusted in the next price-setting period to recover shortfalls.

RPP prices are established by the OEB every year and are intended to recover the actual costs of providing the electricity to consumers, such that, overall, the price of electricity reflects the cost and no subsidy occurs. However, some claim that electricity prices are indeed subsidized in Ontario, amounting to billions of dollars annually.[17] This occurs through, for example, the government's charging below-market water royalty rates for hydroelectric generation or below-market returns on equity for Ontario Power Generation.

To the extent that the price of electricity is subsidized and is lower than the cost, price signals fail, and consumers are encouraged to consume more electricity than they might if prices reflected costs. This makes consumers less sensitive to electricity charges and energy efficiency, and more willing to purchase larger, less energy-efficient houses. The distribution charge, as it covers the costs of building and maintaining local infrastructure, will also be relevant to urban development patterns. Other electricity-related costs (such as transmission and some administrative costs) are not sensitive to urban form factors.

Distribution charges have two elements. A "customer service" charge takes the form of a fixed monthly rate or fee and covers the utility's administrative costs, such as meter reading, billing, customer service, and accounts. The "distribution charge" is based on the amount of electricity used and covers the local utility's costs to deliver the electricity to the home or business. It includes the costs of building and maintaining the infrastructure (e.g., wires and hydro poles).

The current method of allocating costs to customer classes, along with the rate structure, does not result in electricity distribution rates reflecting distribution costs as they vary within and across the urban landscape. The methodology to be used for establishing distribution charges is laid out by the OEB. Indeed, at present, under the *2006 Electricity Distribution Rate Handbook*, costs are allocated to the different customer classes (residential, commercial, etc.) based on their respective shares of revenue.

Given that the distribution charge is based on the amount of electricity used, and is standard across a given utility, it cannot reflect the cost impacts of urban form, especially the effects of variations in density. The costs of building and maintaining underground cables, above-ground wires, and hydro poles will be higher per unit for businesses and homes on larger lots than they will be for those on smaller lots for the simple reason that the former require more cable, wire, and hydro poles per building. This is true irrespective of how much electricity one home consumes compared to its neighbour. Yet, these infrastructure-related cost variations are not reflected in electricity prices.

This situation is merely another variation of the problem that occurs when prices reflect average costs rather than marginal costs. The result is the same as for other types of network infrastructure that is subject to average-cost-based prices: the more efficient customers end up subsidizing the less efficient, more expensive-to-service customers. A cross-subsidy exists within the local utility's customer base, most typically flowing from those customers in higher-density areas to customers in lower-density areas.

Local utilities' service areas are not monolithic in urban form. There tend to be significant density variations within the service area of any given local distribution company (LDC). And distribution costs can vary drastically within a given service area as a result of other urban-form-related issues, such as greenfields development versus reurbanization or discontiguous development. Yet, standard distribution charges ignore these variations and apply across a local utility's service area and, therefore, do not reflect actual cost variations within LDCs.

The possible exception involves a handful of LDCs that have density-based charges. Because its customer base extends across Ontario and therefore covers a wide range of conditions, Hydro One Networks does have a distribution charge based on density. It has three density classifications: Urban Density (areas with 3,000 or more customers, and a line density of at least 60 customers per kilometre); High Density (areas containing at least 100 customers, and with a line density of at least 15 customers per kilometre); and Normal Density (areas with densities lower than those of the preceding classifications). Hydro One notes: "Our rates reflect the cost to serve customers in each density classification, which means that rates are higher for customers in less densely populated areas."[18] Indeed, Hydro One distribution charges do vary by density classification, which may capture to some degree cost differentials between different types of communities, but not likely reflect cost differentials within larger urban areas.

Unlike other regulated electricity charges, which are standard across Ontario, distribution charges vary from local utility to local utility, including the monthly service charge and the distribution charge. Just the local distribution charge can be a significant portion of the bill. In Toronto and Brampton, for example, local distribution accounted for about 17 percent of the total bill.[19] In these municipalities and others, the amount of the distribution charge exceeds the transmission charge. It has also been noted that distribution rates have been rising much more quickly than other components of the typical energy bill.[20]

It could be argued that, because they are established on the basis of individual local utilities, distribution charges do broadly reflect geographic variations in cost. However, this overlooks the great variations in cost causation that occur within the boundaries of a given LDC – even those that are primarily urban.

Aside from the usual capital, operating, and maintenance costs related to network infrastructure, some other costs would also be expected to vary with urban form. One example is meter reading. The OEB acknowledges that "it is generally more expensive to read individual meters for customers that are farther apart than the meters for customers that are located in close proximity."[21] In allocating meter-reading costs to different customer classifications, it recommends use of a factor that takes density as well as meter-reading frequency into account.[22] This methodology, part of a broader review of how costs are allocated to different customer classes, has not yet been implemented. Meter-reading costs are currently reflected in the monthly customer charge, a fixed fee that does not vary based on density or other urban form factors.

In short, costs that vary significantly with urban form (network infrastructure, maintenance, meter reading) should have associated charges that reflect these variations. The current situation results in an implicit cross-subsidization of higher cost-generating customers by lower cost-generating customers and inaccurate price signals that contribute to over-investment in infrastructure and inefficient urban development patterns.

Explicit subsidies are provided to higher-cost, low-density, primarily rural and remote areas through the Rural and Remote Rate Protection Program. The amount of subsidy in this program is about $150 million annually.[23] The funding for this program is raised from all consumers and is included under regulatory charges. The other cross-subsidies that occur within LDC areas, however, are implicit and hidden.

It should be noted that the OEB was, at the time of writing in the fall of 2006, in the process of completing its Cost Allocation Review. The Cost Allocation Review initiative re-examines the way electricity distribution costs are established and allocated to the different customer classes. Despite the fact that the OEB intended rates to be better aligned with cost causation of the different customer groups,[24] the impact of urban density on cost causation was not a part of the Cost Allocation Review process. A review of how distribution rates are designed – the Electricity Distribution Rate Design Review – was scheduled to begin in early 2007. However, given that the Cost Allocation Review did not take urban form factors into account, it is unlikely that these important cost determinants will be reflected in the review of distribution rates design.

Natural Gas

The cost components for natural gas service are typically broken down in a manner similar to those for electricity. They are comprised of the commodity cost (i.e., the cost of the gas itself); the transportation costs (i.e., the costs involved in transporting the gas from the source [in the case of Ontario gas, typically from Alberta or the Unites States]); and the costs of distributing the gas to the final consumers within Ontario. As in the case of electricity, what is of most interest for our purposes are distribution costs as these are most likely to be influenced by urban development patterns. Distribution costs are significant – it is estimated that, in the Province of Quebec, for example, they account for 37 percent of the cost of delivered gas.[25] Moreover, 70 percent of distribution costs are associated with the capital costs of the pipelines.

In general, less research has been conducted on natural gas costs than on electricity costs and this is also true regarding the relationship between urban form factors and gas distribution costs. However, the research that has been undertaken shows a strong relationship between the latter two. In one analysis, Guldmann finds that an increase in population density is related to a decrease in distribution capital costs. Moreover, a marginal gain in density has a higher impact in the higher-density ranges, where apartments and other multi-storey buildings entered into the equation: "In highly dense urban areas, the same pipeline layout serves a given layout of buildings, whatever the number of stories and gas customers involved, hence the significant economies of scale achieved with additional stories."[26] The author concludes: "These results show rather dramatically that economies of scale in gas distribution are to be achieved through service densification rather than through service area extension," that is, by adding customers within existing service boundaries rather than by increasing the overall number of customers by expanding the service area.[27] Indeed, research in Quebec shows that the marginal cost of adding to daily demand is very low (estimated at less than 1 cent per cubic metre) and well below average cost, while the marginal cost of adding pipeline length is high, ranging from $93,000 to $167,000 per kilometre.[28]

Gas supply has been gradually deregulated in Canada and Ontario, beginning in 1985, with the deregulation of commodity prices and, later, the introduction of wholesale and retail competition. The regulated gas supply refers to the sale of gas by regulated utilities, primarily to their core, small-volume customers. The two large regulated gas utilities in Ontario are Enbridge Gas Distribution Inc. and Union Gas Limited.[29] Regulated gas currently accounts for one-third of the gas volume and 60 percent of customers (mostly residential).[30] The price of the gas itself as well as transportation, storage, and distribution rates are reviewed and approved by the OEB for the regulated utilities. Prices charged by retail natural gas marketers are not regulated.

Both Enbridge and Union Gas currently employ a cost-of-service approach as the basis for rate-setting, but there is no consistent methodology mandated by the OEB (as there is for establishing electricity rates). Gas charges are broken down into different components. In the case of Enbridge, for example, charges are comprised of:

- a gas supply charge (i.e., the charge for the gas commodity itself, levied on the basis of the amount of gas used per cubic metre);
- a delivery charge, which includes both transportation (the cost of transporting the gas from the source to the local distribution system) and delivery (the delivery of the gas through the utility's distribution system to final consumers); and
- a customer charge, based on a fixed monthly fee.

Because, in this case, the delivery charge includes both long-distance transportation costs and local delivery costs, the cost impact of urban form (which relates only to the local delivery portion) cannot be isolated. So the costs of gas distribution, as they vary with urban form, are not apparent in the rates charged.

Moreover, some of the other costs that vary with urban form are covered in the fixed monthly charge, which is uniform across all areas. These urban-form-sensitive costs include emergency response, meter reading, and equipment maintenance.[31] In all, given the pricing structure in place, the urban-form-related variations in delivery costs are not accurately reflected in Enbridge's gas distribution prices.

Union Gas uses a similar rate structure to that of Enbridge, with the significant exception (from my perspective) that storage, transportation, and delivery charges are itemized separately on residential users' bills. This allows the customer to isolate the amount charged for local delivery compared to other charges. Unfortunately, the delivery charge is also expressed in terms of usage only and, therefore, does not reflect actual cost variations associated with urban form. Union Gas does, however, recognize some geographical variations in costs at a more macro scale, and it applies different rates across the five zones that make up its service area. This rate structure reflects the differing costs of transporting natural gas to the various zones (which extend across the Province of Ontario). Per-cubic-metre delivery costs are also higher in the north and east "due to higher operating costs associated with fewer customers spread over a larger area" as well as to higher construction costs and greater distances to gas storage facilities.[32]

For example, delivery charges range from 2¢ to 5.7¢ per cubic metre in southwestern Ontario compared to a range of 8¢ to 9.7¢ per cubic metre in the northern and eastern Ontario zones.[33] Unfortunately, the fact that substantial cost variations also occur *within* each of the zones is not recognized.

Given current pricing structures in the regulated utilities cited above, prices do not adequately reflect actual cost variations related to urban form. This is because they are based on usage levels and a flat monthly rate, both of which are divorced from these cost variations. While at the aggregate, system-wide level, delivery rates may reflect delivery costs, the substantial variations related to urban factors such as density and contiguity of development pattern are not accounted for.

More generally, another study conducted by Guldmann compares costs of distribution based on common cost allocation methodologies with marginal costs. It finds that pricing based on conventional cost allocation methods leads to price discrimination and cross-subsidization[34] – between rate classes, within rate classes, and between communities. The policy implication is that pricing practices should move away from company-level pricing to locally differentiated pricing, in which prices can more accurately reflect actual costs.[35] Further, the analysis of marginal distribution costs in Quebec cited earlier led the authors to conclude that pricing structures should pay less attention to maximum daily demand and more attention to the way consumers are located along the pipelines since it is pipeline length that is most important in determining marginal costs.[36]

The OEB is moving away from cost-of-service-based rates to "incentive rate (IR) regulation." The "incentive regulation methodology" focuses on ensuring incentives for efficiency. From my perspective, a potential weakness of incentive regulation is the further decoupling of rates from costs. Current proposals aim to mitigate the breakdown of the relationship between costs and rates by requiring "rebasing" before setting rates for a given period. Each IR plan is to begin with a "robust set of cost-based rates."[37] We must wait to see how, ultimately, gas distribution prices do or do not relate to actual costs, as they vary with urban form, in Ontario in the future.

Telephone

Today, a complex array of telephone services is available, offered by a wide range of providers. Reviewing all of these services is beyond the scope of this book, so my focus here is on the illustrative case of basic local telephone service. Basic local telephone service is delivered over an extensive physical network of cables, wires, and switches, the costs of which would reasonably be expected to vary with urban form. For example, it has been estimated that, in providing land-based telephone service, as opposed to serving customers in the central business district, it costs twice as much to provide service to customers in the rest of the central city and ten times as much to serve those at the urban fringe.[38]

The sensitivity of service delivery costs to density is also shown by the differential costs between rural and urban areas. It is estimated that, in the United States, the subsidy to rural phone users was $8.7 billion in 1991.[39] This was an implicit subsidy, paid for by urban customers through the mechanism of uniform pricing. In other words, every household pays the same monthly fee for basic phone service regardless of the cost to deliver the service. If phone pricing were "de-averaged" such that the prices reflected actual cost variations, urban customer bills would decrease by $77 per line per year, while rural customers would pay $316 more per line per year.[40] In other words, rural customers were each paying $316 per year less than it cost to provide service to them, while urban customers were each paying $77 extra per line per year to subsidize the former.

In reality, of course, this would not be the outcome of such a straightforward de-averaging: some rural customers would likely give up the service altogether. Further analysis shows an interesting result: most rural customers would still pay for the service, even at the higher rates, with the price increase raising revenues by $8.0 billion. About 7 percent of rural customers would drop the service – either because they could not afford it or would choose not to pay it. Providing financial support to maintain phone service for that 7 percent would cost $0.7 billion.[41] In other words, the same level of service and market penetration could be maintained for a $0.7 billion explicit subsidy rather than for the $8.7 billion implicit subsidy provided through prices based on average costs.

Until fairly recently, telephone service in Canada was delivered through a limited number of companies that were regionally based, regulated monopolies. Rates were regulated to ensure that they were just and reasonable, while also allowing companies a reasonable rate of return: "This regulatory approach, coupled with price averaging and value of service pricing, were used to set affordable rates while, at the same time, allowing incumbent local carriers to extend, improve and maintain service ... Profitable areas (usually urban) and profitable services (long distance, optional services) subsidized local service and areas with high operating costs (usually rural or remote)."[42]

Thus, the goal of universal access (access for all to basic telephone service at a reasonable price) was achieved by implicit and invisible subsidies, specifically a cross-subsidy paid by customers in low-cost areas to customers in high-cost areas through a regulated price for local phone service.[43] This arrangement relied on regional monopolies with a large enough customer base to enable and sustain the cross-subsidization. With deregulation and the introduction of competition – first with respect to long distance and then with respect to local service – this situation was unsustainable. New entrants might target those customers paying prices that were significantly higher than costs, leaving incumbent companies with a smaller base with which to support the majority of high-cost customers who were the beneficiaries of the cross-subsidies.

One of the major aims of deregulation was to bring prices for different services more in line with costs. However, a particular problem in Canada as elsewhere is that some areas are much more expensive to serve than are other areas. In a deregulated environment, implicit cross-subsidies could not be relied upon to provide the revenue shortfall that existed in high-cost areas.

A new targeted and explicit subsidy system was introduced in 1992, replacing implicit subsidies through price averaging. It was modified to the current system in 2000.[44] Basic residential telephone service in high-cost areas is now subsidized through the National Contribution Fund, to which all major telecommunications service providers (TSPs) contribute a percentage of revenues.[45] The TSPs were required to establish "rate bands," based on areas with similar costs.[46] Costs within each band were to be as homogeneous as possible. The Canadian Radio and Television Telecommunications Commission (CRTC) approved a uniform banding structure for the large incumbent companies,[47] in which telephone exchanges are classified as follows:

- Band A: which generally includes exchanges in the core areas of major urban centres (e.g., core exchanges in Toronto, Montreal, and Ottawa);
- Band B: which generally includes non-core exchanges of major urban centres such as Montreal and Toronto, and exchanges in other major urban centres such as London, Hamilton, or Markham, Ontario, as well as some core exchanges in smaller urban centres (e.g., central Kingston);
- Band C: which generally includes exchanges with more than 8,000 lines as well as smaller urban centres such as Kingston (minus the core exchange), Kanata-Stittsville, Cornwall, or Coburg, Ontario;

- Band D, which generally includes exchanges in smaller communities with between 1,500 and 8,000 lines, and local loop lengths (i.e., distance from the wire centre to the home) of less than 4 kilometres (such as Bolton or Bracebridge, Ontario);
- Band E: wire centres or exchanges with less than or equal to 1,500 total lines;
- Band F: wire centres or exchanges with greater than 1,500 and less than 8,000 total lines, and where the average loop length is greater than 4 kilometres; and
- Band G: remote wire centres or exchanges (e.g., without year-round access or found in remote parts of a company's serving territory).

Bands E, F, and G were designated as high-cost bands.[48] High-cost bands E and F tend to include small settlements, while Band G includes remote communities without year-round road access, including northern communities. Within Bell Canada's serving area, examples of Band E communities include Baysville, Centralia, Killarney, and Bloomfield, Ontario. Band F includes places like Arthur, Brooklin, Caledon, Creemore, Kemptville, and Bancroft, Ontario. Band G includes places like Big Trout Lake, Ontario, and Obedjiwan, Quebec.

Areas classified in high-cost bands (reflecting "high-cost serving areas" [HCSAs]) were to be identified by TSPs according to a common definition. To compensate for providing basic phone service at affordable (i.e., lower-than-cost) levels in these areas, TSPs would be paid a subsidy based on the number of residential lines in the three high-cost bands, with subsidies reflecting cost variations. The subsidies paid are based on calculations submitted annually by each of the TSPs, using a common methodology, but they ultimately vary by provider according to their particular cost profiles. For example, for 2005, Bell Canada received a subsidy of $5.48 per month for each residential line in Band E, $3.14 per line in Band F, and $23.64 per line in Band G. SaskTel received $22.91, $15.55, and $33.48, respectively.[49] In the Bell Canada serving area, almost 940,000 lines were subsidized,[50] and 164,000 were subsidized in SaskTel's area.[51] In all, about 15 percent of residential lines are considered to be high cost.[52] The total national subsidy paid through the National Contribution Fund to TSPs for providing below-cost service in high cost areas was about $250 million in 2005.[53]

From a cost, fairness, transparency, and efficiency point of view, this new system of a targeted, explicit subsidy is better than the old system of implicit subsidies. The overall cost of the subsidy has been significantly reduced, and it is more clearly targeted to the highest-cost areas. However, the system is still not perfect, particularly from the point of view of its effect on urban sprawl. There are several reasons why this is the case.

First, a major problem with the current situation is that the subsidies are still poorly targeted (albeit this is somewhat improved by the National Contribution Fund). In the high-cost areas to which explicit subsidies are paid, a uniform low (and generally below cost) price means that customers who do not need subsidies still receive them. Some customers may be willing and able to pay higher, cost-based rates. The subsidy is not based on ability to pay, only on being a customer in a designated high-cost area. The flip side of this point presents another dilemma, namely, that people who actually may be more in need of subsidies, such as low-income people who do not live in the designated high-cost areas, are not eligible for subsidies in Canada.[54]

Second, though now targeted, the subsidies to high-cost areas are not transparent – either to the subsidizers or to the subsidizees. In other words, it is unlikely that either consumers who are being subsidized or those whose rates contribute to the subsidy fund are aware of the subsidies. Consumer prices in high-cost areas are still artificially low (with TSPs being compensated for shortfalls from the National Contribution Fund) and do not accurately reflect actual costs; therefore, they fail to properly inform consumers' decision making.

Third, prices for basic local phone service are still regulated and do not substantially reflect costs, especially as they vary within and across urban regions. Though some of the most extreme cases of cross-subsidization have been made explicit through the contribution regime for high-cost areas, low-cost customers continue to subsidize higher-cost customers within and between the low-cost bands A through D. This is an implicit subsidy, of which most consumers are unaware.

Price regulation for basic local residential telephone service is still in effect in Canada. It is a very complicated system. The CRTC approves all rates, which are based on the band structure described above. Again, these bands are supposed to reflect areas of homogeneous costs. However, the phone rates across the bands do not vary much. For example, in the non-high-cost bands in Bell's serving areas, the rate structure is shown in Table 8.1. This pricing structure shows a limited degree of price variation between the major bands A to D. The main difference is the existence of higher-priced sub-bands within bands B, C, and D. It is true that the maximum prices in Band A (which is presumably the lowest cost band) are lower than those in any other band, and the maximum price in Band D (presumably the highest-cost

Table 8.1

Monthly rates for basic local residential telephone service, Bell Canada ($)

Rate band	Flat rate (individual line)
A1	19.00
A2	19.80
B1	19.00
B2	19.80
B3	23.25
C1	19.00
C2a	19.80
C2b	23.25
D1	19.00
D2a	19.80
D2b	24.85
D2c	25.30

Source: Bell Canada, General Tariff, Item 70.

band) is the highest of any band. But prices in bands B and C are exactly the same. And there is a greater degree of variation within each band than across different bands, especially given that bands are intended to reflect homogeneous costs.

If we examine the rate structure above as it applies to Toronto, for example: Toronto is a B2, except for four central wire centres, which are A2. In any event, the rates for A2 and B2 are the same, so the price for basic residential service across Toronto is standard, at $19.80 per month, regardless of location. Prices in sub-bands A1, B1, C1, and D1 are the same, at $19.00 per month, less than what is charged in bands A2 and B2. If the rate bands reflect costs, does this mean that costs to provide basic residential service are lower in places like Brantford (B1), Trenton (C1), or Manotick (D1) than they are in the centre of Toronto and, indeed, the rest of Toronto (A2 and B2)?

The companies themselves have argued that cost is very closely related to density. Bell argues that "density is closely correlated with the cost of providing primary exchange service in the Company's operating territory."[55] Moreover, Bell notes that there is an inverse relationship between density and costs of providing basic residential service: "Overall, the results show that the average cost per residence line increases with decreasing levels of density."[56]

There are significant density variations between urban areas included in the rate bands. Brantford (B1) has a density of 340 persons per square kilometre; Trenton (C1) has a density of 130 persons per square kilometre; Manotick (D1) has a density of 100 persons per square kilometre; and, in Toronto, population densities associated with wire centres generally range from 3,000 to 9,000 persons per square kilometre.[57] Given that the density in Band A can be up to ninety times greater than that in Band D, and that density is closely related to cost, one might reasonably expect more significant price variations between bands, particularly given that bringing prices closer into line with costs has been an explicit objective in the deregulation process. The fact that these variations are not present suggests that low-cost areas continue to implicitly subsidize high-cost areas *within* and between the so-called "low-cost bands" (in addition to the explicit subsidies from low-cost bands to high-cost bands E, F, and G).

In other words, significant urban-form-related cost variations exist within each band, and between bands, that are not reflected in the prices, which remain relatively uniform across bands. Through these average prices, the lowest-cost areas continue to subsidize the higher-cost areas within and between bands A through D. The lowest-cost areas are the higher-density areas in these bands, including business districts and urban cores, while the higher-cost areas are the lower-density areas and smaller towns.

One example of this involves the question of apartment buildings (or what the phone companies like to refer to as multiple-unit dwellings [MUDs]). The companies have noted that MUDs are inherently cheaper to service than are ground-related dwellings. In fact, Bell petitioned the CRTC to have MUDs removed from subsidy calculations.[58] This was "in view of the likelihood that the costs of serving MUDs are relatively low and prices above cost," with the result that MUDs were not seen as in need of subsidy.[59] Indeed, in its recent Final Report, the Telecommunications Policy Review Panel noted the problem that exists when uniform prices are required "across a broad class of customers, even though costs of service vary greatly within the class (a continuing regulatory practice)."[60] It cited as an example that all customers in Band B are charged the same, whether they live in a multi-unit dwelling or in a single, detached house. One could add that, similarly, all customers in high-density urban cores, low-density suburbs, and small towns are charged the same, even though the costs they incur vary considerably. The CRTC not only denied Bell's request to remove apartments from subsidy calculations but also denied a subsequent request by several companies to de-average prices further within a given band in order to respond to new competitors whose service area covered only a portion of a band.[61]

Though density and costs have an inverse relationship, this is not to say that density and cost necessarily vary in exact lockstep (i.e., that a 50 percent increase in density results in an exactly commensurate 50 percent decrease in costs). The reasons given for the close relationship between density and costs are that low-density areas require longer loops (the linkages between the switching centre and the home) and have higher maintenance costs, including increased cost of travel time for installation and repair. The number of lines within a serving area and the nature of the terrain have also been noted as cost factors.[62]

With increasing use of cellular telephone technology, some might argue that density becomes less a factor in driving costs. But the inverse relationship between density and per line capital costs for residential phone service applies equally to conventional wire-based service and wireless phone technology. Bell itself notes that, "regardless of technology, density will continue to be inversely related with per line capital costs. This is because of the economies of scale associated with serving higher density areas which will continue to be present irrespective of the technology used to provide service."[63] As it now stands, the prices charged for basic phone service do not reflect costs as they vary with urban form.

Cable TV

Ninety-nine percent of Canadian households have at least one colour television.[64] Fully two-thirds of Canadian households subscribe to cable television,[65] delivered by cable companies that provide programming content and distribute it over a network to homes and businesses. The distribution network typically consists of a "headend" – a location where the programming is first aggregated and then disseminated – and a network connecting to customers' homes. In recent years, many companies have invested heavily in upgrading their distribution networks, from coaxial cable to fibre optics, and switching from analog to digital systems. This has permitted more channels, better picture quality, and the ability to deliver broadband internet access.

Given that cable infrastructure includes a substantial physical network, one would expect the costs associated with creating, operating, and maintaining the network to be sensitive to urban form factors in the same way as are the costs of telephone, water infrastructure, and other types of similarly linear infrastructure. However, there appears to be no published research that looks explicitly at the relationship between cable infrastructure costs and urban form. This is indicative of the merely partial accounting of the actual costs of urban sprawl.

In Canada, the CRTC regulates the monthly rate for basic cable services provided by companies with at least six thousand subscribers. The basic service is the standard package of services provided to all subscribers within a company's service area. It includes a number of mandatory Canadian programming services – such as the English and French CBC – as well as other services and networks. Prices for other "discretionary" TV services (e.g., specialty channels or Pay TV) are not regulated, but the CRTC nonetheless expects these to be "reasonably priced."

However, where there is competition within the provider's service area, a cable company can apply to be no longer subject to the regulation of prices. As a result, many of the major cable companies have taken this opportunity with the result that, in many larger urban markets, basic cable prices are, in effect, no longer regulated. Typical prices for basic cable service range from $25 to $43 per month, with some regional variations.[66]

In the absence of rigorous empirical studies of cable costs and prices, it is difficult to draw definitive conclusions. However, one would reasonably expect costs to vary with urban form factors, as they do for other network industries. And, given relatively uniform prices, particularly within a given market, it is unlikely that prices reflect actual cost variations related to urban form.

Broadband Internet

Access to broadband or high-speed internet does not fall under the CRTC's basic service objective for universal access, which requires only that dial-up internet access be provided at local rates. However, high speed access to the internet is increasingly viewed as being essential to economic and social development as well as, of course, to expanded entertainment services such as movies on demand or high-definition television. With the introduction of voice over internet protocol, it may also become an important method of providing telephone service. Canada has one of the highest rates of broadband subscribers in the world, at twenty-two subscribers per one hundred inhabitants.[67] One recent survey suggests that about half of all Canadian households have high speed access, compared to 14 percent with dial-up access.[68] In Canada, most subscribers receive their high speed access either through the cable network or through the telephone network (at present, there is an almost even split between these two).[69] Internet access is provided by the major incumbent telephone and cable companies as well as by a number of other internet service providers (ISPs).

There appears to be no published research that looks explicitly at how the costs of delivering high-speed internet access might vary with urban form factors. However, to the extent that the broadband network architecture is the same as is that for the telephone network, it would not be unreasonable to assume that costs would vary in a manner similar to that shown for telephone infrastructure. As for high-speed internet access delivered via the cable network, given the lack of specific research into cable network cost variations and urban form noted above, there is no empirical basis upon which to draw parallels. But, to the extent that the cable network is a linear one, it would not be unreasonable to expect costs to vary with urban form factors in broadly typical ways.

Prices for standard high speed access are generally in the range of $40 to $50 per month, introductory offers and bundling aside.[70] The retail prices of internet access are not regulated by the CRTC. However, the prices charged by incumbent cable companies to other ISPs are subject to CRTC approval.[71] They are to be based on costs plus a mark-up. The resulting "third-party internet access service rates" do not vary locationally but do vary by company and by the speed of internet access offered, stated in terms of a monthly rate per end user.

Retail prices, as they are unregulated, are not bound to follow the wholesale structure and price levels; however, in practice, they tend to do so, both on the part of the major cable companies and other ISPs. As such, it is unlikely that prices for high-speed internet service reflect variations in cost associated with urban form.

Postal Service

Postal service is another example of a network industry, and, this being the case, it is not unreasonable to expect the costs of mail service to vary with urban form factors. In fact, several studies have sought to identify the major cost factors in postal service. In this discussion, the focus is on the provision of standard mail on the part of government organizations or government-regulated organizations rather than on the part of private courier companies.

One study undertaken for the European Union analyzes cost drivers across all EU member countries, looking for the existence of economies of scale, economies of density, and economies of scope in the postal service.[72]

Economies of scale are said to exist if unit costs fall when output and network size increase in the same proportion (i.e., if proportional increases in the size of the network and the amount of mail decrease the costs of delivering a letter); economies of density are said to exist when adding mail over a fixed network lowers the unit cost of mail delivery; and economies of scope are said to exist when expanding the product range (say, adding parcel delivery to letter delivery) lowers unit costs.

Overall, the study finds that there are broadly constant returns to scale (i.e., expanding the network and the volume of mail together did not affect unit costs either positively or negatively) but significant economies of network density. In other words, adding to the mail volume over a fixed network lowers the unit cost. Specifically, increasing mail volume by 10 percent increases total costs by only 6.5 percent (thereby lowering per unit costs).[73]

Postal service can be thought of as having the following major components: collection, outward sorting, transport, inward sorting, and delivery. Of these, the most significant cost component is delivery to the final address. For EU countries, on average, delivery accounts for about half of total postal costs: "Given the relative importance of delivery with respect to other activities the cost characteristics of the provision of postal products is going to be highly influenced by the delivery activity."[74] The EU study finds that, keeping the network constant, a 10 percent increase in volume increases delivery costs by only 6.4 percent, thereby lowering unit costs.[75]

With respect to the impacts of geographic factors on postal costs, a study by Cazals et al. measures the impact of the density of delivery points (i.e., the addresses of homes and businesses to which mail is delivered) along a given length of route with the expectation that, for a given length of route, the greater the number of delivery points, the lower the actual cost per delivered item. The study finds that this relationship holds and is significant: a 10 percent increase in address density results in a 2.7 percent reduction in unit costs.[76] This relationship between density of delivery points and lower costs is confirmed in other studies.[77] In fact, economies of density are found in all of the other major components of the mail service, including mail collection, sorting, and transport.

Studies also assess the extent to which the degree of urbanization affects postal costs. One would expect that the higher the percentage of urban population, the greater the efficiencies and the lower the cost. Indeed, this has been found to be true: a 10 percent increase in urban population results in a 6.7 percent reduction in per unit costs.[78] Looking at collection costs only, a 10 percent increase in the share of urban population would lower unit costs by 9.7 percent.[79] A UK study finds that the most important factors influencing geographical cost variations are the travel distance between delivery points, the average volume of mail per delivery point, and the remoteness of the area from major hubs.[80] Thus, the evidence is strong that postal service costs are sensitive to urban form factors, such as the density of delivery points and collection points, as well as to the percentage of urban population. For a network industry, this is by now not a surprising result.

When we look at the pricing side for standard letters, uniform rates are in effect and do not change either with the distance the letter must travel or with urban densities. In fact, "postage stamp pricing" is a generic term used in many industries to describe flat, or uniform, rates that hold regardless of factors such as distance-related costs.

In Canada and most other Western countries, postal service is subject to a universal service obligation, which typically mandates uniform rates as well as basic service standards. In Canada's case, mail is delivered by a government-owned Crown corporation (Canada Post), which maintains a monopoly on letter mail. The price of first-class letter mail is subject to a price cap formula, which permits stamp-price increases of no more than two-thirds the consumer price index.[81] The more expensive, lower-density routes are subsidized from Canada Post's general revenues through an implicit subsidy system "buried in overall postal rates."[82] The extent of the subsidy is not available, if indeed it is known at all. This is similar to the situation that existed with respect to basic telephone service before the introduction of an explicit, targeted subsidy for high-cost areas and, thus, likely involves higher than necessary subsidy costs and overall costs.

Because postal service is very much under review in many countries, there is considerable discussion of alternative pricing mechanisms. This includes zonal or geographic pricing, in which prices vary with distance or density. In the United Kingdom for example, Royal Mail applied to introduce a zonal pricing system for select retail bulk mail services that were not subject to the universal service obligation. Under the proposal, five zones would be established based on population and business density at the destination (rather than on distance the letter travels), with prices reflecting cost variations. Each zone encompasses areas with similar delivery costs. In the above-average density zones, prices would fall, and in the lower-than-average density zones, prices would increase, as is shown in Table 8.2. These figures give an indication of the actual cost variations between zones of different density in the United Kingdom. If applied, prices in commercial centres and urban zones would drop, and prices in rural areas would increase.

Table 8.2

Royal Mail's proposed zonal pricing

Zone	Description	Variation from national average price (%)
A	Business district	−4.6
B	High density	−1.6
C	Average density	0 (existing tariff)
D	Low density	+4.5
E	Very low density	+7.3

Source: Royal Mail, "Application under Licence Condition 21 for Approval to Offer Geographic Zonal Prices for Bulkmail Services," 5 July 2006, p. 11, from Table 2.1 (p. 8) and Table 2.4 (p. 11), http://www.psc.gov.uk/.

They suggest the level of implicit subsidies at work and the degree to which denser areas cross-subsidize less dense areas.[83] In other words, these figures imply that, under current uniform pricing, mail to business districts is overcharged by about 5 percent, while mail to low-density, primarily rural locations is undercharged 5 percent to 7 percent.[84]

Average Prices: Efficient Development Subsidizes Inefficient Development

The services described above are all network industries, characterized by a physical network of infrastructure that extends over geographic space and/ or includes travel over the service area, be it by truck, car, or on foot (in the case of some postal delivery). The services are united in their use of average pricing, in which standard prices apply across service areas. These prices do not reflect how cost varies significantly with the geographic and urban form characteristics of the service area, especially distance and density.

As we know by now, the effect of average pricing is to overcharge those customers that incur below-average costs and to undercharge those who incur above-average costs. As has been shown above for each of the services considered, below-cost customers tend to be those in denser, urban areas, and above-cost customers tend to be those in less dense, more distant, or more rural locations. This creates a situation in which inaccurate price signals and hidden cross-subsidies influence consumers' and businesses' decision-making processes, especially when one considers the cumulative financial impact of the distortions that exist across all of the services reviewed above. This leads to an inefficient allocation of resources within the industries themselves, especially, to higher than necessary levels of subsidy where subsidies are implicit rather than explicit and to overinvestment in infrastructure in inefficient areas. The price structures send false signals that systematically underprice inefficient development, making it relatively more attractive, and overprice efficient development, making it less attractive. These mis-prices are a critical factor in the promotion of urban sprawl.

Housing, Infrastructure, and Energy
More Mis-Pricing and Mis-Incentives

The widespread mis-pricing of municipal services, utilities, and other network services, primarily through the application of average cost-based pricing, is detailed above. There are, however, yet more instances of public policies creating mis-pricing and other types of mis-incentives that encourage urban sprawl. These are found in policies to encourage homeownership, in infrastructure and energy policies and programs, and in the case of "bundled goods," all of which are discussed below.

Housing and Mortgage Policy
Homeownership is a valued central tenet of the North American way of life. Houses generally appreciate in value over time and provide a major, if not the largest, source of wealth creation for most families. Many government programs, extending back decades, have sought to make home ownership available to a wider slice of the population. In the United States, the federal government has insured mortgages for homebuyers since the creation of the Federal Housing Administration in 1934. Also in the United States, mortgage interest and property tax are eligible as income tax deductions.

Canadian initiatives of the same era were similar, but ultimately their influence was not as widespread as that of the powerful US programs. In Canada, the Veterans' Land Act, 1942, helped to provide housing to veterans returning from the Second World War and assisted in the creation of some fifty thousand homes.[1] Following the model of the US Federal Housing

Administration, the Canadian government instituted the Dominion Housing Act in 1935. By providing a government guarantee or insurance, this act encouraged lenders to provide long-term amortized mortgages to homeowners. In 1946, the newly created Central Mortgage and Housing Corporation took over the administration of the mortgage insurance program.

These and other similar initiatives were well-intentioned programs aiming to help returning veterans readjust to civilian life as well as to help others who might not otherwise be able to afford to buy a home of their own. The problem is that they had and continue to have unintended consequences, particularly in terms of their impact on consumption patterns and urban development patterns. The scale of these impacts has increased as the extent of the programs has broadened and deepened, and as cities have grown and problems such as congestion and air pollution have intensified. Moreover, there are new issues to confront today, such as the environmental impacts of development, which were not top of mind when the programs were initiated.

In the United States, mortgage interest and property tax deductibility apply on principal of up to $1 million. Because the dollar amount of the subsidy increases proportionately with the size of the mortgage, this has become known as the "mansion subsidy."[2] Mortgage subsidies are estimated to cost the US federal government $100 billion per year.[3]

In Canada, we do not have mortgage interest and property tax deductibility. But we nevertheless have homeownership programs that result in unintended consequences for urban development patterns, often in ways that undermine planning policies for compact, sustainable communities. To illustrate these mis-policies, some of the major Canadian programs and their impacts are discussed in detail below.

Mortgage Loan Insurance

Today, the Canada Mortgage and Housing Corporation (CMHC) offers mortgage loan insurance for homebuyers (and for rental buildings) allowing borrowing of up to 95 percent of the cost of a new home – compared to a maximum of 75 percent, which is typical in the private mortgage market. The aim is to promote higher levels of home ownership, particularly for first-time buyers who may have difficulty saving a 25 percent downpayment.

However, particularly in the case of affordable homes for first-time buyers, much of the supply is primarily on greenfields sites, especially for single detached dwellings, as comparable housing in more central, already-urbanized areas tends to be more expensive. So the Mortgage Loan Insurance program can inadvertently spur demand for greenfields housing, with its attendant costs. As has been shown earlier, the more distant a house is from the centre of a city, the more cars are likely to be owned and the more kilometres travelled, with commensurate impacts on GHG production.

Historically, the CMHC set a maximum house price above which a potential homeowner was not eligible for loan insurance. That ceiling was lifted as of 2003. There is now no limit on the price of a house that is eligible for mortgage insurance. While this does eliminate a barrier for first-time buyers who choose to live in areas where housing is more expensive, it also in effect allows people to buy larger homes than they otherwise might be able to, including those who are "trading up." Larger homes often come with larger lots, in suburban locations, and higher levels of energy use. In fact, research undertaken for the CMHC notes that the size of homes has been increasing at the same time that household size has been falling. It also notes that GHGs are closely linked to house size: for every square foot of housing occupied, on average 5.9 kilograms of GHGs are emitted every year.[4]

Government policy and mortgage insurance make it easier for people to consume more land and housing without placing any limits, regardless of impacts on energy consumption in the home or impacts on energy used for travel to and from the home. As structured, this CMHC policy flies in the face of the agency's other initiatives, which are aimed at building sustainable urban communities and energy-efficient green homes. Policies such as these need to be reviewed within the broad context of their impact on sustainable urban growth and energy use.

Also recently introduced is a policy of providing mortgage insurance for second homes, such as cottages or recreational properties, potentially encouraging sprawl in more rural or ex-urban locations. The impacts of this initiative on energy consumption both within the home and in terms of increased auto travel to and from the second home are not addressed. It is difficult to understand the policy rationale for this initiative: why is encouraging ownership of a second home a matter for public policy and government involvement?

In the post-Kyoto era, it is hard to imagine a rationale for government intervention that extends beyond helping potential buyers to purchase their first, energy-efficient home or to undertake energy-efficient renovations. At least, it is hard to imagine a rationale that is consistent with sustainable community objectives. The CMHC does offer incentives to buy an energy-efficient home or make energy-efficient renovations, but gains from these could be easily negated by other incentives that support increasing the size

Table 9.1

Travel characteristics and costs, and urban location, 1996

	Older urban region	New suburban region
Average travel costs	$7,000	$13,700
Average housing costs	$10,100	$13,600
Housing costs as a percentage of income	18.8	18.3
Travel costs as a percentage of income	13.0	18.4
Average number of cars per household	1.07	1.84
Transit modal share (average daily, all purposes)	22.7	5.5

Source: Miller et al., *Travel and Housing Costs in the Greater Toronto Area: 1986-1996*, Technical Report, vols. 1 and 2. Data in first four rows from Table E.1, p. viii; in fifth row from Table 6.2, p. 24; in last row from Table 6.4, p. 35.

of the home and/or encouraging moves to areas that require more driving and infrastructure. Not only does this kind of conflicting and inconsistent policy, within the same organization, have limited effectiveness from a sustainability perspective, but it is also doubly expensive: it is paying both for increasing GHGs and for reducing them.

Conventional Mortgage Policy

It is well established that, when comparing houses of similar floor area and lot size, houses located in central neighbourhoods tend to be more expensive than houses that are farther away from the city centre simply by virtue of the added amenity and accessibility that centrality brings. These central areas also tend to be well served by transit, where walking and cycling are viable forms of transportation. As a result, central households tend to own fewer cars, on average, than houses that are more distant from the city centre (see Table 9.1). In fact, there is a clear distance/car-ownership gradient: car ownership increases by 0.0045 cars per household for every kilometre away from the centre of the city the household is located.[5]

Of course, car ownership and distances travelled by car are closely linked. The more cars you have, the farther you are likely to drive. It has been shown that, on average, distances travelled increase by 15.1 kilometres per day for every additional car owned by a household.[6] And the farther away from the city centre a household is located, the farther its members travel on a daily basis – an estimated additional 0.68 kilometres per day for every kilometre of distance a household is located from the city centre.[7]

So the farther away a household is located from the central city, the more cars its members are likely to own and the further they would travel every day. Thus, their transportation costs are likely to be greater than those of members of households located nearer the city centre. On average, a household in the City of Toronto spent $7,000 per year on urban travel costs in 1996. Households located in the surrounding suburban municipalities spent, on average, between $10,000 and $14,000 – up to twice as much as those located in the central part of the metropolitan area.[8]

Indeed, transportation costs can account for a very significant portion of a household's budget. In two of the four suburban Toronto regional municipalities, household transport costs were, on average, about equal to housing costs, while in the two others, transport costs were about 85 percent of housing costs.[9] In comparison, transport costs were about 70 percent of housing costs in the City of Toronto. Table 9.1 compares key data for the older urban region (the City of Toronto) with a newly urbanizing suburban region (the Region of York).

Households that live in areas where fewer cars are needed and where total vehicle-kilometres travelled are lower, and where transport costs are thus correspondingly low, could afford to spend more of their income on mortgage payments, without increasing the risk of default. However, when a family goes to the bank to apply for a mortgage for a new home, the bank considers the household's income as well as how much debt it has. At present, most mortgages are conditional upon house-related monthly costs (gross debt service) not exceeding 32 percent of gross monthly household income, and total debt payments (including gross debt service and other debt service – total debt service [TDS]) not exceeding 40 percent of household income. TDS would include car and other consumer loans, for example, but not other transportation-related costs, such as vehicle-operating costs. Even excluding auto loan payments, the costs of operating a vehicle can be very substantial – about $4,500 per year for a basic car driving an average distance (and excluding parking costs).[10]

The conventional mortgage analysis does not factor in lower overall transportation costs in areas that are well served by transit or where walking and cycling are possible. Households located in these areas would spend less on transportation and, therefore, be in a position to spend more on mortgage payments. The fact that the conventional mortgage analysis does not take transport costs (except debt) into account is surprising, especially given their magnitude. The maximum TDS ratio of 40 percent allowed under conventional mortgage lending practice does not allow higher shares of income to be spent on housing, even if transportation costs are substantially lower. This, in effect, constitutes a bias against households that spend less on transport but that may need to spend more on housing in central locations, where comparable housing tends to be more expensive than it is in suburban locations. In other words, conventional mortgage analysis has an inherent bias against those who choose to live in more sustainable urban environments, consume less energy, and create less air pollution.

This is particularly important for the first-time homebuyer, who is often forced to suburban locations and new greenfield housing because of higher costs of even starter homes in central locations. For example, the members of a typical household with an income of $60,000 and a minimum 5 percent downpayment would be able to afford a home priced at a maximum of $186,000. In many larger urban centres, their choices would be extremely limited. They would be more likely to find a home in their price range, or be able to buy more house and land, if they purchased in suburban locations.

If, on the other hand, the mortgage lending process recognized that they might spend less money on transportation living in a central location, and allowed a TDS ratio of 50 percent instead of 40 percent, for example, they could now borrow a higher amount of principal and have a wider choice of homes and locations open to them – including those that may be more expensive but that have significantly fewer environment impacts. These considerations can only become more important in the medium to longer term as gas prices increase, along with other vehicle operating expenses, such as insurance. Fortunately, there are practical ways of dealing with this issue (see Chapter 12).

Tax Policies

In addition to mortgage-related policies and programs, there are a number of special tax policies aimed at encouraging homeownership. The most significant of these is probably the capital gains exemption for primary residences. Under this provision, gains in the value of a home are exempt from capital gains tax, provided that the home is a primary residence. This exemption speeds the capital accumulation process and allows homebuyers to buy houses that are more expensive than they might otherwise be able to afford without the exemption, in particular, for successive home purchases after the initial one (once some capital has been accumulated through the sale of the first home). Given that there is no ceiling on the price of an eligible home or on the amount of capital that is not taxed, it also has the potential effect of encouraging the purchase of more expensive homes as a means of maximizing non-taxable earnings and accumulating capital. Though not limited to expensive suburban homes, to the extent that more valuable homes are larger homes on larger lots, the policy can be seen as contributing to urban sprawl. Interestingly, in the United States, though there is mortgage interest and property tax deductibility, there is a ceiling on the amount of capital gains associated with the sale of a primary residence exempted from taxation (currently set at $250,000 per single person and $500,000 per couple). In Canada, the amount of federal revenue that was foregone as a result of this tax policy (also known as a "tax expenditure") is estimated at $8.65 billion for 2006 and projected to be $6.2 billion for 2009.[11] This is one of the government's largest personal income tax breaks.

A number of special policies are related to the federal goods and services tax (GST). GST treatment of housing is especially complicated. Newly constructed homes are subject to GST when sold to the homebuyer. But purchasers of such a home are eligible for the new housing rebate – a rebate of 36 percent of the GST paid on houses that sell for a maximum of $450,000. This rebate initially came about as a result of pressure from the construction industry to maintain the effective tax rate on housing at the same level that existed before the GST was introduced. It argued that applying the full (then) 7 percent GST would have negative impacts on affordability.

If, on the other hand, you renovate an existing house, the costs of that renovation are, for all intents and purposes, subject to GST. If a homeowner wants to create an accessory rental unit within her home, for example, she will be charged the full GST on the cost of the necessary renovations. She will also be charged the full GST on costs of making her home more energy-efficient, such as updating furnaces or installing energy-efficient windows. A homeowner would have to essentially rebuild her existing home, or create an addition larger than the existing house, in order to be eligible for a GST rebate on renovation-related costs under the new housing rebate.[12]

Though resale housing is not subject to GST, the inequal tax treatment of new homes versus renovations may put the purchase and renewal of existing homes at a competitive disadvantage when compared to new homes, which, more often than not, are found on greenfields sites. For example, of the roughly 225,000 housing units awaiting planning approval in the GTA in 2001, about 15 percent were slated for already-urbanized land, with the remaining 85 percent headed for greenfields sites.[13] This is especially important in terms of the impacts on energy use – such as the added energy used for transportation when suburban locations are chosen or in terms of the relative incentive to choose a transit-oriented neighbourhood and renovate an existing home to make it more energy efficient rather than to choose an auto-oriented neighbourhood.

The new housing rebate is a fairly expensive tax break. The cost of the exemption is estimated at $720 million for 2007, with a projected value of $515 million for 2009.[14] Though the tax code does not explicitly incentivize energy-efficient renovations, the federal government does offer grants under the ecoENERGY retrofit program.[15] Funding for this program totals $220 million over four years, including grants to small organizations for non-residential retrofits.[16]

Another common type of homeownership incentive is provided through the use of Registered Retirement Savings Plan (RRSP) savings towards the purchase of a home. Under these types of program, a homebuyer is permitted to borrow funds from her RRSP to put towards the purchase of a home. These funds and their growth are tax-sheltered, including with regard to their withdrawal for use in purchasing a home. Under the federal Home Buyers' Plan, first-time homebuyers can withdraw up to $25,000 from their RRSPs per person, without paying income tax on the amount, in order to buy a home (in this case, the program is not limited to newly constructed homes).

Where incentives employ flat amount ceilings, as is the case with the maximum RRSP withdrawal, or a maximum house price of $450,000 for a new housing GST rebate, significant variations in house prices that occur within and across urban areas are not accounted for. For example, a family with a $25,000 downpayment will be able to afford a larger house and lot in a greenfields location than in an urban area and, in fact, may be incentivized towards the former. One response to this might be to allow homebuyers to borrow higher amounts from their RRSPs when they purchase in areas that offer higher levels of sustainability and incur lower transportation costs but have higher house prices.

Other incentives intended to increase home ownership levels exist at the provincial level. For example, the Province of Ontario offers a land transfer tax rebate for first-time homebuyers when they buy a newly constructed home. First-time homebuyers who may want to purchase a resale home do not benefit from this tax break, which is intended, in part, as a boost to the residential construction industry. All or part of the land transfer tax may be refunded, up to a maximum refund of $2,000. It is estimated that this rebate cost the province $33 million in foregone revenues in 2006.[17]

A number of incentives are aimed at increasing levels of home ownership, allowing accrual of personal wealth and the stability that homeownership brings. However, the way these instruments are structured is not sensitive to their potential to unintentionally encourage urban sprawl, higher infrastructure costs, and higher levels of energy use for transportation and running a home. Several instruments may inadvertently encourage the purchase of larger homes, which are often located in suburban areas where more energy is needed for transport and auto dependence is greater. Some instruments are aimed at new construction only, which can skew demand towards greenfields sites over already-urbanized areas. And frequently, these instruments, as currently structured, contradict other public policy objectives related to the reduction of energy use and GHGs and to the creation of sustainable communities. Tax breaks and mortgage loan insurance programs encourage larger homes, sprawl, and energy use, while grants are issued to promote energy-efficiency retrofits – a double expenditure whose effects cancel each other out. It is not uncommon for this to occur even within the same organization, where lack of a consistent approach calls into question the wise use of fiscal resources. For example, within the CMHC, reductions in mortgage insurance premiums for energy-efficient homes are aimed at curbing energy use, while providing mortgage loan insurance for second homes will act to increase energy use. Two programs are being funded, though the effects from an urban sustainability perspective are contradictory. While laudable in intent, policies to encourage home ownership must now be examined within a broad context of interrelated public policy objectives on urban sprawl, energy use, GHG emissions, and the wise use of public funds.

Transportation and Infrastructure

Housing and business location decisions tend to be made in conjunction with transportation considerations. The financial cost, mode of travel, and travel time are all considered when deciding on where to buy a home or locate a business. A household's cost of travel can be very significant, as is shown above. And the cost of travel relative to the cost of housing tends to increase as the location of the home moves farther and farther from the centre of the city and as greater reliance on auto travel, longer distances, and more vehicles per household come into play.

Tax Policies

In influencing the cost of transport, tax policies affect the mode of travel, how many cars people own and their type, how far people travel (which is closely linked with how many cars they own), and location decisions, all of which, together, shape the demand for infrastructure – its type (e.g., roads versus transit), the overall amount (e.g., total lane-kilometres of road needed), its cost, and its environmental impacts. In influencing location decisions, costs of transport therefore play a key role in shaping urban development patterns.

A large part of the cost of travel is the cost of fuel. Gas prices are heavily influenced by a number of public policies, including taxes and subsidies. Both the federal and provincial governments, for example, levy a separate excise tax on gas sold at the pump, currently at 10¢ per litre federally and at 14.7¢ per litre in Ontario. The federal and provincial governments both exempt alterative fuels from their excise tax. GST is applicable, but sales tax is not charged on energy sources in Ontario, a measure estimated to cost the province some $4 billion per year (though the provincial fuel excise tax is higher than the federal rate).[18] This means that taxes account for a little less than one-third of the price of gas, when the total price is at around one dollar per litre.[19] Not surprisingly, the gas tax is a significant source of revenue for governments: the federal government raises about $4 billion per year from gasoline tax, and $1.6 billion from the GST on gas and diesel fuel.[20]

Both the federal government and the Province of Ontario have recently agreed to devote a portion of their gas tax revenue to environmentally sustainable infrastructure for cities (in the former case) and public transit (in the latter). For the federal government, it is estimated that this will provide $4.4 billion in funding over four years to 2010,[21] and an additional $8 billion to 2013-14.[22] Ontario currently provides two cents per litre for transit funding. It is estimated that, by 2010, this will have provided $1.6 billion in transit funding since the program's inception in 2004.[23]

Given its considerable negative externalities, taxing gas and reinvesting proceeds (at least part of them) in more energy-efficient, less polluting alternatives makes sense. Price signals encourage behaviour consistent with policy objectives (e.g., reduced GHG emissions). One would expect that higher prices would moderate demand for gas and for travel while investments would improve availability of alternatives to car travel. This is smart policy. Price signals moderate demand for unsustainable activities, and pricing provides revenue to invest in more sustainable alternatives. Some argue that higher gas taxes should be implemented as a proxy for road tolls, with the result being that the more you drive the more tax you pay. Though significant, fuel taxes in North America are still considerably lower than in

Europe, where, in many countries, the taxes exceed the cost of the fuel itself, often substantially (see Chapter 12).

On the other side of the equation are incentives to the energy sector. These incentives have the effect of lowering the price of gas for vehicles as well as for fuel used to heat and cool homes and business premises. To the extent that energy is underpriced because of government subsidies or tax breaks, consumption levels rise. This means that, being less sensitive to prices, people may drive greater distances, buy less fuel-efficient vehicles, or buy larger, more distant and energy-consumptive homes.

Current tax incentives for the energy sector are mostly in the form of accelerated capital cost allowances. These incentives allow companies to claim a larger share of a capital investment earlier, compared to those expenses that would normally apply, thereby lowering their taxes in the first year or years following the investment (in essence, accelerating the deductibility of the expense). These breaks are intended to encourage investment, for example, in exploration or development of new sources of energy. The total cost of the tax expenditure associated with accelerated capital cost allowances is difficult to estimate, even for the federal government, which offers the incentive.[24]

One review of federal tax policies for renewable versus non-renewable energy investments concludes that treatment is "reasonably similar," with a few important exceptions.[25] The most significant of these involves tax concessions for the oil sands. Oil sands are subject to the mining provisions of the Income Tax Act rather than to the oil and gas provisions. The mining provisions allow for more generous write-offs for property and pre-production development expenses as well as for special provisions for assets used to extract bitumen. The Department of Finance estimates the value of this concession at between $5 million and $40 million for every $1 billion invested.[26] Based on capital investment in the oil sands, it has been suggested that this translates into a tax expenditure of between $200 million and $1.6 billion between 1995 and 2005.[27]

Other tax policies relate directly to various modes of transportation. For example, in 2006, the federal government introduced a tax credit for the cost of transit passes, with the intention of increasing transit ridership. This measure also corrected a previous situation in which both employer-provided transit passes and parking spaces were treated as taxable benefits; however, in practice, most drivers were not taxed, while the transit-riding employees were.[28]

Another example of taxation related to transportation is the Province of Ontario's phasing out of sales tax on automobile insurance premiums. Originally levied at 5 percent, premiums are now exempt from sales tax, a measure estimated to cost the province some $800 million per year in foregone tax revenues.[29] The aim of the tax elimination was to increase the affordability of auto insurance premiums, which had been rising. One of the main causes of the rising premiums was identified as the higher cost of vehicle repairs and replacements due to the rising price of vehicles and greater use of electronics, which are expensive to repair, and a rising share of more expensive light trucks and SUVs.[30] The particular execution of this initiative provides a subsidy that lowers the cost of driving, thereby providing an incentive to auto ownership and car travel. In addition, it provides this subsidy to all drivers, regardless of whether affordability is an issue or not, while doing nothing to address one of the main causes of rising premiums – costly and fuel-inefficient vehicles.

These are some of the policies related to purchasing and running a vehicle that influence the cost of travel and, in so doing, affect decisions regarding location of homes and businesses. Higher travel costs mean less willingness to drive, creating a greater demand for different types of activities to be closer together and more accessible, including by non-auto means. Other policies that affect the costs of infrastructure are also important.

Infrastructure Grants and Loans

Earlier chapters review how DCs, regulated prices, and other fiscal policies provide revenue for urban infrastructure of various kinds and affect their pricing, in turn influencing decisions that shape urban development patterns. Another source of funding for urban infrastructure is government grant or loan programs, usually in the form of grants made from provincial or federal governments to municipalities.

In recent years, the federal government has begun to provide funding for municipal infrastructure projects through programs such as the Infrastructure Canada Program (at $2.05 billion) and the Canada Strategic Infrastructure Fund (at $4 billion). Funding is used for a variety of projects, including highways, urban expressways, transit, and sewer and water infrastructure. These programs are not governed by criteria regarding their environmental impacts or impacts on urban sprawl, with the exception of a portion of the Infrastructure Canada Program, which is earmarked for "green" infrastructure. Also included here is the $12 billion federal Gas Tax Fund created through gas tax revenues, noted above, and intended for "Environmentally

Sustainable Municipal Infrastructure." There is also the one-time Public Transit Fund, at $400 million for 2005-06, $155 million of which was earmarked for Ontario and allocated within the province based on transit ridership.[31]

The major source of infrastructure funding in Ontario is through the Re-New Ontario program. Introduced in 2005, this is a five-year infrastructure investment plan, with funding totalling $30 billion, 90 percent of which is to be direct investments from the government. This program includes $1.4 billion in funding from the province's 2¢ per litre gas tax revenues, to be directed towards transit investments.[32] Funds will also be directed to highway improvements, sewer and water infrastructure, affordable housing, schools, hospitals, and court buildings. Transportation infrastructure investments account for $11.4 billion of the total, including $4.5 billion for transit expansion and $6.5 billion in highway and border crossing improvements. In addition, the 2006 budget announced the Move Ontario initiative, a one-time, $1.2 billion source of funds for transit improvements in the GTA as well as for improvements to municipal roads and bridges primarily in rural and northern communities.[33]

Investment in urban infrastructure has been deferred and neglected and is much needed. It is laudable that the federal and provincial governments are finally recognizing the importance of healthy cities to citizens, the environment, and the economy, and are investing substantial sums of money to maintain and improve quality of cities. However, as always, there is the potential for unintended consequences that stem from the structure of the funding programs.

First, by creating physical infrastructure, the programs obviously have a direct impact on urban development patterns. Depending on the type and location of the project, some of the investments may promote urban sprawl. For example, investments in urban roads, highways, and expressways, if not undertaken within the context of a carefully crafted transportation and urban development plan that ensures transit support, can promote urban sprawl and further auto dependence. Investments in metropolitan expressway ring roads in Edmonton and Calgary were made under the Canada Strategic Infrastructure Fund. Investments in extensions to sewer and water networks into previously unurbanized locations can support sprawl development in those areas.

Unless carefully undertaken, there can also be a disconnect between different types of investments. For example, some investments in road improvements or extensions can work at cross-purposes with transit investments, rendering the latter less effective. The federal government has taken some steps under the more recent Gas Tax Fund and Public Transit Fund to ensure that investments are clearly in line with environmental objectives, including reduced GHG emissions. These include a requirement for fund recipients to have or develop an integrated community sustainability plan in the former case and a transit ridership growth plan in the latter.

In Ontario, the *Places to Grow* plan, intended to govern the growth of the Toronto region from some 8 million inhabitants currently to 11 million inhabitants in 2031, was brought into law in 2006. In theory, all major provincial infrastructure investments are to be made in support of the *Places to Grow* plan (e.g., with an emphasis on priority areas identified, such as urban growth centres). In practice, there has as yet been little in the way of formal mechanisms implemented to ensure consistency between *Places to Grow* and the now significant infrastructure investments getting under way. For example, serious discrepancies have been noted between *Places to Grow* and the province's initiatives in the same region under the $3.4 billion *Southern Ontario Highways Program 2006 to 2010*.[34]

Second, as investment takes the form of a grant from upper-tier governments to municipalities, the full cost of the investment is not borne by the users or beneficiaries of the investment. This in effect constitutes a subsidy from a broad group of taxpayers (federal, provincial, drivers) to local residents and businesses. This leads to underpricing development that benefits from the investment – in the form of lower property prices, property taxes, or utility prices than would otherwise have been the case.

Especially now that substantial sums are being invested in infrastructure, it is critically important to ensure that these investments support planning objectives and the creation of sustainable, efficient communities. The examples reviewed above show how transportation and infrastructure policies play a role in shaping urban development patterns. Some programs and policies inadvertently contribute to sprawl, while others attempt to mitigate it (e.g., through investments in transit). Here consistency of approach is critical: to avoid duelling subsidies and to achieve tangible results, it is essential to ensure that one set of policies is not undermining another.

"Bundled" Goods: Parking and Local Roads

Parking is a significant component of urban sprawl, especially surface parking. Given the high number of parking spaces provided at malls, offices, and theatres, it is a major impediment to achieving higher densities. In suburban locations, it is not uncommon for the footprint of the building to take up only a quarter or even less of the area of a lot, with over 75 percent of the site devoted to a surface parking lot. Provision of off-street parking spaces is mandated through local zoning bylaws for virtually all uses – single detached homes, apartments, shopping malls, office buildings, restaurants, or factories. When the price of land is low, surface parking is most often provided (land is cheaper than building parking structures). Only for more expensive land does structured parking become economically viable.

Parking requirements are generally based on a calculation of the demand for a given building type at the peak time – the worst-case scenario. Given that parking is typically not paid for by the driver and is therefore under- or unpriced, the demand is further inflated. Needless to say, the result is a vast oversupply of parking spaces. The total number of spaces is not tracked nationally. Several attempts at estimating the total number have been made. Delucchi and Murphy estimate a range from 125 million to 200 million spaces in the United States just for non-residential, off-street, unpriced parking in 1990-91.[35] Residential spaces and street parking are on top of this. Another estimate suggests that there are 232 million parking spaces in retail malls alone.[36] This implies that, on average, there are several spaces for each vehicle. There are about 230 million cars and trucks in the United States,[37] and there are over 18 million cars and light vehicles in Canada.[38]

From a sprawl perspective, the core of the problem is that parking is rarely paid for by the user (i.e., the driver), particularly in suburban areas, where parking is typically "free." In fact, it is estimated that, in the United States, 95 percent of automobile commuters regularly park for free at work, mostly the result of free parking provided by employers. When car travel for all purposes is considered (except trips that end at home), it is estimated that motorists take advantage of free parking for 99 percent of all trips.[39]

Of course, parking is not really free because it comes with high costs, and these costs must be paid somehow. These include capital costs (land, construction) as well as maintenance, lighting, landscaping, snow clearance, security, and insurance. Construction costs for parking spaces can vary considerably, depending on factors such as whether it is a surface lot, an above-ground garage, or a below-ground garage. Spaces in surface lots may cost around $2,000 each, while spaces in an underground garage could easily cost $20,000 or more, not including land.[40] When capital costs (including land) are converted to monthly equivalents, and maintenance and operating costs are added, the cost of a single parking space may range from $30 to $200 a month.[41] When the number of parking spaces that exist in Canada and the United States is considered, it is easy to see that the aggregate cost of parking is huge. For the United States, Delucchi and Murphy estimate the total cost at roughly between $79 and $226 billion per year in 1991.[42] Another estimate places the annual cost of parking at $500 billion in 2000.[43]

For residential uses, the costs of parking spaces and garages are recouped in higher house prices for detached, semi-detached, and townhouses. For multi-unit buildings and condos, the purchase of one or more parking spaces is sometimes optional. In other cases, however, condo buyers must purchase a parking space whether they own a car or not. And so with residential development, to the extent that homeowners are also drivers, one could say that the driver does cover the cost of residential parking and there is no subsidy.[44] However, providing parking spaces and garages adds to the cost of the home as well as taking up land area, adding to sprawl. In the vast majority of cases, the number of parking spaces that must be provided on a property is mandated through municipal zoning bylaws, regardless of the actual number of cars owned by any one household, often to avoid "unsightly" street parking.

In the case of non-residential uses, the costs of parking are recouped through higher property prices, which are in turn passed along into the prices everyone pays for goods and services. The costs are incorporated into the prices of goods and services delivered from factories, warehouses, shopping malls, offices, and the corner convenience store. To the extent that governments do not charge the full cost of parking at their own facilities, parking costs will be regained through higher taxes too. Thus, the costs of "free" parking are actually shared among all consumers and citizens. However, not all consumers and citizens use parking to the same extent: some people drive less often than others; some take transit, cycle, or walk; some do not drive at all. Thus, a cross-subsidy is created, with less frequent or non-drivers subsidizing frequent drivers. All shoppers at the mall, for example, end up paying for the "free" parking provided in the price of the goods and services they acquire there, regardless of whether they drove and parked, took a taxi or bus, walked or cycled.

Given the extent of parking and its high cost, and that the vast majority of it is not paid for directly by users, it is not surprising that the parking subsidy for non-residential uses is astronomical. It is estimated that only 5 percent to 13 percent of the costs of parking are covered by parking charges.[45] Given the magnitude of parking costs, as suggested by the estimates above, this amounts to a subsidy of hundreds of millions if not billions of dollars annually.

Lack of pricing for parking has several serious consequences. First, because parking is not subject to a price signal, demand is unrestrained and parking is oversupplied, which only further elevates the costs and expense. This is a classic inefficient allocation of scarce resources, predicted by economists in the case of inaccurate pricing (or, indeed, a complete lack thereof). The result is overspending on the construction and maintenance of parking spaces, when there are many more productive uses to which the financial resources may be put.

Second, this exaggerated demand for parking – which is not only demand for unpriced parking but demand for unpriced, peak-period parking – is formalized into minimum parking standards developed by traffic engineers and relied upon by planners across North America as the basis for determining parking standards entrenched in local zoning bylaws. Not surprisingly, when parking is free and abundant, people are more likely to choose to drive, initiating a vicious cycle of auto dependence and low-density development.[46] When these inflated parking demand estimates become mandatory minima, high minimum parking standards are a self-fulfilling prophecy in that they beget more demand for driving and parking. As parking requires land (and lots of it!), parking standards have a direct and long-lasting impact on urban development patterns, entrenching low-density development over the long term.

Third, when "free" parking is provided to employees at the workplace, this constitutes a subsidy that is available only to drivers. Commuters who use other, more sustainable modes of travel receive no similar subsidy. Moreover, a considerable body of research has confirmed that unpriced parking results in a higher percentage of commuters choosing to drive rather than to use more sustainable alternatives than they do when parking is priced. It also leads to a higher share of single-occupancy vehicles.[47] In short, unpriced parking artificially lowers the cost of driving and increases the demand. This reduces demand for transit and other alternative modes while promoting lower-density development and overbuilt road infrastructure.

Like parking, local roads can also be considered a bundled good. The cost of the "on-site" roads – that is, those roads that are within a given subdivision or development project area – is recouped by developers through the prices of the houses and other development within the project. Developers typically construct these roads themselves before turning them over to the municipality. Thus, the cost of the road is "bundled" into the price of the house or commercial rents in the corner convenience plaza. They are neither priced nor paid for separately, obscuring their actual cost. Because local road costs are unpriced and invisible to the buyer or renter, they tend to be oversupplied. If homebuyers knew how much of their house price was accounted for by the local road, given a choice they may opt for a narrower lot.

Local road expenses can also be a source of cross-subsidy within a subdivision when, for example, actual road costs, as they vary with house type and type of development, are not reflected accurately in house prices. For example, the pricing of homes may include an overcharge for the road component for multiple-unit dwellings and undercharge single houses on large lots. Delucchi and Murphy estimate the capital cost of bundled, on-site local roads built in the United States in 1991 to be $5 billion to $15 billion.[48] The total cost of all roads paid for by the private sector and recovered in the price of structures, goods, or services was estimated at $12 billion to $76 billion for 1991.[49]

More Mis-Pricing and Mis-Incentives

And so more instances of mis-pricing and mis-incentives are uncovered in yet other areas – in policies to promote home ownership, energy and infrastructure policies, and bundled goods. These are not primarily cases of average cost pricing like those that have been encountered with municipal services, utilities, and other network services; rather, in these areas there are a number of different mechanisms creating mis-pricing and mis-incentives, which are grouped and detailed in the next chapter. The effects on urban sprawl are nonetheless similar to those of average cost pricing: the unintended consequences of public policy encourage sprawl and disadvantage more compact development and non-automobile modes of travel.

10

Driving Sprawl
Pricing and Policy Mis-Incentives

It quickly becomes apparent that there is a wide range of public policies, programs, and fiscal instruments at all levels of government that influence urban development patterns either expressly or (frequently) inadvertently. These interventions affect prices for a broad spectrum of services and infra-structure, housing, commercial development, and transportation in a way that encourages urban sprawl. Mis-pricing, such as when prices charged for urban goods and services do not reflect costs incurred as they vary with urban form factors, leads to underpricing of inefficient development and overpricing of efficient development. This mis-pricing plays a crucial role in encouraging urban sprawl. Here the term "prices" is used loosely to include charges for urban goods and services in their various forms – including free market and regulated prices, DCs, rates, fees, or taxes, as applicable.

Urban development patterns are also susceptible to other policy mis-incentives, such as policies and programs with inherent spatial biases. The instances of mis-pricing and mis-incentives detailed in preceding chapters can be categorized into a handful of common types of policy. These common flaws and their implications for urban sprawl are described below.

Mis-Pricing: A Typology of Mechanisms

Generally speaking, mis-pricing of urban goods and services (as with all other goods and services) stems from two common sources: subsidies and cross-subsidies. A subsidy is "money paid, usually by government, to keep prices below what they would be in a free market ... or to make activities happen that otherwise would not take place ... By distorting markets, they can impose large economic costs."[1] Emanating from government, subsidies can take several forms, including grants or tax forgiveness, special loans or loan guarantees, or other preferential treatment from government.

In contrast to a direct subsidy, a cross-subsidy involves transferring "the burden of covering costs from one area of products or consumers to another," effectively favouring or subsidizing one group over the other, and is *internal* to the firm or agency that establishes and charges the prices.[2] In other words, the cross-subsidy takes place through the price mechanism itself. Another definition holds that a group cross-subsidizes all other consumers if it faces prices that exceed the costs to the group of going it alone – that is, if it pays more than its *stand alone costs*.[3]

As the preceding chapters show, there are many instances of subsidies and cross-subsidies that occur in the provision of urban goods and services, infrastructure and investment. Across this wide range, however, a few common types of mis-pricing become evident.

Government Grants, Loans, Tax Breaks

The discussion above documents several instances of subsidies that play a role in promoting urban sprawl. Many of these are subsidies to homeownership (e.g., new housing GST rebate, land transfer tax rebate, use of RRSPs for home buying), energy, and auto use, all taking the form of tax breaks. The other major type of subsidy is grants for infrastructure, which are provided through federal and provincial programs. Together, these initiatives have the effect of artificially lowering the cost of buying and running a home or non-residential property to the homeowner or business, and encouraging higher levels of consumption – larger buildings, more land, more cars and travel – than would otherwise be the case. The collateral impacts on urban development patterns that these programs and policies impose are not adequately considered.

Duelling Subsidies

The above analysis uncovers some examples in which different subsidies are operating at cross-purposes. This can occur as a result of subsidies emanating from the same government or even from the same organization. This is the case, for example, with CMHC programs such as mortgage insurance that tend to promote demand for larger and more distant (i.e., energy-consumptive) homes, on the one hand, and incentives to purchase "energy-efficient" homes or make energy-efficient retrofits, on the other. In other examples, the federal government subsidizes the production of energy, on the one hand, and provides incentives to conservation, on the other. If not carefully executed, simultaneous investment in both highway infrastructure and transit can also be mutually undermining. In these instances, government is providing incentives and subsidies to bring about an outcome, as well as its opposite, in a bout of double-spending and duelling subsidies. Aside from representing a misallocation of public resources, these incentives affect both absolute price levels for affected goods and services (e.g., housing) and relative prices (e.g., prices of housing in central versus more distant locations).

Apparent Non-Pricing of Public Goods

Another type of mis-pricing involves the non-pricing of certain public or quasi-public goods. This is not to say that the costs of roads or parking, for example, are not paid for – of course, the costs of construction, maintenance, operations, and replacement must somehow be paid for (otherwise they would not exist). But the pricing of these goods and services is not accurately and apparently tied to their use. They are paid for mostly through general forms of taxation or are embedded in product pricing rather than through a more direct user charge that might be levied for each and every use, making the actual costs much more apparent to the user. Not surprisingly, when goods and services appear to bear no cost and seem "free" to the user, there will be undisciplined, excessive demand and higher infrastructure costs overall.

Prices Based on Average Costs

The costs of a wide range of network services, such as water, sewer, roads, utilities, garbage pickup, and postal service, vary with urban form. These cost variations occur both within and between cities and towns. Within a particular city, costs of providing network services can vary substantially from city centre to older suburb to new suburb, depending on the development pattern and specifics of local geography. In particular, factors such as density, location, local context, and type of land use have been shown to influence service costs. Density of development has the greatest impact on per unit servicing costs for network infrastructure and services. Costs can also vary significantly with location of development, depending on factors such as specifics of network architecture, whether there is existing capacity at a particular location, distance to central facilities, as well as topography, geography, or other environmental features of the landscape.

The fundamental problem related to most of the services described above is that prices charged do not reflect costs incurred as these costs vary with location and development pattern. Instead, average cost-based prices apply to all the major utilities reviewed above as well as to infrastructure construction though the DC. Where average prices are such that some consumers, homebuyers, or businesses pay more than costs incurred while others pay less than costs incurred, a cross-subsidy is created. Indeed, this condition is a common definition of cross-subsidy: "A price scheme is said to have cross subsidies if some consumer prices are below average costs and others are above."[4] Inefficient urban development is subsidized, efficient development is overpriced, with commensurate impacts on urban development patterns.

Prices Unrelated to Costs

The property tax presents a variation on the theme in that it is not a case of average prices. With the property tax, "prices" – in this case the taxes levied – are based upon the assessed market value of the property, which bears no intentional or systematic relation to the level of costs incurred for municipal services. Still, for many municipally provided network services – such as roads, road maintenance, snow clearance, sewer and water, garbage and recycling collection – the costs are sensitive to urban form factors such as density. Those who incur lower costs by virtue of living in more efficient urban environments do not necessarily pay lower taxes, given that taxes are related to the value of the property rather than to cost causation. In fact, in some cities, such as Toronto, the denser areas tend to be more central and higher valued. Residents of these areas will pay proportionately higher taxes *and* incur relatively lower costs compared to those in suburban homes. Thus, as a price signal, property taxes are not a good indicator of the level of municipal costs incurred by a particular household or business. As a result, this decoupling of prices and costs also creates the possibility for cross-subsidies through the property tax and price signals regarding the actual costs of services misfire.

Bundled Goods and Services

I also discuss instances of "bundled" goods and services, in which costs are bundled into market prices, which can be a source of cross-subsidy. Of most relevance are bundling of parking costs, as well as local road costs, in house and commercial property prices. In addition to the cross-subsidy issue, a particular problem with respect to these bundled goods is that, because their costs are rolled in with other housing costs, they cannot be isolated and, therefore, consumers cannot make informed choices about them. Other than for the occasional ball hockey game, local roads offer little amenity other than access, which is not improved with more metres of road. If home-owners knew the share of their house price that was related to local road costs, they might choose to live on a forty-foot lot rather than a sixty-foot lot and direct the road savings towards more house. In other words, they might choose a denser development option. As it is, local road and parking costs are wrapped up in the total house price, or in the price of other goods and services, and the consumer cannot make informed choices about them.

Non-Pricing of Externalities

Last, though not the focus of this book, the non-pricing of externalities such as congestion or air pollution is an important pricing flaw. When non-priced, externalities in effect act as a form of cross-subsidy. For example, a portion of the cost of driving – those costs associated with air pollution – are borne by others who must experience the pollution even if they are non-drivers. As noted earlier, non-pricing of externalities is a common source of market failure, noted as a cause of excessive suburbanization and decentralization.

The Wider Costs of Subsidies and Cross-Subsidies

Price averaging is often used deliberately, as an explicit mechanism for cross-subsidization. This was how the universal service obligations for basic telephone service were fulfilled prior to the implementation of the National Contribution Fund, for example. However, the problem with all of the in-stances of mis-pricing noted in these chapters is that cross-subsidization is occurring but is apparently *not* the result of a deliberate policy, is largely hidden and opaque, and has undesirable consequences in promoting urban sprawl. The existence of these cross-subsidies is not widely known either by the subsidizers or the subsidizees.

This is a problem because, by definition, the person who incurs lower costs winds up subsidizing the person who causes higher levels of cost. Through the pricing policies discussed at length above, we have seen instan-ces of mis-pricing causing the following specific types of cross-subsidization:

- those who live on small lots subsidize those living on large lots;
- smaller residential units subsidize larger residential units;
- those who don't drive or drive less subsidize those who drive most;
- land uses that generate fewer trips subsidize uses that generate more trips;
- those who live in less expensive-to-service areas subsidize those who live in more expensive-to-service areas;
- those who live nearer the centre of the city subsidize those who live farther from the centre; and
- urban dwellers subsidize rural dwellers.

Of these, probably the most widespread cross-subsidy and the one with the most significant impacts on urban form is related to density, that is, to lot size (given the degree to which density affects unit costs across the range of goods and services I have discussed).

Naturally, average pricing creates a financial disincentive for the consumer who makes the more efficient, sustainable choice, and an incentive for those who make less sustainable, inefficient choices. It is not surprising that, when consumers are overcharged when they choose a smaller lot, or choose to live in a denser neighbourhood or in a smaller house, fewer will make these choices than otherwise might if pricing accurately reflected the lower level of costs incurred. Similarly, consumers who choose larger lots and homes, or who choose to live farther away or in auto-oriented settings, are encouraged by average pricing because they underpay. They do not pay the full direct cost of their choices. So we get many more people choosing less sustainable options than would be the case if we had accurate price signals.

Because of inaccurate pricing, critical decisions about where to live, how large a lot and house to acquire, and related transportation choices (such as whether to use transit or car and how many vehicles to own) are all systematically influenced in a way that contradicts sustainable community objectives. This also applies to business location decisions. Average prices and other forms of mis-pricing are contrary to sustainable urban growth policy objectives across the board.

Average cost-based prices are used over and over. When the cumulative impact of overcharging on all the relevant urban goods and services is considered, the overpayment by those who live or conduct business more efficiently and sustainably is substantial. The evidence presented above has shown that, through average pricing and other mis-pricing, those who incur below-average costs would be overcharged for the following goods and services:

- water and sewer services
- roads
- parking
- electricity
- natural gas
- basic telephone
- cable TV
- broadband internet
- postal service
- municipal snow clearance
- recycling collection
- garbage collection.

Where mis-pricing prevails, a household living in the central city, in a denser, mixed-use neighbourhood, for example, is likely overcharged for the services listed above. Conversely, those who live in low-density, auto-oriented suburban locations will tend to be undercharged.

These overcharges occur through the various forms of mis-pricing discussed above, relating to DCs, property taxes, user fees, prices, and utility rates. Some of these costs (like DCs) are embedded in one-time prices, such as the price of a house, while others represent ongoing charges, such as property tax and utility costs. It is not hard to see how inaccurate prices for this broad range of items might skew decision making regarding home purchases, business locations, and transportation choices.

For a segment of consumers, both subsidies and cross-subsidies lead to underpricing of certain urban goods and services and, ultimately, to underpricing of inefficient development patterns. Underpricing leads people to consume more of a good or service than they otherwise might. If we were talking about a private good or service that had no negative externalities, then we might not care. For example, if, due to a subsidy, someone buys a more expensive laptop than she otherwise might, we might be indifferent because, aside from the cost of the subsidy itself, it has no further implications for the public at large. However, with respect to subsidies for the urban goods and services under discussion here, there are significant societal impacts – in the form of negative externalities and public goods – that result from the price distortions.

First, the cumulative impact is that underpricing leads to overconsumption of land and/or building and/or auto use in the form of urban sprawl. This, in turn, implies the need for more extensive infrastructure, with higher costs than would be the case with accurate pricing. As seen in previous chapters, study upon study documents the higher infrastructure costs associated with sprawl development. Inaccurate price signals are a primary source of demand for more and more expensive infrastructure. Accurate price signals would shift demand, reduce sprawl, and bring down infrastructure costs and tax levels.

Second, mis-pricing, such as average cost-based pricing, represents a very crude implementation of what can be a very sophisticated instrument. In its crude form, it can provide a subsidy where one may not be needed. Everyone who incurs above-average costs gets a price break, whether they could afford the good or service otherwise or not. (On the other hand, some of those who incur below-average costs but pay average costs may be in need of a subsidy.) As we saw with basic telephone service prior to the introduction of a targeted subsidy program, the costs associated with this across-the-board subsidy are much higher than need be, raising overall costs of the good or service.

An economist would use other language to describe this, saying that average prices lead to a misallocation of scarce resources. "Efficient" pricing is needed to ensure that markets are not distorted and that resources are not wasted. The economically efficient price is the one that exactly recovers the full economic costs incurred to provide one more unit of service – that is, that covers the incremental cost, say of servicing one more subdivision (the marginal cost-based pricing described in Chapter 6).[5] Average prices do not typically achieve this.

Third, there is also the issue of whether we, as a society, should be subsidizing non-essential goods and services. Everyone can understand the need for universal access to basic phone service, health service, and shelter, for example. However, the subsidies and cross-subsidies described above often go well beyond subsidizing basic needs and cross into the territory of subsidizing particular preferences or lifestyle choices. There is an important distinction to be made between subsidizing affordable housing for low-income households, for example, and subsidizing affluent households that choose to live on a large lot. In the telecoms sector, it is assumed as a basic tenet that everyone should have access to a telephone at a reasonable rate – but not that everyone should have a right to affordable movies on demand. Yet, in our approach to many services and urban development, we don't make a similar distinction. In effect, we provide subsidies to inefficient development. People who could otherwise pay don't, and people who overpay may be less financially able to or, in any event, are most likely unaware that they are subsidizing someone else's lifestyle choice. "De-averaging" of prices and smarter, more efficient approaches to subsidies are huge issues in many industries, most notably telecommunications, but also in the natural gas sector. Not so in urban development.

Finally and crucially, underpricing of sprawl – along with its flipside, overpricing of compact development – leads to other attendant costs associated with an inefficient development pattern. This includes not just higher infrastructure costs than necessary but also all of the external costs, such as congestion, air pollution, GHG emissions, public health costs, and so on. Some of these external costs are paid for through higher taxes (e.g., public health costs), while others are currently not paid for at all in monetary terms but, rather, in diminished quality of life.

Policy Mis-Incentives

So far I have identified common policy flaws that are related to pricing and that contribute to urban sprawl. There is a final type of problematic policy. It cannot be thought of as a subsidy as it is not characterized by a flow of money; rather, some government policies and programs have built-in biases, incentives, and disincentives that influence certain kinds of behaviour and/or urban development over other kinds of development and/or behaviour. Unfortunately, the kind of behaviour and development favoured is usually inconsistent with creating sustainable communities, while the incentives created encourage sprawl and discourage compact forms of development. Together, these could be called policy mis-incentives. They tend to be policies that were developed without taking into account the realities of the urban landscape and geography in which they operate, and the inadvertent spatial outcomes and impacts on development they would engender. These spatial outcomes continue to be ignored. Thus, they send the wrong signals. At best, these are missed opportunities.

Examples of these include:

- One-size-fits-all policies, such as those that use absolute amounts as criteria, without exploring their impacts in different locations and urban settings. A flat-ceiling withdrawal of $25,000 from RRSPs is one example.
- Conventional mortgage policy, which ignores consistent, measurable geographic patterns in spending on transportation versus housing and, in so doing, creates a bias against those who spend less on transportation and against more sustainable neighbourhoods.

- Property tax generally, which, based on market value, discourages densification on individual sites.
- Commercial DCs, which, charged per square metre of floor area, similarly discourages densification.

With a little forethought, these instruments could all be refined and redesigned to be much more effective and efficient in their impacts, and they could be brought into line to encourage the evolution of sustainable communities rather than to undermine them.

What is apparent is that there are many, many of these hidden incentives, disincentives, and mis-incentives, in both policy and pricing, that act upon the decision making that shapes cities. Indeed, the review above is more illustrative than exhaustive. They may be the result of the "silo" problem – that the economists who develop fiscal and pricing policy are unaware of the impacts they might have on urban development patterns and that the planners whose policies are intended to shape cities do not know enough about fiscal policy. However, planners and planning can no longer afford to ignore the economic and fiscal context in which cities evolve and, in particular, the raft of subsidies, mis-pricing, and mis-incentives that undermine the evolution of compact, sustainable communities.

Taken together, the impact of the policies described above is enormous, accounting for billions of dollars of direct and indirect subsidies to urban sprawl. And, when the cumulative impact of mis-pricing across the range of urban goods and services described above is considered – from house prices to property taxes to utility rates to auto insurance – it is easy to see how homebuyers or business decision makers are influenced to make less sustainable choices than they might under accurate pricing and better policy.

PART 4

WHAT TO DO

11

Principles for a Market-Oriented Approach

Preceding chapters reveal some of the problems, issues, and flaws in much of the policy and many of the financial instruments that govern urban development patterns. A new approach is clearly needed, one that removes existing distortions and that allows an unbiased market to play a more central role in supporting efficient urban development. In seeking a more effective approach to curbing sprawl, in developing alternative policies or retooling existing ones, there are a few simple but key principles to be kept in mind. These are outlined below, with specific tools being discussed in Chapter 12.

Market-Based Approaches

Why use market-based approaches? First, because regulatory approaches alone have been ineffective in curbing sprawl, and they will continue to be so because they insufficiently acknowledge the financial and broader economic forces that drive urban development patterns. Market-based approaches address the economic drivers of sprawl directly rather than by simply trying to treat the symptoms. Market-based approaches affect pricing, which, in turn, influences the crucial decisions that cumulatively shape urban development patterns – where to live, how much land to consume, where to locate a business, how much building to build. Introducing accurate pricing brings rationality to bear in these decisions, resulting in efficient outcomes and efficient urban development patterns. In the past, planning has relied heavily on regulation to achieve its objectives. For some issues in some contexts, regulation can provide good outcomes and may be the preferred policy approach. However, in dealing with urban sprawl, market-based approaches are not only desirable, they are necessary. Without introducing the rationality and discipline of prices based on real costs for those decisions that together shape urban development patterns, planning will never succeed in curbing urban sprawl.

Second, regulatory approaches can come with significant costs pertaining to the regulation itself as well as to unintended or collateral consequences, which are not generally accounted for. As is shown in Chapter 4, they can lead to market distortions, economic inefficiencies such as overspending on infrastructure, and other undesirable outcomes (e.g., promoting higher levels of socioeconomic segregation within cities).[1] There is a keen need to deliver planning benefits more efficiently and effectively, reducing both the indirect and direct costs of planning. In the appropriate circumstances, the use of good market-based approaches harnesses the power of market forces to produce planning benefits in an efficient way – removing or reducing the costs of market distortions associated with regulation-based planning.

By more closely aligning price signals with planning objectives, market-based approaches have the potential to reduce the costs of planning itself – that is, the direct costs associated with implementing and administering planning, including public and private costs. For example, by providing the right incentives to direct development to desired locations, market-based approaches could allow broader use of as-of-right approaches to zoning. Proper pricing may provide incentives to efficient development that allow it to substitute for an urban growth boundary and, thus, reduce or remove the costs of market distortions that have sometimes been linked with that particular regulatory tool.

Third, regulatory approaches, such as zoning, can themselves be a source of sprawl, as is noted in Chapter 2. In many instances, there is a need to reform regulation in order to allow more efficient and compact urban forms. The key is finding the right combination of market-oriented policies and regulatory policies, and having these two policy streams work together.

True Cost Pricing

As applied to the public elements of urban development through instruments such as DCs, property and other taxes, user fees and the like, approaches to pricing have been very crude and their impact on urban development patterns an afterthought (if thought of at all). The potential for pricing to bring about significant change in urban development patterns has thus gone untapped. Yet, it does not have to be this way. In other areas, pricing is applied in a very strategic and sophisticated manner, as anyone who has purchased an airline ticket lately will know.

As already discussed in Chapter 6, economic theory tells us that resources will be allocated efficiently when prices are equal to marginal costs. Marginal costs are those associated with an increment in supply – the cost of producing one more widget or the cost of providing roads to one additional subdivision or water pipes to one more housing unit. The central idea behind market-oriented mechanisms as proposed in this book is "true cost pricing." As intended here, true cost pricing means that prices – for all those urban goods and services that form part of development and locational decisions – reflect marginal costs *as those costs vary with urban form factors such as location, density, local context, and type of land use.* Thus, prices for urban services such as water, for example, should accurately reflect not just the amount of water used but also the degree to which the property in question precipitates infrastructure costs (including capital, operating, and maintenance) as those costs vary with the location of the property, lot size, and the other relevant urban form factors. Conventional pricing tends to ignore the significant cost variations linked with these factors.

> True cost pricing means that prices – for all those urban goods and services that form part of development and locational decisions – reflect marginal costs *as those costs vary with urban form factors such as location, density, local context, and type of land use.*

We can also explain efficient pricing in terms of what we are not talking about. We are not talking about "full cost pricing." Full cost pricing is based on marginal *social* cost – that is, the cost to society as a whole of supplying one additional widget or housing unit. In other words, full cost pricing includes the cost of externalities such as, for example, air pollution, noise, or loss of farmland or open space. While there is certainly a compelling rationale for prices reflecting social costs, that approach goes beyond what is discussed here. True cost pricing is about accurately reflecting costs that are already covered by prices – that is, costs for which a monetary value is already established and charged but that are *inaccurately* reflected in prices, leading to subsidies, distortions, and inefficiencies.

The adoption of true cost pricing is therefore not a radical proposition. It does not entail adding to prices costs that currently go unpriced. It merely means adopting a system of prices such that existing costs are redistributed more accurately in order to ensure the efficient allocation of resources. In other words, the idea is to create a situation in which the market works more efficiently and accurately than it does now.

Nor does the approach under discussion here involve artificial financial incentives that go beyond marginal cost pricing to achieve a particular outcome, such as explicit subsidies to encourage sustainable urban form. Of course, this tool has its place in the policy maker's arsenal, particularly in instances in which market forces – even based on accurate pricing – will not deliver broader social benefits. There may be many circumstances in which this approach is both warranted and desirable (e.g., for brownfields remediation) but that is not my focus and it is not what I mean by true cost pricing. With true cost pricing, the focus is on creating a neutral, level playing field.

It should be noted that I use the term "prices" loosely to mean any type of monetary charge associated with development. In addition to what one would normally think of as prices (e.g., monthly fees for telephone or internet service) are DCs, property tax or other taxes, user fees, utility rates, parking fees, and so on. The central idea behind true cost pricing is to closely, accurately, and visibly link actual costs with prices charged. When costs vary because of location, prices covering those costs should vary by location; when costs vary because of density, prices should vary with density; when costs vary because of the type of land use, prices should vary with the type of land use; and when costs vary because of usage, prices should vary with usage.

In implementing marginal cost pricing, a balance must be struck between achieving accuracy, such that the price is equal to the marginal cost, on the one hand, and achieving a practical and workable pricing mechanism, on the other (or, stated another way, a balance between theory and practice). Practical considerations in implementing marginal cost pricing are discussed in the following chapter. On its own, the introduction of true cost prices, if implemented intelligently in DCs, user fees, utility rates, and so on, would go a long way towards stemming urban sprawl.

Think Spatially

One of the major flaws with many of the policies and programs described above is that they simply fail to consider how the policy will play out in the real world of urban landscapes. The proverbial featureless plane is assumed, but, of course, in the real world, the urban context is anything but. This a-geographical approach is particularly true of any one-size-fits-all policy that makes use of a universal policy threshold. The most glaring example of this is, of course, the use of prices based on average costs – applied across a landscape of differentiated costs – and its serious implications in terms of subsidizing urban sprawl.

Another example described earlier is the use of a single flat-ceiling withdrawal – applicable across Canada – of $25,000 from RRSPs for a first home purchase. If geography were taken into account, the ceiling would recognize the substantial house price variations not only from city to city to rural area but also – indeed, especially – between central, suburban, and exurban locations. As it is, a single, nationally applicable maximum withdrawal amount is inherently biased against central urban locations, particularly in larger urban centres, where house prices are highest and most urban growth tends to be occurring, and, therefore, the need to curb sprawl is the greatest.

These biases can be removed and more geographically sensitive policies adopted. One simply needs to consider, at the design stage, how a particular policy or program will play out in different geographical contexts, both inter- and intra-urban – city, suburbs, centre, small town, or rural area.

Tax Shift

Many of the policies causing distortions and promoting sprawl that I note earlier are taxes of various kinds imposed by all levels of government. The good news is that these policies can be corrected to create fewer market distortions and to impart a less salutary effect on the promotion of urban sprawl. New taxes or other pricing mechanisms can also be introduced to support more compact urban form. However, implementation of new taxes or other pricing mechanisms should not be undertaken piecemeal but, rather, in the context of a broader program of "tax shifting."

What does tax shift mean? Traditionally, first and foremost, taxes are seen as a means of raising revenue. However, this approach ignores the fact that tax policy will inevitably have impacts on behaviour of various kinds – whether intentionally or unintentionally – by in effect altering the relative "prices" of those things that are taxed. When prices are higher, we tend to demand less of a good or service. Similarly, when prices are lower, we tend to demand more of it. At present, we mostly tax those things that, as a society, we view as desirable and refrain from taxing those "bads," of which we want less. For example, we tax income, investment, payrolls, and development; we do not tax pollution or GHG emissions.

Tax shifting is the strategic, systematic, and gradual reorganization of the tax system in order to get it into alignment with policy objectives, thus shifting the burden of taxation from economic goods to environmental or other bads. In this way, taxation encourages the kinds of outcomes we want to see and actively discourages behaviours and outcomes we want reduced. Sometimes called ecological fiscal reform, tax shifting has been adopted in many European countries.

An important aspect of tax shifting involves the fact that new environmental taxes can be offset by reducing other taxes, especially those on "goods," thus achieving revenue neutrality. Also, a tax shift can increase or decrease net revenues, depending on the approach desired. The point is that this is a deliberate decision made as part of an overall strategy.

Tax shifting has been shown to be effective in bringing about significant environmental improvements, such as reduced GHGs.[2] Removing taxes from economic "goods," such as labour or income, can also result in economic benefits, such as higher levels of employment. The environmental and economic benefits associated with tax shifting are known as its "double dividend."

An important characteristic of tax shifting is that, when executed intelligently, it should enable citizens to reduce their overall tax burden by changing their behaviour. For example, when the costs of garbage pickup and disposal are buried in property taxes, there is no incentive for people or businesses to reduce their garbage. However, if garbage services are charged separately and at their true cost, and property tax reduced accordingly, then homeowners and businesses should have the ability to reduce their total payments to the city, *and* the amount of garbage produced, *and* municipal collection and disposal costs.

A recent example from the City of Toronto illustrates what not to do. Acting upon newly won taxation powers, the city proposed two taxes – one on vehicle registrations and the other on transfer of ownership of land. The new taxes were viewed simply as sources of revenue that could stem ongoing municipal budget shortfalls. While it could be argued that the vehicle registration tax might somewhat discourage driving, a land transfer tax – which would amount to $5,725 on a home valued at $500,000 – discourages purchases of homes within the city (which is at the centre of the Toronto urban region and fully urbanized – therefore, any development in the city is by definition reurbanization). The land transfer tax could act to shift housing demand away from the city to surrounding suburban municipalities, where no such tax is in place. Analysis shows that the land transfer tax could delay development and redevelopment, and discourage denser development.[3] This counters the city's own policy of aggressive reurbanization and of attracting major population growth. These new taxes could and should have been implemented within the context of a broader tax-shift strategy.[4]

Ideally, major changes to taxation policy, or the introduction of new taxes, should be considered as part of a broader strategy of tax shift. Taxes will inevitably have an effect on behaviour, whether it is intentional or not, so it may as well be intentional. We can no longer afford to have a wasteful and unsophisticated approach in which one set of public policies (i.e., taxes) undermines another set (in this case, planning policies).

Cost Transparency

One of the problems exposed in the earlier analysis is that, even if true cost prices were employed in relation to the many decisions that shape urban form, they are often hidden from view. This prevents decision makers from making fully informed and efficient choices. Not only should prices reflect true costs but these true costs must also be visible to the decision maker. In other words, the connection between cost causation and price must be made both accurate *and* apparent. It is only if the true costs are apparent to the decision maker that they can affect the decision-making process and bring about more efficient development patterns.

One example of hidden costs discussed above involves bundled goods and services. The costs of infrastructure, local roads, and parking are bundled into the price of a new home. The homebuyer has no way of knowing what portion of the price of her new home is accounted for by these infrastructure costs and no way of reducing these costs by making alternative house choices. Unbundling the costs of infrastructure that affect urban development patterns can lead to more informed, efficient decisions. For example, parking spaces could be priced as separate, add-on, or upgrade items as part of the purchase of a new home (in the same way that kitchen upgrades are priced now).

Wherever possible, prices should be charged directly for the good or service that is causing the cost rather than through a proxy price. For example, there has been much discussion in Canada (and recent practice) of earmarking a share of the gas tax for municipal infrastructure. The theory behind this is that, to some extent, this is a charge aimed at those who generate the costs – namely, drivers who use roads and create demand for roads. Also, the amount paid in taxes increases with amount driven. While there is some logic to this, it is at most a second-best solution because the tax is buried in the price of fuel. It still presents a separation between the action (driving) and the costs it generates (the need to repair, maintain, and build new roads). It renders drivers less aware of the actual costs they are causing for themselves and for society as a whole by driving. A better approach would be the use of road pricing, which clearly links the use of roads and the cost that incurs to a price to be paid. Examples of implementing cost transparency are discussed in more detail in Chapter 12.

Fairness

True cost pricing and transparency will not only help to create more informed decisions and a more efficient development pattern but they will also result in a pricing system that is both more accurate and inherently more fair. True cost pricing removes the many existing subsidies and cross-subsidies so that everyone pays for what they consume rather than some groups subsidizing other groups – usually more efficient development subsidizing less efficient development – without even being aware of doing so.

The principle that people should pay the true cost of their choices and not pass them on to others is central to achieving more efficient development patterns. This is especially true in the case of implicit subsidies, where the subsidizers are rarely if ever aware that they are the ones doing the subsidizing. Where subsidies are warranted, targeted and explicit subsidies should be used.

Choice

The market-oriented approach outlined in *Perverse Cities* is less prescriptive than are conventional regulation-based planning approaches. The underlying assumption is that, once the market mechanisms are working effectively (i.e., based on transparent true cost pricing), the market itself will promote efficiency. Regulatory approaches tend to be prescriptive, specifying or placing limits on many aspects of development (e.g., minimum densities, maximum densities, uses, setbacks, parking requirements, etc.). Once effective true cost-based pricing is in place, an opportunity is created to relax some of this structure and to streamline regulatory frameworks. A situation is created in which a developer or consumer can respond to price signals in a number of different ways. For example, faced with a DC levied per hectare of land (rather than the conventional approach of levying on per housing unit basis), a developer has a number of options open to him. He could maximize the density, thereby minimizing the infrastructure cost per unit, which would support the development of denser, more affordable housing. Or he could build a smaller number of luxury homes, with a higher infrastructure cost per unit. The point is that, first, the developer can respond to the price signal of the DC as he sees fit. Under either scenario, the municipality is assured that the DCs will actually cover the infrastructure costs incurred.

Importantly, the bias inherent in the conventional, per unit DC against more efficient development is removed and incentives to densification are provided. This should increase the range of choice of housing types and densities available in the marketplace, in particular, increasing the supply of more efficient, compact development. This occurs not as the result of regulation but, rather, as a rational response to accurate price signals. At any rate, it is very difficult if not impossible to achieve higher densities through regulation alone, particularly in the absence of accurate, transparent pricing. Minimum density regulations are exceedingly difficult to implement: unless the development economics supports efficient densities, more compact development cannot simply be regulated into existence.

The bias against more efficient development that is inherent in the kinds of pricing mechanisms I describe above has limited its supply. Creating a level financial playing field, through accurate price signals, will remove this bias and make possible (and competitive) these more efficient forms, thereby broadening the range of development choices available to homeowners and businesses. So, rather than restricting choice and limiting development forms (as regulation is prone to do), this approach supports choice and the responsiveness of the development industry to market conditions.

This is not to say that regulation is not needed. There are some issues, for example, that the market itself cannot adequately address, such as incompatible neighbouring uses. And regulation may be needed to guide the character or design of development. But with a market-based approach, a lighter hand in regulation is made possible. Smart, focused regulation is needed, working in concert with the market-based approach. Achieving the right mix of regulation to complement transparent true cost-based pricing is the art of this approach.

Consistency

As I show earlier, not only do financial policies work at cross-purposes with planning policies generally, but often, due to a lack of coordination between programs or departments, this occurs within the same organization. A classic example occurs within municipal governments, when the finance department unwittingly puts policies in place that have an impact on planning objectives. For example, the finance department enacts a DC that has the unintended consequence of subsidizing low density, greenfields development. Meanwhile, down the hall, the planning department is busily putting in place a smart growth strategy aimed at curbing sprawl and encouraging compact development. Another example is the duelling subsidy phenomenon described above.

This situation can come about because municipal finance professionals have little expertise in planning, and planners have little expertise in municipal finance. These professional strictures might be overcome with the proper mechanisms within the organization (e.g., interdisciplinary policy teams or integrated strategic planning) to integrate these areas. Attempts at integration are sometimes made, but often these are one way. For example, development proposals are often required to produce a financial impact assessment, but municipal finance proposals are rarely required to produce a planning impact assessment. An important principle is, therefore, to ensure consistency across the range of policies and instruments that affect urban development patterns, be they financial or planning-oriented, so that one set of policies does not cancel out the effect of another.

Context

In Chapter 4, I note that the impacts of any given policy or set of programs depend both on the nature of the regulation itself and on the specific context in which it is applied. Though the tools and instruments described in the following chapter have wide applicability across a range of cities and countries, they cannot always be adopted holus bolus from one context and plunked down in another. If my analysis of tools thus far has shown anything, it is the need to pay close attention to the specific design of instruments, taking into close consideration the physical, spatial, economic, institutional, social, and environmental context in which they are to operate.

Take, for example, the congestion charge implemented in London, England. The specific design of this instrument works well in its context, where congestion in the inner part of the London region is a particular concern and the centralizing tendencies of development are very strong. In Toronto, however, traffic congestion is not just an issue in the core but across the region, and the geographical dynamics of economic growth suggest that, while a congestion charge would have significant benefits in reducing and allocating demand as well as raising funds for improving transit, the correct approach in this case would be to introduce a charge across the regional expressway network that serves the urban region as a whole. Drawing a charge cordon around the centre could further deflect commercial development to suburban locations. Clearly, policies need to be customized to meet local conditions and objectives.

Ease of Implementation

In implementing new tools and policies in support of efficient development, the ease of implementation is of course an important consideration. Generally, regulation can be lightened or streamlined if true cost based pricing is put into place, such as the greater use of as-of-right zoning. Moreover, many of these instruments can provide a simpler approach than their regulatory counterparts. For example, replacing market-value-based property tax charges for network services with a lot size- or lot frontage-based charge would be immensely easier to implement as it would require minimal updating and no modelling of theoretical property values. When contemplating implementing marginal cost pricing for capital costs of network infrastructure, the intention is to do so in a very practical, workable way – by identifying zones or types of development that share common cost profiles and not, of course, on a unit-by-unit basis. Of course, as part of the policy deliberation, the costs and benefits of using a pricing regime must be considered and compared with the costs and benefits of using regulatory approaches.

Costs and Benefits

And speaking of costs and benefits, one of the issues discussed in Chapter 4 concerns the fact that the costs of planning tend to be ignored and the benefits are simply assumed to exist. In implementing new measures, both the costs of implementation and the benefits derived should be more rigorously considered. At the municipal level, for example, the fiscal impacts of major development proposals are often evaluated. But the impacts on development patterns (and related impacts on infrastructure costs) of fiscal policies are rarely considered. Similarly, the direct and indirect costs of introducing new planning measures are rarely considered. The potential administrative and market impacts of measures to control density, for example, or to introduce an urban growth boundary or new parking standards are rarely well evaluated. Even a very simple cost-benefit analysis should form a standard part of the evaluation of proposed instruments – or, indeed, an evaluation of existing ones.

These are some basic principles to keep in mind when implementing new or refined policies, programs, or prices. Some examples of specific tools and instruments that would support more efficient urban development patterns are described in the following chapter.

12

A Toolbox of Market-Oriented Instruments

Earlier chapters detail a number of problems with financial instruments that are used every day to pay for urban goods and services. The problems identified have not so much to do with the instruments themselves as with being poorly designed and failing to take into account important impacts on promoting inefficient urban development patterns. In other words, there is nothing inherently wrong with DCs – indeed, they are an excellent tool for paying the costs associated with new urban growth. The problem lies in the way they are presently designed, which leads DCs to work in opposition to planning objectives for more compact urban growth and reurbanization. DCs and other instruments can, however, be refined and redesigned so as to be brought onside as powerful tools capable of working in concert with policy objectives. Mostly it's a matter of fixing instruments that are already in place but that are badly flawed – in terms of their role in generating inefficient urban development patterns. However, in some cases, new instruments may also be needed in order to introduce pricing where services currently go unpriced or are not directly paid for by the user.

Pricing Options

The fundamental problem with many of the financial instruments reviewed above is a poor approach to price-setting – specifically, that the marginal cost pricing recommended by economists for efficient use of resources is virtually never used in setting prices for urban goods and services. More efficient infrastructure and urban form could be realized through greater use of marginal cost pricing in appropriate circumstances. Kitchen suggests that marginal cost pricing is best used when the beneficiaries can be clearly identified, costs can be accurately derived, services do not generate spillovers or externalities, and income redistribution is not involved.[1] These parameters suggest that marginal cost pricing is appropriate for a wide range of urban services and utilities. These services meet Kitchen's criteria, and marginal cost pricing is generally not in place for them now.

In implementing marginal cost pricing, often a balance must be struck between achieving accuracy and a practical, workable pricing mechanism. Sometimes costs can be complex and difficult to estimate and to allocate to users. However, engineering cost studies and other cost allocation methods have been developed and can be employed to do this. In many cases, cost allocation studies are already regularly undertaken. Introducing a marginal cost approach simply means calculating those costs in a way that allows a different allocation methodology – specifically, one that takes location, density, land use, or other relevant urban form factors into account as drivers of cost.

Of course, the costs of implementing better price-setting should not exceed the benefits of doing so. In other words, if it costs more to determine the marginal costs and to collect them than is realized in the savings that result from increased efficiency and reduced spending on infrastructure, then it doesn't make sense to implement them. The appropriate pricing approach will vary depending on the good or service that is being priced and the major cost components. It is unlikely, however, that in pricing network infrastructure, for example, a specific price would be calculated for each additional housing unit within a subdivision – that is, it is unlikely that perfect marginal cost pricing would be achieved in practice.

When textbook marginal cost pricing is not possible, a practical alternative is an "average-incremental-cost" approach. This approach combines marginal and average cost pricing, allowing full cost recovery while maximizing efficiency: "The idea is simply to allocate each element of costs, fixed and variable ... to a particular incremental decision that results in the provision of a service and then to assign to each additional user the incremental cost attributable, on average, to his or her usage."[2] In an urban context, levying DCs on a subdivision-by-subdivision basis could be considered an example of this approach, with each new subdivision being the "increment" charged its site-specific servicing costs, with average-cost-based charges for development within the subdivision. While not perfect, as a first step, even this change would be a significant improvement over municipal-wide DCs. In defining increments one could also look for categories of development that share common cost profiles, particularly with respect to land use, location, or density. For example, certain types of commercial development may share cost causation characteristics, such as low-, medium-, or high-trip generation rates. While not textbook marginal cost pricing as an economist would describe it, these are practical and reasonable approaches that represent a significant improvement over current pricing practice.

A second pricing alternative, already employed in many private or quasi-private industries, is the "multi-part tariff." Multi-part tariffs assign different prices or pricing strategies to different cost components of the service. As such, they are particularly well suited to pricing services that have substantial infrastructure costs. With a typical two-part tariff, for example, an access charge might be levied to cover infrastructure costs, with a per unit charge applied to actual consumption. As we have seen above, multi-part tariffs are common for network industries such as electricity or natural gas. Hydro fees are often comprised of monthly "customer service fees" (administration charges), "delivery" (infrastructure) charges, and a charge based on the amount of electricity used, for example. Ideally, each component of a multi-part tariff should reflect incremental costs, where these vary. In practice, network access charges, unfortunately, are typically flat rates and, as such, do not reflect infrastructure cost variations associated with location, density, or land-use patterns.

Perfect marginal cost pricing may not be possible, but, as Bird and Tsiopoulous point out, "it is better to be roughly 'right' – that is, to charge some form of roughly economically sensible price ... – than to be clearly wrong,"[3] as is often the case with existing pricing structures surrounding urban development. Some key tools and reforms are outlined below. These suggestions address the issues raised in Part 3. This is, of course, by no means a complete inventory of the possible tools that can be harnessed to support efficient development. It is merely meant to provide some examples of how to move towards better pricing in order to support efficient development patterns.

Structuring a Smart Development Charge

Chapter 7 outlines a number of problems not with the DC itself but, rather, with the particular design of the charge. As currently structured, DCs result in a situation in which efficient uses are overcharged while less efficient uses are subsidized, creating distortions in the land development process and promoting sprawl. Several issues relating to the design of the DC were raised. The solution lies in altering the design to create a DC that is fair, creates efficient allocation of resources, and reduces overall infrastructure costs. In other words, a charge that removes cross-subsidization and works in concert with, rather than against, planning policy objectives of compact, mixed, sustainable urban development patterns.

Any restructuring of DCs should be based on the principle that the charges reflect actual servicing costs *as they vary with location, development pattern, and type of use* – that is, based on true cost pricing. In order to do this, the first step is to identify the cost zones within the municipality – the areas that share similar cost profiles, whatever the underlying reason, be it excess capacity in certain locations, the development pattern itself (e.g., the presence of mixed uses or higher density), topography or soil conditions, proximity to existing infrastructure, or any number of other local factors. Then, *within each of these zones,* the costs are allocated to development and charged in accordance with the degree to which the development generates the costs – in particular, based on the density of development and type of development – be it the type of use or housing type.

Taking Location-Related Cost Variations into Account

Network infrastructure costs typically vary from area to area within the municipality. If costs vary from zone to zone within a municipality, so, too, should the DC. Both commercial and residential DCs should vary in this way. This does not have to be complicated. We are not generally talking about identifying micro-zones of cost variation, say, on a block-by-block basis. But there is a need to identify the main geographic zones associated with differing costs. This can take many forms – on a subdivision-by-subdivision basis or based on rings related to cost, or other appropriate types of zone. For example, in the City of Ottawa, three zones have been identified – the inner urban area, the suburbs, and the rural fringe – each with its own DC (see box). The point is that the zones should correspond to patterns of major cost variation in whatever form they may take in any given municipality. Often this means at least two zones – one in the inner, older urban area and one at the edge where new growth requires all new infrastructure.

Not only network infrastructure costs but also the costs of other facilities can vary by location. In Chapter 7 we see how schools in older urban areas have excess capacity, while new schools are being built at high cost in new suburban areas. In municipalities where a similar condition exists, an efficient education levy would establish zones (at least two at any rate) with

Development Charges in the City of Ottawa

The City of Ottawa has a greenbelt that was implemented in the 1950s. Inside the greenbelt, the urban area is virtually entirely built out. Suburban development is taking place at the outer edge of the greenbelt and beyond in rural areas.

The city employs a development charge based on three zones – inside the greenbelt, outside the greenbelt, and rural (which is divided into serviced and unserviced). Within each zone, charges are levied based on housing type for residential development and floor area for commercial development. As of 2008, the charge for a single detached house inside the greenbelt was $10,745, outside the greenbelt $19,148, and rural (serviced) $7,646. Most of the difference is accounted for by higher road, water, and sewer costs in suburban areas.

In order to encourage transit-oriented development, the roads portion of development charges can be reduced by 50 percent for apartments within 500 metres of a transit or light rail station, if parking restrictions of one space per unit are met. In addition, an area-specific stormwater charge applies, based on drainage areas. These charges vary by dwelling type and tend to be in the range of $3,000 to $4,000 per unit for a single detached house.

Unfortunately, non-residential development is charged on a floor area basis, and no distinction is made between areas inside versus areas outside the greenbelt.

differing and true cost education levies. The costs of other facilities, such as libraries or recreation centres, may also vary by location where excess capacity exists in some areas. The DC should reflect these location-related cost variations.

Unlike conventionally structured DCs, which average costs out across the municipality and render the developer (and, ultimately, the purchaser) indifferent to cost variations, this approach actively encourages development to take place in the lowest-cost locations first and removes cross–subsidies paid by low-cost areas to high-cost areas.

Taking Development Pattern-Related Costs into Account

As is demonstrated over and over in earlier chapters, network infrastructure costs are closely related to the extent of the land area serviced and, therefore, the length of pipe, roads, wires, or other linear infrastructure required. Thus, per unit costs – the costs per house, say – are tied, in part, to the size of the lot and, therefore, to the density of development. Conventional DCs, based on dwelling unit type and not on lot size, therefore cannot accurately reflect the costs of network infrastructure. Today, DCs almost universally ignore cost variations associated with development patterns. If, on the other hand, we structure a charge such that it reflects the extent of the land area to be developed, we have a much more accurate mechanism, more closely aligning costs with charges. For network infrastructure costs, a smart DC would therefore be levied not per dwelling unit or per square metre of commercial floorspace but, rather, on the basis of land area. For example, a charge for municipal water, sewer, stormwater management, and roads could be set at $300,000 per hectare (or whatever the actual cost is).

Basing the charge on land area and actual costs in a given location allows the developer flexibility in determining how to build and recover his or her costs. One response may be to build more densely, thereby generating a greater number of units or floor area over which to spread the costs, lowering the per unit cost of infrastructure. In other words, unlike conventional dwelling unit-based charges that discourage density, here there is a built-in incentive to build more densely. Or the developer may choose to build a smaller number of high-value units. That is also okay as the municipality is assured that the actual costs of development will be covered either way. A few municipalities have adopted this approach for some area-related costs. For example, the City of Vaughan, Ontario, charges for some sewer and water infrastructure costs on a per hectare basis, varying from district to district within the city.

The overall amount of land to be serviced is dependent upon the density of development and determines the *extent* of the network – the overall length of network services required and the total number of linear kilometres of roads, wires, or pipes. Other costs are related to the required carrying capacity of the infrastructure (i.e., the diameter of a pipe or how many lanes a road needs to handle the traffic).

Development pattern also influences some capacity-related costs. For example, as is shown in earlier chapters, lower-density, single-use development patterns result in higher levels of auto ownership, a greater share of trips by car versus other travel modes, longer trips, and more motorized travel per person than are found in denser locations. In other words, lower density generates more car travel and a greater demand for roads and road capacity. But DCs do not reflect the role development pattern plays in generating demand for roads and road costs incurred. In fact, transportation costs are usually allocated on a per capita basis and are included in charges based on house type – completely overlooking the role development pattern plays in the causation of these capacity costs.

Development pattern can influence capacity costs for other types of network infrastructure too, as is shown above. For example, low-density development patterns were found to require more pumping capacity for water networks and encouraged homeowners to use more water for their lawns. These factors should be reflected in the DC itself. How? Well, because these costs are related to the amount of land area developed – or lot size – they could simply be included in the per hectare DC.

Taking Development Type-Related Cost Variations into Account
Capacity costs of network infrastructure also vary with the type of development – that is, with the type of land use, or housing or building type. For example, the number of automobile trips generated varies widely with the type of use, as is shown in Chapter 7. Yet, because they don't recognize that different categories of development place different levels of demand on infrastructure, non-residential DCs rarely reflect these significant cost variations. A true cost based DC would create categories of use according to the degree to which they contribute to road or other infrastructure costs.

These use-related cost variations are at least in part recognized in the Region of York's DCs. They acknowledge the different levels of cost causation for retail uses compared to other non-residential uses.[4] On a per square metre of floorspace basis, retail uses were found to have higher levels of water consumption than industrial, office, and institutional uses as well as higher levels of trip generation. Transportation costs are now allocated according to Institute of Transportation Engineers trip generation estimates for each use. Although retail accounted for only 22 percent of projected non-residential floor area (the usual basis for charging non-residential DCs), it accounted for almost half of all projected trips.[5] Thus, using the usual floor-area basis for determining the total charge would create a situation in which office, industrial, and institutional uses were significantly subsidizing retail uses. Ultimately, water and sewer capacity costs may be allocated according to actual usage; however, as an interim measure, the share of employment accounted for by each category is used. As it stands, the relative charges for each type of infrastructure, and the total charge, are shown in Table 12.1.

Other capacity costs for network infrastructure are really related to demand, which, in turn, is related to population – the number of people being

Table 12.1

Regional Municipality of York non-residential development charge rates ($ per square metre of gross floor area)

	Industrial/Office/Institutional	Retail
Water	22.07	30.03
Sewer	38.11	57.80
Roads	35.31	134.88
Transit	2.15	7.32
Subway	7.10	26.05
General	2.70	3.88
Total	107.44	259.96

Source: The Regional Municipality of York, *Regional Municipality of York Development Charges* (brochure), 21 September 2009. These charges effective 21 September 2009 to 17 June 2010.

served. For example, water and sewer main pipe sizing depends upon the number of people being serviced and the amount of water they use. As DCs must charge a fee against development (as opposed to the number of residents in each dwelling, for example), dwelling type is used as an approximation of occupancy. The use of house type as the basis for DCs is in many instances simply a convenient proxy for population, with single detached homes assumed to have more people per unit. It makes sense to include these capacity-related costs in per dwelling unit charges as they lack a spatially variable cost component.

For some non-residential uses, demand would be related to the number of employees, but there may be significant deviations for certain types of industry that use large amounts of water, such as some manufacturing, for example. Here the best approach may be that suggested in York Region, which is to allocate costs of water and sewer infrastructure based on actual water consumption levels by broad type of use.

To this point I have been talking mostly about network infrastructure. Costs for some types of infrastructure, however, particularly those that are non-linear, are primarily related to the number of people served, and these costs should be charged on this basis or on as close an approximation as one can get. This would include costs of facilities such as schools, recreation centres, or libraries, for example. It might also include water and wastewater treatment facilities (exclusive of the network to which it is connected), though development pattern can still have some influence here (e.g., with low densities increasing water pumping costs).

Type of dwelling unit is most often used as a proxy for population when charging residential development. This is fine so long as, in order to avoid the issue of small units cross-subsidizing larger units, the occupancy figures used for the various unit types are accurate. For this reason, DCs covering population-related infrastructure should not impose a single average cost across all types of units, as is often the case with education charges. Education levies are charged on a per dwelling unit basis regardless of type, even though the larger unit types have higher levels of occupancy on average and,[6] therefore, likely higher numbers of children. Education levies should thus be distinguished by housing type and should vary by location according to costs. Even population-related costs can vary from location to location, depending, for example, on the existence of excess capacity, and these variations should be reflected in the charges.

Capacity-Related Costs for Non-Residential Development

Another essential problem with using floor space as the basis for charging DCs is noted in Chapter 7: by charging for every square metre of development built, a deterrent to densification is created. How can this deterrent be avoided in charging for capacity-related costs? Finding a workable solution to this issue is difficult. There are really only two options for charging non-residential DCs: they can be charged against buildings or against land. At present they are mostly charged against floor area, on the theory that floor area reflects occupancy and that that is what drives capacity-related costs. However, floor area-based DCs reflect occupancy quite poorly, given that floor space per employee varies so much between types of non-residential use. This leads to cross-subsidization between types of non-residential use.

However, one can just as easily use land area as floor area to reflect occupancy, provided it is done correctly. This would mean differentiating between major categories of non-residential use, thus taking varying occupancy into account. Now, however, we must deal with another factor that the floor space approach automatically accounts for, and that is the size of the building. To do this we can use typical densities for each type of development to construct an estimate of square metres of land area per employee for each category of use. The DC would then be charged on a land-area basis, weighted by these land occupancy factors.

For purposes of illustration, assume that retail development typically occurs at 30 percent coverage in a single floor and that there are 50 square metres of floor space per employee. Typically, then, there would be 60 employees per hectare of retail land. Offices might typically be built at 50 percent coverage and three stories, with an occupancy of 25 square metres of floorspace per employee. One hectare of office land would therefore contain 600 employees. The DC would use factors such as these as well as other factors, such as trip generation rates, to charge capacity-related costs against land rather than floor area.

Charging against land area has the significant added benefit that it inverts the current equation – that is, it provides an incentive to densification rather than the disincentive associated with the current floor area approach. Given a fixed DC based on the area of the property, the builder could benefit by constructing more building.

Putting It All Together

What would a DC charge based on the concepts outlined above actually look like? In reality, apart from the fact that the charges imposed would be arrived at differently and structured differently, it would be no more complex than existing DCs. One option is to implement a two-part charge, with network infrastructure – whose costs are related to the amount of land area serviced – being charged on an area basis and infrastructure whose costs are related to population being charged on a population basis (or close proxy thereof), all varying (as necessary) by location. The Town of Markham, Ontario, has developed a system along these lines (see box). The Markham approach is a significant improvement over the standard DC.[7] Many structures are possible, depending upon local conditions. Another approach, which shows how a DC might be structured if all the ideas described above were implemented, is shown in Table 12.2 and Table 12.3. The tables are meant to show the structure of the charge: the figures are purely illustrative, the numbers used being hypothetical. (As an aside, it should be noted that DCs structured in this way represent practical examples of implementing true cost marginal pricing, as described in Chapter 11.)

Ensuring Transparency

These improved instruments deal with most of the types of cross-subsidization embedded in conventional DCs. The one issue that, in some instances, may still not be adequately addressed by this approach is small lots subsidizing large lots and smaller units subsidizing larger units – not through a true cost DC but, rather, in the developer's price-setting of the individual units.

Town of Markham Development Charge Structure

The Town of Markham, Ontario, is a rapidly growing suburban municipality in the Toronto area. Its development charge combines an areal basis with a dwelling-unit charge for residential and with a floorspace-based charge for non-residential.

There is a standard town-wide charge for some hard infrastructure, including roads, structures, traffic management, and erosion control. The "soft infrastructure" charge covers recreation, fire, and library services, and is also standard across the town, as is shown in the following table.

	Town-wide charge	
	Hard	Soft
Residential		
Single/semi	$8,699 per unit	$10,008 per unit
Townhouse	$6,845 per unit	$7,857 per unit
Apartment (2+ bedrooms)	$5,383 per unit	$6,186 per unit
Apartment (1 bedroom)	$3,235 per unit	$3,715 per unit
Non-residential	$182,286 per net hectare	Office/industrial/institutional: $8.24 per m² floor area Retail: $8.96 per m² Mixed use: $5.65 per m²

Source: Town of Markham, Development Charge Information Package (rates as of 1 July 2009).

In addition, area-specific charges apply to both residential and non-residential development. They cover linear infrastructure costs such as roads, stormwater management, sanitary sewers, water supply, and mains. They are on a per net hectare basis and vary by location, ranging from $3,000 per hectare to over $900,000 per hectare, illustrating the substantial degree to which these costs can vary.

In addition to these charges, Region of York development charges are also applicable in Markham, at $24,189 per single or semi-detached unit, and non-residential charges are as are shown in Table 12.1.

Take the case in which a single developer develops a large subdivision that is to include different residential types and houses of various sizes on differently sized lots. He pays the per hectare DC based on the area of the whole subdivision, incurring an aggregate cost, which he is free to allocate

Table 12.2

Efficient residential development charges: An illustration

Zone	Charge		
1	$50,000 per ha.	+	$5,000 per single detached unit $4,000 per row house $2,000 per apartment
2	$120,000 per ha.	+	$25,000 per single detached unit $20,000 per row house $12,000 per apartment
3	$100,000 per ha.	+	$20,000 per single detached unit $16,000 per row house $10,000 per apartment
4	$95,000 per ha.	+	$17,500 per single detached unit $14,000 per row house $ 6,000 per apartment

Table 12.3

Efficient non-residential development charges: An illustration ($ per hectare)

Zone	Office	Institutional	Retail	Manufacturing	Warehousing/ distribution
1	100,000	90,000	100,000	60,000	90,000
2	500,000	450,000	500,000	400,000	450,000
3	400,000	350,000	400,000	300,000	350,000
4	275,000	275,000	300,000	200,000	250,000

as he wishes in the pricing of the different types of residential units. There is no guarantee that, for any given size of house or lot, the ultimate selling price of the house will reflect the actual DC costs. In other words, while the developer will have paid the true cost for the subdivision as a whole, cross-subsidization can still occur between various house types and sizes within the subdivision through the final selling prices he establishes.

One way of dealing with this issue is to require that the actual DC cost associated with each unit is identified as a separate cost item for the consumer to see. It would be calculated for each unit by the municipality and paid directly to the municipality by the homebuyer at the time of purchase, with the infrastructure items it covers stipulated. As such, it would be treated as an explicit and separate component of the price of the house, much the same as GST or land transfer tax is now.

For per hectare charges, the actual cost for each unit would be calculated by simply pro-rating the areal charge applicable for that location to the lot area of the specific unit. So if the area-specific charge was $500,000 per net hectare, and the house in question had a lot area of 300 square metres, then it would have incurred a cost and charge of $15,000 for network infrastructure. For apartment buildings, the pro-rated lot cost would then be divided by the number of units in the building to arrive at the per unit cost.

This approach not only ensures that the DC is accurately reflected in the final price of the individual home or apartment unit, but – equally important – it renders it transparent. Now the consumer can see the cost makeup of potential homes and make a more informed decision about the particular mix of infrastructure, land, and building that she might want. Two equally sized homes might be located within the same subdivision on two different sizes of lots – one large, one small. At an area-specific DC of $500,000 per net hectare, the DC on the smaller 300-square-metre lot would be $15,000, while on a 600-square-metre lot it would be $30,000. Providing this information to the buyer allows her to judge for herself whether she is willing to pay the additional *actual* costs (assuming that the DC does indeed fairly reflect the actual costs of development for that unit) of infrastructure associated with a larger lot. This would be a powerful tool in improving fairness and transparency, while allowing the market to create more efficient development patterns.

Property Tax

Property tax is the primary source of revenue for most municipalities in Canada, and it is a financial instrument that has important implications for urban development patterns. Conventionally structured, using market value as the basis for assessment and thereby decoupling prices (i.e., taxes paid) from actual costs incurred, it acts to encourage urban sprawl, as is shown in Chapter 7. There are, however, several options for reforming and restructuring property tax to turn this important instrument into a force that supports efficient development patterns.

There are two common views of taxes. A general tax is based on a broad measure of a taxpayer's economic capacity or "ability to pay," for example, as reflected in the value of a specific asset.[8] General taxes are mandatory and are not related to any specific benefit or government service.[9] Alternatively, the benefits view suggests that taxes are paid in exchange for benefits received. They are "mandatory or voluntary levies imposed on persons deriving particular benefits from specific categories of publicly provided goods and services."[10]

Regarding the property tax, whether it is a general tax or a benefits tax is a subject of considerable discussion. As a general tax, it is a capital tax levied against house value, as reflected in the market value of the property in question. As a benefits tax, property taxes can be seen as charges levied for municipal services rendered. Regarding property taxes generally, neither a benefits tax nor a general tax approach to property taxes is specifically advocated here. Ultimately, the appropriate approach will vary depending on a number of factors, including the nature of the services that the charge is paying for. Indeed, part of the difficulty in structuring a fair and efficient property tax lies in the wide range of services it covers. For example, some municipal services have a redistributive component, such as various social services, affordable housing, transit, perhaps libraries. Here a beneficiary pay principle is inappropriate, and the use of market-value taxation by municipalities to fund these services may be the best available option.

But insofar as it relates to impacts on urban sprawl, and the pricing of services with urban-form-sensitive costs, what is advocated here involves sticking as closely as possible to the true cost pricing principle: that tax prices reflect cost causation, including long-term capital costs (as they vary with urban form factors) and consumption.

The benefits approach is frequently linked to marginal cost pricing. Kitchen, for example, argues that, for efficiency to be achieved, taxes must reflect marginal costs:

> The underlying principle of the benefits model is simple: those who benefit from municipally funded services pay for them. Economic efficiency is achieved when the user fee, price, or tax per unit of output equals the extra cost of the last unit consumed ... Prices or taxes ration output to those who are willing to pay and signal suppliers (local governments or their delivery agents) the quantity and quality of output desired.[11]

Thus, the benefits model is linked with marginal cost pricing. But this raises the question: "how can a property tax, based as it is on market value of property, be seen to reflect marginal costs?" The short answer is that it doesn't.

But some economists argue that the benefits of municipal services (e.g., parks, roads, transit, parks, etc.) are capitalized into the value of the home or property: the more benefits, the greater the house value, the higher the tax paid.[12] They argue that, in this way, property taxes paid reflect benefits received.

This may be true, but such an approach is clearly not the same as a marginal costs approach. In discussing the benefits approach, there is some confusion between "benefits" and "costs." In the literature on the benefits view of property tax and efficient tax prices, "costs" and "benefits" are often used interchangeably. This is confusing and incorrect. While the property tax is often viewed as a benefits tax, when it comes to establishing taxes to be paid, an important distinction must be made between a property tax that levies according to benefits received and one that levies according to public costs precipitated.

These two bases would not result in the same charges. For example, the benefits of garbage collection to the household depend primarily on how much garbage is picked up every week, but the collection costs are also related to the lot frontage. Can we say that a house achieves greater benefit from roads if it has a larger frontage, which will certainly increase the degree to which it precipitates municipal road costs? In practice, a tax designed to reflect benefits will not yield the same levels of taxation as a tax based on cost causation. If the objective is to promote efficient use of municipal resources, and efficient land-use patterns, then only a true incremental costs-based approach that accounts for location, development pattern, and land use-related cost variations should be applied to services whose costs are influenced by these factors. A property tax as a form of payment for benefits received may be all right if applied to municipal expenditures that are not particularly influenced by urban form (such as administration, policy development, and implementation or shared amenities such as public parks). However, if efficiency of service delivery and urban development pattern are the objectives, it should not be applied to cost recovery for services whose costs are influenced by urban form. Thus, what I advocate is the linking of taxes more closely with cost causation, where urban form factors influence cost (and, of course, only for the non-redistributive services). There are many options available for doing so, some of which are described below.

Fix Inherited Distortions

A number of flaws and distortions embedded in the current property tax system in Ontario and related to the creation of inefficient development patterns are outlined in Chapter 7. A first and obvious step in aligning municipal fiscal policy with compact form objectives would be to undertake reforms to remove the biases. With respect to urban sprawl, one of the key reforms would involve the province's implementing a constant education tax rate on non-residential properties across all municipalities. Aligning the tax rate charged for multi-unit buildings more closely with their share of costs incurred is also critical. This would likely mean reducing the tax rate for multi-unit buildings from one that is two to four times that levied on low-rise housing to one that is equal to or even lower than the rate for low rise. For the City of Toronto, which undertaxes residential development relative to non-residential more than most, achieving more accurate property taxes might mean raising tax rates on low-rise housing while holding the rate for multi-unit buildings steady.

These examples are taken from Toronto and Ontario, but other jurisdictions have their fair share of idiosyncrasies that have an important effect on urban development patterns. In all cases, a systematic tax reform to remove the built-in biases that militate against compact development is needed.

Tax Land Not Buildings

As discussed earlier, property taxes levied on the basis of the assessed market value of properties act as a disincentive to densification as any improvements or additions will tend to increase the value of the property and, therefore, the tax liability. An alternative to market value assessment is land value taxation (LVT) (sometimes called site value taxation). This is not a new idea: in fact, it is widely attributed to Henry George, who lived during the nineteenth century. LVT has been adopted and remains in place in jurisdictions in the United States, Australia, and New Zealand as well as in Taiwan, Hong Kong, Singapore, and elsewhere.

Under this approach, only the value of the land forms the basis for determining the assessed value of the property for taxation purposes, and the value of buildings or other improvements to the property are disregarded. By switching the tax burden to land only, improvements, investment, and densification are encouraged, resulting in more efficient land development patterns. It becomes considerably less attractive to hold land in an underutilized state or speculatively because the same tax must be paid regardless of the amount of development it supports. By encouraging development on underutilized land and discouraging long-term speculation in already-urbanized areas, development pressure at the urban fringe can be reduced. LVT is thus seen as an effective tool for encouraging efficient development patterns, densification, and regeneration of underutilized or derelict urban areas, and it is consistent with the tax-shift theory of not taxing "goods" (in this case, development).

In short, LVT forces landowners to examine more actively and closely the development opportunities afforded by their land to make sure it is optimally developed and to consider acting on them more quickly. This is precisely the kind of behaviour that is needed to secure efficient development patterns but that is discouraged by the market value tax. According to McCluskey and Franzsen: "[LVT] would have substantial effects on the incentives to develop and improve land. It would make possible a greater participation of scarce land resources in the urban and sub-urban real estate market [by] utilizing land in accordance with market forces and demand, instead of ignoring this demand in anticipation of ever greater unearned increments."[13] There is also a certain logic to recovering costs of land-related services on the basis of a land tax, particularly in cases where the costs of network services are recouped through taxation rather than hived off as separate user fees.

On the other hand, the pressure LVT places on landowners to ensure that their property is optimally developed can have undesirable consequences for sprawl at the urban fringe. If "highest and best use" is used to value land, active farmland and conservation lands at the urban edge can be subject to higher taxes than non-fringe farms and fields, straining the economic viability of farming and adding to pressures to convert these lands to urban use. In most areas, this is dealt with by implementing policies that prevent this from happening (e.g., by mandating that farm properties be valued only as if they are maintained in agriculture, excluding their future potential to be turned into urban use).

It is also sometimes claimed that the land value basis cannot generate enough revenue because the value of land is not high enough, and tax rates would therefore have to be set at an unacceptably high level relative to the value of the property, though this is debated.[14] This is unlikely to be true in developed countries, particularly in growing urban areas with high demand for developable land – the very places where rationality in land development and densification are required.

Evidence of the impact of LVT on land development patterns can be tricky to assess – even in places where there is a significant history of using this form of property tax – given the difficulties in isolating the effect of the tax from the other factors that shape urban growth patterns. Nevertheless, research in metropolitan Melbourne has shown that the site value taxation system in use there beginning in the 1920s had a considerable impact on development. Melbourne provided an interesting laboratory, given that about half the local governments that comprise the metropolitan area used site value taxation, while the other half used a capital value assessment. The areas subject to site value taxation exhibited residential densities, population densities, and residential values per acre that were each about 50 percent higher than those in the areas using a capital value assessment.[15] The evidence suggests that site value taxation caused development to occur sooner than it otherwise might have done and that this advantage persists in the long run. (Over a very long period of time, however, as the urban area filled in, this development-precipitating effect was thought to have eroded somewhat.)

Land Value Tax in Sydney and New South Wales

In New South Wales (NSW), the state levies a tax on land ownership (among other taxes). It is based on the value of all land, excluding buildings and other improvements, above a threshold of $359,000 (in 2008). A rate of 1.6 percent is applied against the net land value. Interestingly, principal residences are exempt from the tax. NSW also levies a per space parking tax in some areas, the revenues of which fund regional transportation. Water and sewer services are provided for the entire region by Sydney Water, a corporation owned by the government of NSW.

The state government also sets the framework for local land taxes. In Australia, local governments raise 83 percent of revenues from their own sources on average.[17] Property taxes are the only source of tax revenue available to local governments. A wide range of user fees make up a significant and growing portion of local revenues. On average, 45 percent of local government revenues come from property tax, 35 percent from user fees, with the remainder coming from other sources such as fines, developer fees, etc.[18]

Local governments in NSW are permitted to charge a land value tax as well as a wide range of user fees and other charges. These include charges for water, sewer, drainage, and waste management. Rates (taxes) are charged against the unimproved capital value of land.

The City of Sydney is at the centre of the Sydney metropolitan area. Rates are calculated as a minimum flat amount per property, plus a rate applied to land value (in the range of 0.1 to 0.2 percent, depending on the type of property). The city raises about 55 percent of its revenue from land tax and annual charges (including the Domestic Waste Management Annual Availability Charge), and 18 percent from other charges and user fees.[19]

However, reforms to the Local Government Act in the late 1980s permitted greater flexibility in charging differential tax rates (to different types of properties) if a "capital improved value" were adopted as the basis for valuation. As a result, most local governments switched to a capital improved value. By the 1990s, and following a period of local government restructuring that saw amalgamations and a dramatic reduction in the number of local governments in Melbourne and the rest of the state of Victoria, only a handful of local councils used site value taxation.[16] LVT continues to be the dominant form of taxation elsewhere, however, including in Australia's largest city, Sydney (see box on previous page).

A variation on the LVT is "split rate taxation," sometimes called a "graded tax." In split rate taxation, both the land and the buildings are valued, but they are taxed at different rates, typically with the land component being

Split-Rate Taxes in Pittsburgh, Pennsylvania

The City of Pittsburgh, Pennsylvania, is the largest US city to use split rate taxation. It had a graded tax system in place since 1913. Land was taxed at twice the rate of buildings, until taxes were restructured in 1979/80, such that the rate on land became five times that applied to structures.[20] It should be noted that during the restructuring, tax was not removed from the buildings component; rather, the taxation rate applied to buildings was held constant, while the rate applied to land was significantly increased. In other words, this was not a revenue-neutral tax shift.

The most thorough review of the impact of split rate tax in Pittsburgh was conducted by Oates and Schwab. They compared development in the City of Pittsburgh (which used split rate taxation) with development in the rest of the metropolitan area and other Pennsylvania towns (which did not) before and after the 1980 reform. They document a marked increase in commercial building activity in particular in the centre of the city in the period following the reforms, compared to reduced building activity in the suburbs and other towns.

After considering other factors that could account for the increase in commercial building activity in Pittsburgh post-reform, Oates and Schwab conclude that the split rate tax "played a significant supportive role in the economic resurgence of the city." Other empirical studies have also found support for the use of a land tax in Pittsburgh.[21]

In 2001, however, land value taxation was rescinded, amidst a mayoral campaign, property reassessment, and proposed changes to the tax system.[22]

taxed at a rate several times that of the capital improvements. Split rate taxation can thus be seen as a middle ground between a tax purely on land value and a traditional tax on the combined value of the land and capital improvements.

Banzhaf and Lavery are the first to test the effect of a split-rate tax on density, in this case using Pennsylvania as the example. They examined density before and after the introduction of split-rate taxes in Pennsylvania municipalities and found that the split-rate tax did increase the capital-to-land ratio, as theorized. This increase took the form mostly of an increase in the number of housing units in a given land area, as opposed to simply larger houses. They found that there was a 2 to 10 percentage point increase in the number of dwelling units per unit of land area in the first two decades, compared to areas that did not have split-rate taxation. Population density increased up to 7 percent.[23]

Oates and Schwab's explanation of the role of land taxation is important. They argue that the unique role of LVT lies in its neutrality, and that the land tax can only be understood in the context of other tax alternatives (see box on previous page). For example, higher taxes on structures or on wages were considered as options in the Pittsburgh case. Assuming a context of demand for development – in Pittsburgh or elsewhere – the essential neutrality of land taxation avoided any distortions that alternative taxes might have imposed. It did not prevent, postpone, reduce, or distort development, as other conventional tax instruments might: "land value taxation provides city officials with a tax instrument that generates revenues, but has no damaging side effects on the urban economy. In this way, it allows the city to avoid reliance on other taxes that can undermine urban development."[24]

Pittsburgh was facing a financial crisis and had to raise taxes in some form in order to increase revenues. So it did not remove the existing tax on structures but simply maintained it at its existing level while increasing the tax rate on land. In cases where revenue neutrality is possible, another strategy would be to remove tax on structures and increase the rate on land – a pure land tax. Under these circumstances, one might expect any impacts to be more pronounced than in the Pittsburgh case.[25]

In short, if a tax is to be imposed, LVT is a good one. Like any tax, it cannot in and of itself create demand where none exists. However, in avoiding distortions, disincentives, and penalties that alternative taxes impose, it could render some borderline projects feasible, encourage capital intensity and density of development, reduce long-term speculation, and encourage development to occur sooner than might otherwise be the case.

Unit Value Assessment

Another approach to property tax involves "unit value" or "area" assessment. Under this approach, property is assessed on the basis of area of the lot or floor area of the building(s) or both. For each property, a standard per-square-metre assessment value is applied to the lot area and/or the floor area of the buildings. So the assessed value for property tax purposes is in direct proportion to the size of the lot and the buildings upon it. Today, unit assessment is mostly used in places that do not have a well-developed property market or where transactions are too few to establish reliable market values.

To the extent that services paid for through property tax are development pattern-sensitive, unit value assessment can be seen as an approach that more closely aligns cost causation with property tax due and is therefore more supportive of efficient development patterns than is market value assessment. It disregards factors such as the quality of the building and levels of finish that might contribute to the value of the property but have little impact on demand for services and cost causation.

Sometimes adjustments are made to the per-square-metre rate to reflect factors such as location, zoning, or quality of the structure in order to more closely approximate market values. However, when the adjustments become too complex and detailed, the unit assessment starts to take on the characteristics of a market value system, in which case it is preferable to simply move towards the latter because it will provide a more accurate basis.

Where unit assessment is applied to both land and buildings, care must be taken not to overcharge the building component or a disincentive to density will be created. Land-related costs (e.g., network services) would be best recovered with the land component and population-related costs (e.g., soft services, administration) reflected in a buildings component. Of course, it is also possible to use only a land valuation component, with the tax taking on the characteristics of a land value tax.

Parcel Taxes

A next step beyond unit assessment in the spectrum of efficient property taxes would be to eliminate the property valuation component altogether and simply charge taxes directly against the property itself. This is, in effect, what parcel taxes do. Parcel taxes are separate taxes that can be charged for a specific service or group of services.

They differ from property tax in that they are based on the parcel itself rather than on an assessed value. They can be charged on a per-parcel basis or according to lot size or frontage. They differ from user fees in that they are a tax that can be charged provided the service is available to a property, regardless of whether or not a particular property makes use of the service. Parcel taxes are used in some municipalities in British Columbia, applied to single services or groups of services, where they are enabled under the community charter legislation.

From the perspective of promoting efficient development patterns, parcel taxes are undoubtedly superior to market value assessment, assuming that the property tax is paying for development pattern-sensitive services. Parcel taxes and area assessment also have a distinct advantage in ease of administration. The size of lots and buildings change relatively little and is easy to keep track of, compared to property values under market value assessment. This means simplifying the process and reducing the administration costs of maintaining a market value-based system. Assessing constantly changing market values of millions of properties is complex and costly. In the Province of Ontario, it costs the public about $155 million per year to do so.[26] Of course, this excludes the costs incurred by those businesses and homeowners who often must respond to incorrect assessments. This is a significant sum that, instead, could be used to provide targeted subsidies to those who might have difficulty paying their taxes under a more efficient scheme.

In addition, the municipal tax rates applied must be constantly adjusted to compensate for the changing assessment base. Also, significant inequities can emerge when properties in some neighbourhoods of a municipality appreciate much more quickly than those in other areas. This situation is emerging in the City of Toronto, for example, where properties in the denser central city are appreciating more quickly than are those in the lower-density suburbs.

Choosing the Best Approach

The best approach to the property tax depends, in part, on a municipality's objectives and, in part, on what services the property tax pays for. If the property tax pays, in large part, for services whose costs are sensitive to development patterns (with network service costs accounting for 38 percent of municipal expenditures in Canada),[27] then it makes sense to move to a taxation system whose tax prices can capture these cost variations accurately.

If a municipality's expenditures cover both population-related and urban-form-related costs, then that is a good rationale for a split-rate system. At a minimum, the ratio of taxes levied against lands versus buildings would be weighted to reflect the ratio of land-related versus population-related shares of municipal spending. If the municipality has an explicit objective of reurbanization or improving the efficiency of land development patterns, then moving towards a land value tax makes sense.

If the property tax recovers spending primarily for services whose costs are not particularly sensitive to development patterns, such as social programs, administration, policy, or parks, then a conventional market value system may be perfectly fine. For example, if the costs of network and other services whose costs are development-pattern sensitive are hived off to user fees or parcel taxes, and the remaining services to be covered by the property tax have costs that are primarily related to population, and recovering the localized benefits of municipal investments is a priority, then a market value approach may be more acceptable.[28]

In any event, if more compact development and less urban sprawl are among a municipality's objectives, it may be desirable to remove many development pattern-sensitive services from the property tax and charge a parcel tax or user fees for them instead.

Of course, any switch to a different property tax system must be well considered and involve a transition period, phasing in changes over a period of time to allow households and businesses to adjust. In certain cases, transition assistance and targeted subsidies may be needed to deal with redistributive impacts. And any transformation of property taxes should be part of a broader tax-shift strategy.

User Fees

User fees can be seen as a specific form of benefit taxes; however, while benefit taxes are seen as levies applied to those who benefit from government action generally, user fees are more precise, being "levied on consumers of government goods and services in relation to their consumption."[29] User fees "can be distinguished from other benefit taxes by the accuracy with which the beneficiaries of a public good or service can be identified and the precision with which the amount of the benefit can be measured."[30] User fees are fairly common but, typically, not well designed, and they rarely align with planning objectives. There is also scope for them to be used much more than is currently the case.

User fees offer several advantages, and these are in part why we are seeing evidence that municipalities are more and more interested in pursuing them as a means of financing local services. Critically, compared to property taxes, in which a lump sum is paid to cover a variety of services, user fees make the real cost of services visible and transparent. If properly structured, user fees ensure that services are provided efficiently – that there is not an over- or under-demand or supply because of lack of accurate price signals. They can thereby encourage modifications to behaviour that can allow households, businesses, and, ultimately, municipalities to reduce costs. As such, they can play an important role in a broader tax-shifting program. Over time, if properly structured to reflect development-pattern-related cost variations, they can lead to different location and development choices, and create more efficient urban development patterns, with more intensive use of already-urbanized lands, less sprawl, and more compact greenfields development.

When should user fees be used? As Bird suggests, "Wherever possible, charge. For efficiency, charges should be levied on the direct recipients of benefits, whether residents, businesses, or 'things' (real property)."[31] In particular, user fees are best employed for services in which individual beneficiaries can be identified, associated costs can be quantified, and non-payers can be excluded.[32]

The use of user fees is especially recommended for those services for which costs vary with urban form factors. User fees make the link between the provision of the service and the cost much more accurate as well as apparent to the user, including the cost variations associated with location and urban form.

User fees could be applied to several services that would typically be funded through the property tax. Examples of network services that would benefit from being removed from property tax and paid for directly with user fees include ongoing road maintenance costs (maintenance, repair, cleaning, snow removal), garbage, and recycling. Many municipalities are already moving towards special charges for garbage and recycling.

Getting the prices right is key to realizing the benefits from user fees. There are many options for structuring fees. Unfortunately, at present, they rarely conform to the true cost principle of fees reflecting costs as they vary with urban form and location. In addition, they are rarely undertaken in the context of a broader strategy of tax shifting and, as such, represent a missed opportunity. An example of efficient pricing is outlined below. In this case, pricing roadways illustrates some of the principles.

Pricing Roadways
The costs of roads are presently paid for in different ways, depending on the type of road and the type of cost. This section addresses only the direct costs

of roads: construction, maintenance and repairs, operation, and traffic services. Not included are external costs such as congestion, pollution, or
health-related expenses.

Most roads are paid for primarily through general government revenues
and therefore through different types of taxes, including income taxes, corporate taxes, sales tax, and property tax. As seen earlier, a portion of fuel
tax can sometimes be directly targeted to transportation infrastructure.
Tolls pay only a small portion of road costs – one estimate puts it at 5 percent.[33] The combination of revenue sources will vary from jurisdiction to
jurisdiction.

Most of the ongoing costs of urban roads are covered through general
property taxes. Urban roads are rarely subject to user fees, with the exception of an occasional bridge or expressway toll. Construction costs for
regional roads may also be paid for through DCs or impact fees. And, in new
greenfields developments, the capital costs of local roads are usually embedded in the selling price or rents of houses and commercial or institutional
development.

The problem with these sources of revenue for roadway costs is that they
are unrelated to the degree to which different payers actually precipitate
costs. Indeed, many of those taxed may not even own a car, or may have
minimal or only occasional use of roadways, while others will be heavy
users. The fuel tax bears a stronger link with cost causation – the more fuel
consumed, the more driving is likely to occur – though it is still imperfect,
given significant variations in fuel efficiencies between types of vehicle. In
any event, current revenue-generating mechanisms fail to send any kind of
accurate price signal regarding the true cost of roads. As a result, demand is
higher than what is efficient, congestion and over-building of roads being
the result.

In other words, the link between cost causation and price is extremely
weak when it comes to roads. Unlike with other network services, such as
cable or natural gas, users are not issued a bill that reflects their use of the
service – in fact, users pay only a portion of the cost of the construction,
maintenance, and operation of roadways. Also unlike other network services, those who pay may not even make much use of the service. Within
urban areas, virtually everyone who is billed for services such as water or
electricity will use them. But with roads, all houses, businesses, and citizens are billed, through property and other taxes, even if they make little
use of them.

In order to create efficient urban development patterns and to reduce infrastructure costs, the pricing of roads needs to be closely aligned with the degree to which costs are incurred. Costs for urban roads can be classified into (1) capital costs and (2) operating and maintenance costs. The former represents the construction costs, while the latter consist of ongoing costs such as repairs and maintenance, snow clearance, and cleaning as well as police services related to traffic and emergency services related to accidents. As with all pricing instruments, as close a link as possible should be made between the prices charged and costs incurred – both in terms of attaching prices to the very factors that determine cost and in terms of ensuring that the price levels reflect costs as accurately as is practically feasible.

For capital or "fixed" road costs associated with new development, if initial construction costs are covered by DCs, then an efficient DC, structured along the lines described above, would result in a more accurate price signal. For existing development, all properties could be charged an access fee, which represents benefits received from having access to the urban road network. This would apply equally to users and non-users as all households and businesses benefit from the road network, even those households without a car. Roads support economic activity and allow goods to be delivered to shops, for example: and every property has road access and frontage. The access charge could also be based on lot area or lot frontage as these factors determine, in part, the extent of the urbanized area and, therefore, the extent of the road network required. It could be an annual charge, included with the property tax bill, for example.

In terms of operating and maintenance costs, or "variable" costs, these can be attributed to two main factors: the extent of the network (i.e., the amount of lane-kilometres) and the amount of travel, which influences the wear and tear on the roads as well as the likelihood of being in an accident. A useful indicator of contributions to the former costs is lot size, while a measure of the latter is distance travelled (i.e., VKT). Costs of road cleaning and snow clearance are related to the extent of the network, which, in turn, is linked with lot size. Other costs, such as repair, policing of roads, and emergency services are linked with distances travelled.

In recouping costs related to distances travelled, even charging a standard road-use fee based on each vehicle owned would be an improvement over the current system because then at least *some* direct and apparent link would be made between cost causation and prices. For example, road maintenance and policing charges could be added to the vehicle registration fee, captured in a municipal charge, or a road charges fee could simply be billed regularly to the owner of each licensed vehicle. This approach takes only car ownership into account, not VKT, although there is a very strong relationship between these two factors.

Perhaps a more accurate approach would involve charging a road-use fee based on actual VKT for each vehicle. This could be calculated either through odometer readings at the time of licence renewal or on a regular basis. These charges would more accurately link the causes of road costs with prices paid, while making the costs much more apparent to the user and promoting more efficient use of roads as well as equity improvements. Or VKT could be estimated based on neighbourhood, using a neighbourhood average VKT per household as that varies from district to district within the city.

A fuel tax is often proposed as a good proxy for road use. However, it is not the best choice if the aim of the instrument is to charge for the direct costs of road use. It is inaccurate, given substantial variations in fuel efficiency of vehicles, particularly at this point of transition to more fuel-efficient vehicles and hybrids. The link between a fuel tax and road use is usually buried within the per-litre price of fuel and so does not provide a clear price signal regarding the true costs of road use. On the revenue side, the link between taxes raised from fuel and spending on transportation infrastructure is also often very weak. However, a fuel tax is appropriate if an emissions or carbon tax is what is really being sought, given the close relationship between fuel consumed and emissions generated.

Another option for recovering road costs involves road tolls. Indeed, road tolls are often used for expressways or special facilities such as bridges. One of the benefits of road tolls is that they can charge for roads in real time, making the true cost of road use very apparent. There are many options for structuring a road toll, including charging for crossing a boundary (cordon charging), charging for driving within a given area (area charging), or charging for use of a linear section of infrastructure (e.g., a bridge, expressway, or tunnel). A number of technologies are available, which permit the free flow of traffic while still imposing a charge. Positioning technology is being developed in order to allow road charges to accurately reflect the distances travelled by a vehicle. Implementing advanced tolling systems may come with substantial costs (though these are likely to fall as the technologies improve and are more widely adopted), which would have to be weighed against the benefits achieved.

The portion of variable road-related costs that is related to lot size (cleaning, snow clearance, and a portion of maintenance and repair) could be established as a separate municipal charge, levied annually along with the tax bill and based on lot size or frontage. A base fee for roads should be charged to all households, even if they are not car owners, or these costs could be included in a property tax that reflects lot size.

Shifting the costs of roads from taxation to specific road charges is a substantial step towards better pricing, promoting more efficient use of the road system as well as greater transparency. It would also remove or reduce existing cross-subsidies between non-, light, and heavy road users, thereby improving equity. In the long run, these reforms will correct current pricing biases that make sprawl attractive, leading to more efficient development patterns.

An important opportunity for tax shifting is also created. If governments cover costs through a user fee, then road costs can be removed from general taxation and tax bills for businesses and households can be reduced accordingly. Given that roads cost are a significant portion of municipal spending, taxes could be significantly reduced. Assuming accurate pricing, revenues produced will, by definition, cover the costs of roads, though charges can be set to also include improvements to the transportation system. Consumers benefit from a clear understanding of road costs and, significantly, from the opportunity to save money and lower their overall costs by changing their travel behaviour. In the long run, this pricing would encourage households, businesses, and developers to take transportation costs into account when making locational or development decisions, and this would result in more compact urban form. This presupposes that viable transportation alternatives exist, an obvious prerequisite when considering implementation of road charges.

Pricing Network Services

The problem with the pricing of utilities, such as water, electricity, natural gas, telephone, cable, broadband internet, and other network services, is similar to that with DCs and other revenue-raising instruments – that is, "prices" are based on average costs, even though actual costs vary with location, development pattern, development type, and other urban form factors. Not surprisingly, the solution is also similar to that for DCs – namely, de-averaging prices so that they vary by location, development pattern, and use, thus accurately reflecting cost differentials.

However, while the DC covers only capital costs, prices for network services can cover capital, operating and maintenance, or replacement costs. This section addresses the pricing of network infrastructure and services costs other than those paid for by DCs or property tax. These include utilities such as electricity, natural gas, telephone, cable, or broadband connections, for example, as well as some specific municipal services such as water.

There has been much discussion lately of implementing marginal cost pricing for utilities such as water and electricity in order to promote conservation of resources and to reduce GHG emissions. For water especially, because it is often charged on a flat fee basis, the marginal cost to the consumer of one more litre is zero. At no perceived cost for more consumption, it is not surprising that consumers use more water than they might if prices reflected marginal costs. Many alternative pricing schemes have been proposed. However, while they might aim to reduce water or electricity consumption, they very rarely account for location, development pattern, and land use. Ignoring these cost variations means the prices continue to act as an incentive to sprawl and, to the extent that sprawl contributes to consumption (larger lots mean more lawn watering), as an incentive to consumption.

The approach to overcoming this flaw is similar to that used with regard to DCs. The first step is to identify those costs that are sensitive to location, development pattern, and development type as opposed to those costs that are not. Taking the case of water provision as an example, and oversimplifying for purposes of illustration, the major costs are categorized in the manner shown below. Let us look at three main components of infrastructure cost for the provision of water: treatment, the network of transmission and distribution pipes, and pumping.

First, one needs to identify those costs that are not at all sensitive to the location of the development being served. For example, considered in isolation from the network of pipes to which a water treatment plant is attached, as a "point" facility the plant's costs would not be expected to be sensitive to the location of the development being served;[34] rather, its costs would be governed primarily by capacity requirements (among other non-spatial factors such as standards, technology, etc.). These costs could, therefore, be covered by a standard system-wide usage charge – so many dollars per cubic metre of water consumed.

Second, unless development takes place on the proverbial featureless plane, other costs can be sensitive to location. Transmission and distribution pipes may be more expensive in one area than in another on a per-metre basis due to factors such as topography. And geological conditions can make pipe installation and maintenance more expensive in some areas than others, or distances from the treatment plant may be greater in some areas than others. Pumping costs may be higher if higher elevations are to be serviced. The second step, therefore, is to delineate the geographic zones that have similar cost profiles.

Then, within each cost zone, aggregate costs are apportioned according to causation factors. Costs of the network of pipes that connects the treatment plant to homes and places of work are sensitive to demand (i.e., how much water will flow through the system and the capacity required to accommodate it). However, costs of the network are also dependent upon development pattern – particularly density. In this case, the costs should be apportioned accordingly, with capacity-related pipe costs included in a usage fee and density-related pipe costs included in an areal charge based on size of lot or frontage. Pumping costs are also determined, in part, by demand (how much water will flow through the system) and, in part, by density (how much terrain is to be traversed and, therefore, how much pumping is required). Again, the demand-related costs would be included in the usage fee, and the density-related costs would be reflected in the areal charge. Development type can also play a key role in determining demand for water, with some uses consuming more water than others. Volume-based usage fees would account for these variations by type.

In this example, we end up with a two-part pricing system: (1) a volume-based charge reflecting volume-related costs and (2) an area-based charge reflecting density-sensitive costs. The volume charge reflects costs attributable to the amount of water used and, therefore, the capacity costs incurred. It could include costs of the water itself, treatment, the capacity-related portion of network costs, and the capacity-related portion of pumping costs. The volume charge might be on a per-cubic-metre basis or on a block basis (e.g., one price for the first one thousand cubic metres, with different prices levied for additional consumption "blocks"). Blocks can have increasing prices or decreasing prices, but if water conservation is an objective, decreasing block pricing is ill-advised.

The second component of this pricing system reflects costs that vary with density, such as the density-related portions of network costs and of pumping costs. These costs are independent of the volumes of water consumed. The charge could be a monthly fee that varies with the size of the lot. This could be on a per-square-metre basis or on a block-pricing basis according to lot sizes. Another option is to charge according to lot frontage. It is possible that both the volume-based charge and the area-based charge would vary by zone. For most customers, administrative costs are generally not related to density, location, or usage, and they would be billed on a flat per-customer basis. An exception to this is the cost of meter-reading, which is sensitive to density and should, therefore, be included in the lot-based charges.

This, of course, is but one possible pricing structure. Myriad options are possible, depending on local conditions, urban form, geography, and other factors. One example of geographic zones being implemented for water pricing may be found in Cleveland, Ohio (see box). I am aware of no current examples of pricing for water or other network infrastructure that incorporate all the principles of efficient pricing as outlined in this book. Much water pricing continues to be on a flat fee basis. There is movement to redesign water prices to a usage-based system. This presents an important opportunity

Cleveland's Zone-Based Water Rates

The Cleveland Division of Water (CDOW) provides water to the City of Cleveland as well as to the surrounding suburbs of Cuyahoga County, Ohio (which includes the city of Cleveland). Since the 1970s, it has employed a zonal pricing system. This came about as the city was expanding at the edge, with new suburbs requiring water services, but the City was unable to afford to extend the system to these areas. The cost of serving these areas was high, in part because the outer areas were at higher elevations, incurring increased costs for pumping, pressurization, and related capital facilities. An agreement was reached whereby the City would extend its water system to the suburbs, subject to the adoption of a zone-based pricing system. Such a system continues to be in place today.

Under the system, four zones were established: the City of Cleveland, the Low/ First High District, the Second High District, and the Third High District. These districts reflect increasing distances from source water (Lake Erie) and progressively higher elevations and therefore incur progressively increasing costs. Prices in the outer zones are calculated as a multiple of those in Cleveland proper. Respective rates for the four zones were $10.63, $17.54, $20.20, and $23.17 for the first thousand cubic feet (MCF) of water (in 2008).

Cleveland also employs an increasing block rate to address the amount of water used. Beyond the first MCF, water is charged at a considerably higher rate, and these rates also vary according to zone. So this pricing system successfully and simultaneously addresses both usage and location-related costs. There is also a quarterly customer service charge on a flat fee basis that is standard across all districts.

to also integrate urban form factors into the pricing equation both in order to reduce sprawl and to promote conservation.

Pricing of any goods or services can be extremely complex. Often, many objectives must be balanced against one another. However, the critical effects pricing has on urban development patterns (and urban development patterns have on costs) have been widely ignored, and they need to be considered by governments at all levels when structuring pricing for government-provided or government-regulated services.

Unlike DCs, and except for some municipal utilities (especially water and sewer services), municipalities do not always control pricing for network services. Most of these network industries are nonetheless regulated by upper-level governments – be they provincial, state, or federal. Here amendments to legislation may be needed in order to mandate efficient pricing.

Pricing the Automobile

How the direct costs of roads are paid for through a variety of instruments, such as DCs or property tax, and how these instruments might be restructured or better designed to bring about more efficient and environmentally sustainable outcomes, has already been discussed. Roads are, of course, a big part of the cost of travel, but other significant costs of travel include fuel and auto insurance.

As noted in Chapter 9, subsidies to the production of oil and natural gas artificially lower the costs and prices of these non-renewable resources. The result is higher levels of consumption than would otherwise be the case as artificially lower prices fail to accurately reflect more expensive extraction methods and higher costs. In addition, governments end up subsidizing both the production of fuels and the mitigation of the negative externalities that result from their use (e.g., smog, GHGs, or global warming). Rationality needs to be brought to bear on these double-subsidy situations. The role of government priorities and expenditures needs to be scrutinized and made consistent in order to stop the double spending of government resources. This being the case, subsidies to energy production need to be seriously reviewed within a larger context of competing objectives, such as the reduction of GHGs and the prevention of global warming.

Another significant cost of car use is insurance. As noted earlier, one example of poor pricing involves the Province of Ontario's eliminating sales tax on auto insurance in an effort to reduce its costs to the driver. Why should auto insurance be singled out for special tax treatment, especially in a manner that does nothing to address the cause of the problem in an efficient way (i.e., rising premiums associated with more expensive and larger vehicles)? While it may help those in an affordability crunch somewhat, the policy creates a subsidy to auto travel and further encourages auto use. Auto insurance should be taxed the same as all other services. If subsidies are needed for some groups because of affordability issues, then a targeted subsidy should be applied.

An alternative approach might be to introduce pay-as-you-drive insurance. It has been shown that the greater the amount of annual travel associated with a vehicle, the greater the likelihood of its being involved in a crash and incurring costs. Instead of paying an annual flat premium that does not reflect how crash risk varies with amount driven, and that creates a cross-subsidy from infrequent drivers to frequent drivers, a policy-holder would pay by the kilometre driven, with different rates still reflecting the other usual variables (e.g., driving record, type of vehicle, etc.).[35] Unlike conventional auto insurance, pay-as-you-drive insurance establishes a clear and visible link between kilometres driven and costs paid. As such, it would help to moderate travel demand and distances travelled – something that conventional insurance, with its flat-fee structure, does not do.

Parking

Free parking is both the most significant and most ignored contributor to urban sprawl. Addressing free parking could bring about very substantial rewards in curbing sprawl. Also, parking lots represent development potential – sites that can be redeveloped and densified. New development can still include parking (priced!) in a structured form, along with other uses, resulting in a double benefit. A property tax shift to a land-area basis (LVT or variant) should help by making it less attractive to hold underbuilt land. However, many other practical and effective tools are also available to deal with the oversupply of parking.

Parking is usually a "bundled" good. The costs of parking provided at a given facility are bundled in other prices – of goods and services sold at the mall, in house prices, commercial rents and property prices, even taxes. Transferring the costs of parking in these ways leads to underpricing and hence over-supply as well as to cross-subsidies between non- or infrequent drivers and frequent drivers. So, in order to make parking efficient, two objectives must be fulfilled: (1) unbundling and (2) efficient pricing. There are many approaches that can be taken to achieve this.[36] Some possible approaches in a few key areas are outlined below.

Unbundling Parking in New Construction

The cost of parking – garages, driveways, and additional land – is typically bundled into the purchase price of new homes. With the exception of some multi-unit buildings and condominiums with shared parking, parking spaces or garages must be purchased whether needed or not. This adds to the cost of the home and to urban sprawl by requiring greater use of land for surface parking. Instead, for new home construction where homes (i.e., single-family dwellings) are sold prior to building and are often built to purchaser specifications, parking spaces could be priced and sold separately as purchase options. This allows homebuyers to buy fewer spaces if they have only one or no cars. This improvement in transparency provides the homebuyer with more and better information on the cost components of her home, giving her the opportunity to make an informed choice about how much money to spend on parking. The same principle can be applied to new-build, non-residential development.

Of course, zoning regulations are an obstacle because they stipulate a high minimum number of parking spaces. These regulations need to be amended and standards reduced, including allowing on-street parking, a practice that is currently illegal in many jurisdictions. Or, for example, lower parking levels could be provided if the property owner enters into an agreement with the municipality to implement a transportation-demand management plan. Where the cost of developing and implementing the plan is less than the land, construction, and maintenance costs of providing parking, this will make economic sense.

"In lieu" fees are another option. These are fees that a developer pays to a municipality instead of building required parking. The municipality can use the fees to provide collective public parking through a parking authority or other similar entity. This can allow for sharing parking among a number of facilities, which can be quite efficient and can reduce the number of spaces required. In lieu fees are in use in many municipalities, including the City of Toronto.

Rationalizing Visitor Parking

"Free" visitor parking is provided at malls, institutions, offices, restaurants, and shops. The substantial costs of providing this parking should be removed from rents (which are then passed along in goods and services prices or taxes) and transferred directly and specifically to the user in the form of parking charges. The prices should be based on the principles of efficient pricing – that is, parking rates should recover all the direct costs associated with providing and maintaining parking spaces.

In regard to periods of high demand, instead of providing parking spaces that exist 365 days of the year in order to ensure that there are enough spaces only for the relatively few peak periods, retailers should consider congestion pricing as a viable alternative. In other words, in the same way that congestion pricing works for roads, parking pricing could vary by time of day in order to encourage more efficient use of facilities. For example, a base parking price could be implemented for parking at the mall, with increased hourly rates during peak periods in which demand would otherwise outstrip supply. This would encourage shoppers with other options to visit the mall at non-peak times or use other modes of travel.

Here a smart financial tool can be used to address a problem that has historically had an engineering solution: physically building more and more parking spaces, thus fuelling the cycle of supply and demand for driving. The financial solution is vastly superior to the physical solution. Congestion pricing for parking is a flexible tool that can respond easily to changing conditions, demand is rationalized, over-supply of spaces and cross-subsidies on the part of non-drivers are eliminated, sprawl is reduced, and revenues are generated that can be reinvested in alternatives to auto travel.

Where businesses that provide parking compete with one another for customers, it may be difficult to implement parking pricing on a piecemeal basis as it could send some drivers to businesses that maintain their "free" parking. However, by transferring parking costs directly to users, businesses charging for parking would be able to reduce the prices of their goods and services, thus maintaining their competitiveness. Alternatively, a blanket regulation may be required at a municipal or state/provincial level, requiring efficient pricing to be phased in for major parking facilities so that no business suffers a competitive disadvantage. Or municipal or state/provincial governments could impose a tax on unpriced parking only, providing a strong incentive for owners of private parking facilities to do so on their own (see below).

Removing Employee Parking Subsidies

Many employers provide "free" parking to their employees, encouraging solo driving and creating a situation that is unfair to employees who do not drive to work. One way of addressing these related problems, of course, involves the employer simply charging a cost-recovery parking rate to the employees who use the spaces. This would not only help manage the demand for driving but also, with parking revenues now covering costs, enable employers to use these savings to increase wages to all employees – a fair and efficient solution. Or the prices of goods and services produced could be reduced (or taxes reduced, if it is a government office).

Another approach that has been used successfully elsewhere is called "parking cash out." Under this scheme, employees are offered a choice of a free parking space or an amount of cash that is equal to the cost of providing the space. This eliminates the cross-subsidy issue as well as providing an incentive to carpool or find other modes of travel to work. And, so long as the employer can reduce the supply of parking spaces in response, thereby reducing their costs (e.g., in the case of rented spaces), she suffers no net costs. In recognition of the employee parking problem, from an equity, traffic congestion, and environmental perspective, the State of California enacted a "parking cash out" law in 1992, which puts driving and other modes of travel on a level footing (see box).

Parking Cash Out in California

The California parking cash-out law came into effect in 1993. Employers with over fifty employees who provide subsidized parking to employees must also offer a cash allowance equal to the subsidy. The law applies only to firms that do not own the parking spaces, so that they can readily adjust the number of spaces provided in response to the program and thus render the program cost neutral to the company. If parking costs are bundled into the company's rent and cannot be identified separately, then the law does not apply. Employers who provide non-rented on-site spaces directly to their employees are also not subject to the law. However, employers who provide additional cash benefits to cover parking costs, or who reimburse employees for their commute-related parking expenses, are subject to the law.

A review of the program does indicate that, where implemented, cashing out is effective in changing travel behaviour. On average 12 percent of eligible employees accepted the offer. Solo driving was reduced by an average of 17 percent. Annual vehicle-trips and VMT were reduced, along with CO_2 emissions. Employees found other ways of travelling to work in order to get the cash benefit (these included carpooling and transit).

However, given that the vast majority of parking spaces in California are owned by the employer (84 percent), and that enforcement has been weak, the law has not been widely applied (an estimated 3 percent of all spaces) and so the aggregate impacts have been small. However, the scheme does illustrate the potential of financial tools such as this.[37]

One area where immediate action can be taken concerns parking at government facilities. "Free" or subsidized parking is frequently provided at government offices. Instead, all levels of government should have a clear policy on providing parking at their own facilities and in facilities that they may finance, in whole or in part, through grants. This includes ensuring that drivers and non-drivers (both employees and visitors) are treated equally from a financial perspective. This could include parking cash out-type programs for employees or the introduction of cost-recovery prices.

Pricing Parking through Taxes

Where private landowners do not voluntarily price their parking for visitors and employees, or where mandating such pricing is not desirable, an array of parking taxes of various forms can be used to achieve similar ends. Parking taxes can be applied to revenues from commercial parking facilities or levied on a land area or per-space basis, with many variations and permutations possible. Many cities impose a tax on commercial parking revenue, including San Francisco, Pittsburgh, Miami, Los Angeles, and Chicago, with rates ranging from 10 percent to 50 percent of transactions.

In other cities, parking taxes are levied on the number of spaces or land area devoted to parking. This approach is commonly used in several Australian cities. In Sydney, an annual levy per stall is charged, while in Perth, those who supply parking must pay a parking licence fee. In Melbourne, long-term parking was targeted in order to promote turnover in the use of spaces and to create more parking supply for visitors and shoppers. A long-stay car park levy is charged to permanently leased parking spaces and long-stay spaces in commercial lots in the city centre. Each of these schemes has produced considerable revenue that is reinvested in improving transportation.[38] The design of the parking tax is critical in determining its success and will depend upon the objectives to be achieved as well as considerations of local economic conditions, travel patterns, urban form, and other factors.

Pricing Parking on Public Lands

A considerable share of the parking supply is in public hands, including parking at government facilities as well as on-street parking. Municipal governments can usually make much greater use of issuing permits for parking on public facilities and metered parking. At present, these tools are mostly used in denser central urban areas. However, there is great potential for implementing them in suburban areas, where there is lots of space for parking on wider roadways but little to no charging. They can provide a revenue source to municipalities as well as rationalize demand for auto travel. New technologies can facilitate ease of payment, while central programming allows changes to the pricing structure to be easily implemented. The City of Seattle uses wireless pay stations to charge for public parking, and it increased its revenues by 60 percent by replacing standard meters.[39]

Housing Policy

A range of issues related to housing policy is described above. In some cases, these consist of mis-incentives created through tax and other financial policies, while, in others, it is the existence of policy biases against compact development that is the concern. Examples of some concrete steps that can be taken to address these biases are outlined below.

Mortgage Loan Insurance

Problems with government mortgage loan insurance programs are outlined in Chapter 9 – namely, that they can inadvertently encourage sprawl and higher levels of energy consumption both for transportation and in the home. At the same time, other programs aim to reduce residential GHG emissions. We can no longer afford to support these mutually nullifying programs. *All* CMHC programs should take overall energy efficiency into account, including energy efficiency associated with locational choice and its impacts on transportation as these make up the lion's share of household energy use. Ideally, programs would be structured to provide incentives for homebuyers to choose energy-efficient houses *and* locations.

For example, the mortgage loan insurance program could be retooled to better address current policy objectives and to do so more efficiently. In order to avoid the mansion subsidy problem, mortgage loan assistance should be pegged at the price of a standard starter home. In order to avoid geographic distortions, it is imperative that the variations in starter home prices *within and across* urban regions be reflected so as to create a level playing field.

Another option might be to make granting mortgage insurance conditional upon selecting a home that meets energy efficiency criteria (including considerations of location and neighbourhood context), providing financial assistance for energy retrofits if needed. This approach would help send a clear signal to developers and homebuilders regarding the design of their product, and it would create a situation in which government programs work to support each other. Or a tiered system could be introduced, with higher mortgage shares of purchase prices granted for more energy-efficient homes and locations. Government-provided mortgage insurance for second homes should be removed altogether.

Location Efficient Mortgages

Biases in conventional market mortgage practices are described earlier. Their aspatial approach and inattention to transportation costs creates inherent biases against central, more expensive, and usually more efficient house choices. Recently, location efficient mortgages (LEMs) have been developed, their purpose being to overcome these problems. They are being tested in several US cities, with the support of the US Federal National Mortgage Association ("Fannie Mae") and others, along with a new "Smart Commute" mortgage.

The idea behind the LEM is that, if households spend less than the average on travel because their members live in a part of the city where a car (or cars) is not needed, then they can afford mortgage payments that are higher than those that would be sanctioned under conventional mortgage lending practice (and a higher than normal mortgage amount). This would help with the purchase of homes in these areas, which are often more expensive, given their centrality and transportation infrastructure. In the US pilot project, the areas within a city that would qualify for LEMs due to their potential to enable people to make less use of cars are identified based on their walkability, level of transit service, mix of uses, and so on. Areas are evaluated and a "location efficient value" is determined for each neighbourhood that represents potential transportation cost savings and, therefore, additional income that can be counted towards supporting a mortgage. Thus, the maximum housing-costs-to-income ratio permitted is higher than normal, as is the total-debt-to-income ratio. Households are permitted to borrow larger amounts than they would under a conventional mortgage. The Smart Commute program is a newer, more simplified version of the LEM.

Rollout in the United States is still limited, and, unfortunately, little assessment has been undertaken regarding the success of this model. A primary criticism so far is that the model could incur a higher risk of default if the transportation savings projected are not realized. This may be true, although the lack of data has made it impossible as yet to prove this, and certainly causing financial stress to homeowners should be avoided. However, other than auto loan or lease payments, transportation spending is not scrutinized for conventional mortgagees. These can be very significant, particularly for households owning two, three, or more cars. These households could be subject to similar levels of financial stress, although because, in this case, costs stem from transportation rather than housing, they are ignored in determining mortgage eligibility. It is assumed that travel costs are more variable than housing costs and so adjustments to transportation spending can be more readily made. This is only partly true. Canadian Automobile Association data suggest that variable costs (including gas and maintenance) are about one-quarter of annual driving costs.[40] Fixed costs, including finance, depreciation, insurance, licence, and registration fees, account for about three-quarters of driving costs. Typical total annual costs are in the range of $9,000 to $12,000 per vehicle. Moreover, households living in car-dependent suburbs often have no transportation alternatives (such as viable transit) and can be hard pressed to reduce the number of vehicles they operate. And spending on housing is spending on an asset that tends to appreciate in value, compared to spending on cars, which tend to depreciate.

As a significant cost, transportation should not be ignored. As is shown in Chapter 9 for the Toronto region, in suburban areas transport spending was about equal to spending on housing. A typical suburban household had two cars and twice the transport costs of a typical urban household, which had only one car. Given the magnitude of transportation costs, it makes sense to look at transport and housing costs in both urban and suburban cases when determining mortgage eligibility and carrying cost as they are inextricably interlinked.

It has also been argued that LEMs do not provide sufficient increase in borrowing power to make a significant difference for new home buyers of modest income.[41] Certainly, in some markets where housing is extremely expensive, this can be the case (as is true in Vancouver, the context within which this critique was made). However, in other housing markets, LEMs may provide enough additional borrowing power to shift a housing decision from a suburban to an urban location. The National Resource Defense Council, a LEM partner in the United States, notes that a household with an income of $50,000 choosing an efficient location and saving $200 per month on transportation could qualify for an additional $40,000 of principal compared to a conventional mortgage.[42]

This raises the issue of the objectives for LEMs. If the objective is primarily to increase affordability for first-time buyers, then LEMs may or may not be effective, depending on local housing market conditions. If, however, the objective is to make LEMs widely available to home purchasers of all types so as to level the playing field generally between housing opportunity in urban and suburban locations and reduce the bias towards urban sprawl, then LEMs can be an important instrument.

LEMs are another tool with the potential to address inherent biases against housing choices in urban locations. As always, local conditions are important: they will work more effectively in some urban and economic contexts than others. As a fairly new instrument, they will undoubtedly continue to evolve and to be refined. In the meantime, the bias against those spending less on driving and wanting to live in more walkable, transit-oriented neighbourhoods might be addressed through other techniques as well. For example, CMHC offers a refund of 10 percent on mortgage loan insurance premiums for energy-efficient homes. Why not offer the same refund for the purchase of homes that are located in energy-efficient neighbourhoods and reduce energy used for transportation? Significantly, over time, this, along with other adjustments described in this chapter, will cumulatively shift demand, pressing developers to look more to urban locations to provide new homes as well as to create more efficient, mixed-use new suburban development.

Tax Treatment of Housing

The failure of conventional mortgage practice to take important locational and urban form factors that affect mortgage eligibility and carrying capacity into account creates an inherent bias against more efficient, transit-oriented, and walkable neighbourhoods. It is ironic but true that, by failing to recognize geographic variations, this aspatial approach ends up creating distortions. The same problem exists when absolute thresholds that apply across a landscape of considerable variation are used as criteria in policy and programs.

For example, as noted in Chapter 9, under the federal Home Buyer's Plan, first-time purchasers can withdraw an income-tax-free amount of $25,000 from their RRSP to put towards a purchase of a home. The problem with a standard flat maximum of $25,000, which applies across the country, is that prices vary significantly from market to market as well as within regional markets, depending on location. As noted earlier, for households preferring an urban location but faced with higher home prices there, the flat $25,000 will not go as far, and it provides an incentive to purchase in lower-priced, often suburban locations. As in the case of LEMs, one response to this problem is to allow homebuyers to withdraw higher amounts from their RRSPs when they purchase in sustainable neighbourhoods and incur lower transportation costs but are faced with higher house prices.

The use of a single national maximum home price cut-off for the federal New Housing Rebate also creates distortions. It can prevent households from buying in expensive but efficient urban areas as well as possibly providing unnecessary subsidies in low-price markets. The maximum should be based on the price of a reasonable starter home as that price varies both within and between housing markets. It cannot be overstated that, in coming to terms with urban sprawl, capturing price variations for comparable housing *within* urban markets is critical.

By ignoring important geographical variations – in house prices, spending on transportation, and other relevant factors – policies that employ uniform cut-offs as criteria can have a distortionary effect. The New Housing Rebate and Home Buyers Plan have an additional problem – namely, that they disregard the energy efficiency of the dwelling itself. Consistent with government GHG emissions reduction objectives, the New Housing Rebate and Home Buyer's Plan should apply only to energy-efficient homes and renovations within sustainable neighbourhoods.

Other programs have more overt distortionary effects, such as the Ontario land transfer tax rebate for first-time homebuyers of newly constructed homes only. This program is inherently biased against older urban areas, where the supply of new housing is relatively small. Either the rebate should be removed entirely or it should be extended to all first-time buyers of sustainable homes, meaning an energy-efficient home in an energy-efficient neighbourhood.

Housing can be made more affordable by making it more sustainable. If the reforms described above – to DCs, property tax, proposals for unbundling, utility pricing, and so on – were implemented, the infrastructure cost component of efficient homes would be reduced. Along with correcting distortionary policies and programs that favour more inefficient forms of housing, these reforms can make houses more affordable while simultaneously reducing government spending and environmental impact.

Infrastructure Grants

Issues with infrastructure programs through which grants of various kinds are offered are noted earlier. One problem is that the grants involved constitute a direct subsidy, which, in turn, leads to underpricing of the infrastructure in question for users and benefits development. In addition, these grants are often made in isolation, without the benefit of an integrated capital investment plan in the receiving municipality, which can lead to misspending of resources or to double-spending (e.g., giving grants both to roads and transit within a municipality in the absence of an integrated transit and urban growth strategy).

In order to deal with the mis-pricing, of course, the need for grants at the local level could be reduced through direct charging for and funding of infrastructure at source. In theory, this is preferable because it involves a more accurate price signal and requires decisions on spending to be made in the same locality in which the money is to be raised, thus increasing accountability and visibility of costs. Of course, some kinds of charging are not permitted legally. In many cases, this would require legislative changes regarding the powers of local municipalities to raise revenues. Also, the costs of some worthwhile projects may exceed local revenue-raising capacities.

NRTEE Criteria for Infrastructure Grants

Recommendation:
That the granting of federal infrastructure funding be subject to a practical, performance-based set of criteria that ensures funded projects make substantial contributions to improved environmental quality in a cost-effective manner. Proponents should be required to submit a Sustainable Community Investment Plan, outlining the needs to be addressed by the infrastructure, and demonstrating:

a) how the proposed infrastructure investment fits into a comprehensive, longer-term investment plan for improving urban environmental quality;

b) how existing infrastructure capacities have been or will be fully exploited;

c) how all options for jointly addressing infrastructure needs with surrounding municipalities or other relevant entities have been explored and fully exploited;

d) a comprehensive approach to managing the demand for the infrastructure (for example, for transportation infrastructure, a transportation demand management plan is required; for water, a metering program);

e) that a range of alternative options for solving infrastructure needs – including other types of infrastructure – have been explored;

f) a life-cycle costing analysis of the proposed project and alternatives;

g) financial contributions and roles of other partners, including provincial government, other agencies and the private sector; and

h) a quantification of the expected environmental improvements in terms of air, water or soil quality of the proposed project and alternatives.[43]

Upper-tier government grants are often necessary for larger capital projects, particularly where the revenue-raising ability of local governments is economically limited or legally constrained. Where grants are used, they should be subject to strict criteria in order to ensure that they represent the best possible use of resources under this financing method. The National Roundtable on the Environment and the Economy (NRTEE) has developed criteria that are helpful in this regard (see box).

Pricing Externalities

Pricing Congestion

Pricing congestion is a different matter from pricing the direct costs of roadway construction, maintenance, and operation. It extends somewhat beyond the scope of this book in that it means establishing a price for something that (with the exception of a few toll roads) is not currently priced at all. At present, congestion is treated as an external cost. Establishing a price paid by road users is a means of rendering the external costs internal. It aims to introduce a price so that a scarce resource (road space) is more efficiently allocated and demand management is introduced. This avoids the "free rider" problem that is at the heart of unpriced goods, in which road use is not rationalized in any way through a price signal. The result is overuse of the common facility and consequent congestion, which imposes high social and economic costs.

The primary aim of a congestion charge, not surprisingly, is to reduce congestion, though the same charge can also include road costs (in which case these costs would be subtracted from any separate road charges, as outlined above). As such, congestion pricing is typically sensitive to time of day and place as well as distance travelled. It can also vary by type of vehicle as larger vehicles contribute relatively more to congestion than do smaller vehicles.

Considerations for vehicle emissions can also be integrated into a congestion charge, as is the case in London, England (see box). When introducing road pricing, it is essential that there be attractive and viable alternatives to the car. A good use of revenues from congestion pricing is to invest in alternative, efficient, and sustainable modes of transportation. Charges can also be revenue-neutral, with revenues used to reduce other less desirable, inefficient, or inequitable taxes. In the short run, a congestion charge will change travel behaviour as people switch to different modes, routes, or

London Congestion and Emissions Charges

Congestion charges were introduced in London in 2003, with a charge being levied for crossing a boundary into the central area zone during peak hours. Since then the zone has expanded and the price of entry has increased to £8 per day. There are myriad ways to pay the charge, including online, by mobile phone, or at a self-service machine.

Congestion levels have been reduced compared to the period before the charge was introduced, and use of alternate modes of travel are up. The scheme produced net revenues of £123 million in the 2006/2007 fiscal year. By law revenues for the first ten years must be reinvested in improving London transport. For example, a £500 million package to improve walking and cycling in the city was announced in 2008.

As of October 2008, CO_2 charges are also implemented in the congestion zone. Under this scheme, low-emissions cars are totally exempt from the congestion charge, while vehicles that produce the highest levels of CO_2 are subject to a higher rate of £25 to enter the zone.

As of February 2008, a low emission zone (LEZ) has also been implemented, superimposed over and extending well beyond the congestion zone to cover most of Greater London. The zone is in effect at all times, not just peak periods. Upon entering the LEZ, vehicle licence plates are checked electronically against a database of registered vehicles to determine whether the vehicle meets emissions standards. If it does not, a daily charge is applicable. The charge does not apply to cars, motorcycles, or small vans, but primarily to older diesel-engined trucks and buses.

travel times. In the long run, and of particular interest in relation to urban sprawl, congestion charging can also alter urban development patterns as people and businesses modify their locational preferences for living and working in response to clear price signals for driving.

The structure of the pricing mechanism is critical and will depend upon specific objectives as well as unique local conditions (such as the morphology of the city in question, regional travel dynamics, and local economic conditions). There is a huge literature on road pricing in all its forms that can be consulted. As global warming and urban sprawl continue to be pressing issues, road pricing of some form is an inevitability. It is just a matter of when and what system to implement. The United Kingdom, for example, along with other European countries, is currently studying the implementation of a nation-wide road pricing scheme.[44]

Supporting Tools

Thus far, I have outlined financial and fiscal tools that support efficient urban development. While necessary, these tools are not always sufficient on their own. Other tools are sometimes needed to support the adoption of market-based policies. There are many, but some key ones are outlined below.

Consistency Audit

A first step for governments and other organizations looking to implement effective policies to curb sprawl is to undertake an audit of existing policies and programs across their entire organization. This is, first, in order to identify those policies and programs that influence urban development patterns (whether intentionally or unintentionally); second, in order to identify those policies and programs that might be inadvertently working against compact sustainable development – especially (but not necessarily only) financial policies, programs, and instruments; and, third, in order to address circumstances in which some policies may be working at cross-purposes with each other (e.g., programs that subsidize energy prices while also subsidizing energy conservation).

For municipal governments, this might mean taking a close look at the structure of their DCs or impact fees, property tax base and rates, and other infrastructure pricing (e.g., water rates) as well as specific financial policies or incentives that may be in place. Provincial, state, and federal governments also need to look at their system of taxes, rebates, user fees, and other charges, programs, and infrastructure spending.

To the extent that provincial, state, or federal governments play the important role of regulator for key industries that are related to urban development, this regulatory role should also be reviewed. For example, regulators of cable, telephone, broadband access, natural gas, and electricity could require that pricing of these services reflect true costs as they vary with location and urban form. This kind of audit will address the fact that it is not now a level playing field for compact development and sprawl. Developers who argue for lack of market intervention benefit from the current distortionary interventions, policies, and public investments that artificially support sprawl in the marketplace.

Identifying Sustainable Neighbourhoods

Many of the reforms and refinements to current policies and programs outlined above suggest that they be targeted to sustainable neighbourhoods and locations or that the relative sustainability of a neighbourhood – based on its form, mix of land uses, and location – be known. This would be the case, for example, with location-efficient mortgages, a location-variable RRSP withdrawal amount for the Home Buyers Plan, or applying the GST new home rebate to energy-efficient homes only.

"Energy efficiency" needs to be redefined to mean not just the energy efficiency of the individual building itself but also the energy efficiency of the building in its urban form context and location, including (especially) the energy use associated with travel to and from the building.

> "Energy efficiency" needs to be redefined to mean not just the energy efficiency of the individual building but also the energy efficiency of the building in its urban form context and location, including (especially) the energy use associated with travel to and from the building.

There are many tools under development to help in the identification of a neighbourhood's sustainability. One is LEED for Neighbourhood Development – LEED-ND. Currently in the pilot project stage, this rating scheme and certification process builds on the LEED building certification process, focusing on neighbourhood location and sustainability.[45] This kind of certification helps to make neighbourhood sustainability easily apparent and understood, and it would provide valuable information to homebuyers looking for more sustainable options but without the ability to assess neighbourhood sustainability themselves.

Cost-Benefit Analyses

Cost-benefit analyses constitute a textbook staple for planners. However, when it comes to practice, they are rarely undertaken, even notionally or on the proverbial back of the envelope. When development scenarios or projects are proposed, often only costs are assessed, and this provides an incomplete and possibly misleading perspective, whether a particular development proposal or long-term growth management options are being considered. When considering development alternatives, different development patterns will affect both costs and revenues, and information on all outcomes is essential in order for an informed decision to be reached.

As well, it is important for both the costs and benefits of planning policy initiatives to be considered. As noted in Chapter 4, the costs and benefits of

planning as a whole are rarely considered or discussed. Yet, planning benefits may not be being delivered in the most efficient way possible. Regulatory
initiatives aimed at curbing sprawl should be costed not only in terms of
implementation but also in terms of any secondary effects that might be
precipitated, and these costs should be weighed against projected benefits.
In addition, alternative approaches (including alternatives to regulation)
should be assessed as part of a spectrum of policy options, including financial and pricing instruments. This will help to ensure that planning benefits
are delivered in the most efficient way possible.

Urban Form Impact Analysis
Many municipalities require that fiscal impact analyses be undertaken in
conjunction with proposals for new urban development. These analyses
typically assess the fiscal impact on the municipality in terms of additional
costs and revenues associated with the new growth as proposed. Different
types of growth, with different locations, densities, mix of uses, layouts,
standards, and street design, can have vastly differing fiscal profiles and financial implications for the municipality or service provider. Municipalities
often require fiscal impact analyses in order to ensure that a particular development proposal will not result in a financial burden.

It is obvious by now, however, that the opposite phenomenon is also at
work – that is, that fiscal policy can have a pronounced effect on urban form
and the attainment of municipal planning objectives for more compact, efficient development. The reason this comes about often has to do with the
fact that municipal financial policy is developed in isolation from planning
policy. These two streams need to be considered and developed together,
through higher levels of integration between financial advisors and municipal planners. This could be achieved through multidisciplinary policy teams.
Or municipalities should conduct an urban form impact assessment on all
pricing proposals relating to their financial instruments, such as proposed
DCs, taxes, service fees, and utility rates.

Targeted Subsidies
In the discussion above, the need to replace various forms of inaccurate
pricing with true cost pricing is reiterated. In implementing this switch,
some will inevitably end up paying more than they did previously, while
others will pay less. Of those who end up paying more, many if not most will
typically be able to afford the extra costs. However, an increase in prices

could result in economic hardship for some groups for some essential services. But by creating accurate price signals and rationalizing demand, the switch to efficient pricing should result in overall cost savings, and some of these savings could be redirected to those faced with difficulty in paying for an essential service. Or a transparent subsidy fund could be created. It is shown in Chapter 8, for example, how, in the case of telephone service, a cross-subsidy embedded in prices based on average costs that amounted to $8.7 billion could be replaced by a targeted subsidy of $0.7 billion, eliminating hidden cross-subsidies of $8 billion. Rather than subsidizing many who may not require subsidies, or supporting cross-subsidies for high levels of service or non-essential services, a targeted subsidy is both fair and efficient.

As Bird and Tsiopoulos suggest:

The appropriate initial position in formulating sound public policy is that any public service with an easily identifiable direct beneficiary should be paid for by that beneficiary, unless sound and convincing arguments in favour of a particular degree of explicit public subsidy can be produced. This starting point is in complete opposition to that which many countries seem to have adopted, namely, that whatever subsidies now exist are right, so that the onus of proof with respect to any change lies with the proponents of change.[46]

13

Perverse Subsidies, Perverse Cities

Mis-Pricing, Mis-Incentives, and Sprawl

In market economies, land-use patterns are determined by a few key decisions made millions of times daily in relation to land, building, location, and the integral issue of transportation. It is these decisions, made by developers, builders, homeowners, business owners, employees, families, and institutions, that, over time, determine the shape of our cities. These decisions themselves are shaped in no small way by prices – both absolute price levels and the relative prices of different types of development in different locations – and of different modes of transport. If these prices accurately reflected the true costs of alternative development choices, then by definition we would have an efficiently operating market, an efficient allocation of resources, and an efficient, sprawlless urban development pattern.

However, at present, prices rarely reflect the true costs of alternative development choices. In fact, they are systemically biased in a way that makes the more efficient choices overpriced and the less efficient choices underpriced. Naturally, this has a significant impact on those key decisions and the nature of demand for housing and business properties. When things are underpriced, we tend to consume more of them than we otherwise would; when they are overpriced, we tend to consume less of them than we otherwise would. Unfortunately, this is the situation that currently applies to land use and related key decisions. Sprawl is underpriced, and so the demand for it is exaggerated. Efficient forms of development – denser development, smaller lots and buildings, low-, medium- or high-rise apartments, mixed use, and central locations – are overpriced, so demand for them is reduced compared to what an efficiently operating market would call for.

The many instances of mis-pricing and mis-incentives are critical to those key decisions around land and buildings that shape urban development patterns: How much land? How much building? In what location? How to travel to and from the property? In fact, it has been shown above that prices for the following urban goods and services are subject to mis-pricing and mis-incentives:

- property prices for land and buildings
- mortgages and mortgage insurance
- parking, gas, car insurance
- home heating, cooling, and water heating (hydro and gas)
- other utilities: cable, internet, telephone, postal service
- water, sewer, roads, garbage collection, recycling, snow clearance.

Taken together, it is apparent that these mis-prices have a significant impact on property decisions, market supply, and demand. These are the decisions that cumulatively shape urban form and determine the specific patterns in which cities evolve.

Why are prices distorted? Prices and policies fail to account for significant cost variations related to location, local context, type of land use, density, and other urban form factors. This applies in some way to all of the pricing instruments discussed above: DCs, property tax, user fees, utility rates, bundled goods, and housing- and automobile-related taxes and tax concessions. Poorly crafted policy also plays a role, such as with mortgage or homeownership programs, as do direct subsidies.

In short, demand is influenced by prices, and those prices are distorted by policies that favour sprawl over efficient development. This creates a biased, fettered market in which the demand for sprawl is inflated, while demand for more efficient forms of development is deflated. Claims that sprawl is simply the result of the "invisible hand" of the market and consumer demand are inaccurate at best. Sprawl is the result of a particular market form – one that is systematically biased and distorted in its favour.

Mis-pricing not only distorts the demand side of the market but also affects the supply side. It renders developers and builders indifferent to the variations in costs of different development forms and locations or provides mis-incentives. A typical DC based on average costs, for example, removes incentives to develop at low-cost locations, to build more densely, and to build less auto-dependent forms of development.

Causes of Sprawl Revisited

I define sprawl as an inefficient development pattern. When a direct and necessary link can be made between a given factor and inefficient development, this factor is a cause of sprawl. Where no such necessary link exists, this factor cannot be seen as a cause of sprawl (though it may be a cause of urban growth). The specific kind of mis-pricing uncovered in *Perverse Cities* – the perverse subsidies that arise from underpricing inefficient development and overpricing efficient development – is a factor that is clearly and directly linked to the creation of sprawl. Though not my focus, the non-pricing of externalities associated with sprawl, such as congestion or GHG emissions, would also be considered a cause.

The types of government policies and programs (highlighted above) that inadvertently favour sprawl can also be directly linked with the creation of inefficient development patterns. Mis-incentives resulting from policies that do not take urban context into account, such as flat RRSP withdrawal limits for first-time buyers, are one type of cause. Many types of land-use regulations also fall into this category, influencing the supply side of the equation by mandating densities that are lower than what an unbiased market would otherwise provide. By limiting alternatives to conventional low-density suburban growth, regulations such as zoning, subdivision controls, and engineering standards ensure that sprawl is the primary form of development and make the suburbs more spread out than would otherwise be the case.[1]

Urban design that creates auto-dominated landscapes and continues to rely on unconnected road systems and segregation of communities one from another is another cause of sprawl. The relationship between sprawl and regional governance is more complex. Lack of regional governance is often cited as a cause of sprawl. Certainly, without a regional growth framework, leapfrogging can be an issue. And some form of regional coordination is necessary to solve a different type of market failure than mis-pricing – the provision of public goods. The protection of environmentally sensitive areas and the provision of regional transportation infrastructure are instances in which government must step in. As Knaap points out, regional coordination is required to, at a minimum, coordinate regional scale infrastructure (such as greenspace networks and transportation) between local jurisdictions and with land use.[2]

And, while lack of regional coordination can contribute to sprawl, experience to date suggests that, where it does exist, it provides no guarantee of curbing sprawl but is still seen as a precondition for compact development.[3] The fact that regional governance has not solved the sprawl problem suggests that there are other sprawl drivers at work – such as mis-pricing, perhaps?

Other forces are often cited as drivers of sprawl, but if sprawl is viewed as the inefficient or excessive use of land, then these should be seen more as drivers of urban growth (rather than of sprawl per se) in that they need not *necessarily* lead to sprawl. These include population growth, rising affluence, and technology. As it relates to sprawl, there is little one can or should do about this group of issues.

> All of what we might call the "true" causes of sprawl fall squarely in the realm of public policy: mis-pricing with respect to public-sector financial instruments or of publicly regulated prices, public policy mis-incentives, and mis-regulation of land use.

Falling transportation costs is also included in this group of "natural" drivers of suburbanization.[4] Falling transportation costs can be seen as a cause of sprawl to the degree that automobile use is underpriced (e.g., through road subsidies). If true cost pricing were in effect for transportation costs, then they need not be considered a cause of sprawl, even when falling.

In theory, the rent gradient need not be considered a cause of sprawl either, provided it is unbiased by distorted prices. An efficiently operating market would be expected to create lower land prices as distance from the city centre increases. However, in practice, land prices and rents are subject to price distortions, creating a distorted rent gradient, with prices higher than they ought to be in the centre and artificially low at the edge.

Thus, all of what we might call the "true" causes of sprawl fall squarely into the realm of public policy: mis-pricing with respect to public-sector financial instruments or of publicly regulated prices, public policy mis-incentives, and mis-regulation of land use. On the one hand, it may be troubling to think that the problem of sprawl – one that governments have been struggling to solve for decades – has, in fact, been largely created by those same governments, however inadvertently; on the other hand, it may be comforting to realize that this means that the sprawl issue is eminently tractable rather than the result of some inexorable force like population growth, rising affluence, or technological advancement. Curbing sprawl in no way means curbing these latter forces.

The Sprawl-Is-the-Result-of-Market-Forces-and-Consumer-Choice Fallacy

It is also often argued, particularly by those supportive of sprawl, that it is really an expression of consumer demand, with the "invisible hand" of the market simply responding neutrally to that demand. In the introduction to *Perverse Cities*, the sprawl defenders' view is summed up with a quotation. We can now revisit that summation to evaluate it in light of the evidence and analysis presented above. To reiterate:

> Development patterns at the beginning of the twenty-first century are the result of market forces that respond to the demands of citizens, as residents, as workers and as consumers. If one understands the role that market forces have played in generating sprawling development patterns, several things become more obvious. First, it becomes apparent that regardless of the merits of altering current trends, it will be difficult for public policy to do so, because market forces will work in the opposite direction. Second, it is clear that there will be unintended secondary effects from anti-sprawl policies that may make people worse off. Third, these development patterns, responding to public demand, may not be so undesirable after all. And fourth, the way in which to design and implement land-use policy to further commonly held goals becomes clearer.[5]

The sprawl promoters assert that sprawl is simply the result of consumer and business preferences being expressed through the market and that, if one understood this, one would understand why we have sprawl. Yes, urban development patterns are the result of the key decisions being played over and over again, and the choices made by consumers, businesses, employees, developers, and others. But the sprawl defenders fail to note that the price and policy context that shapes and guides these decisions is highly skewed. It consists of a set of "market forces" whose price signals are distorted by a wide range of perverse and largely hidden subsidies, along with poorly designed policies that skew decision making and entrench and perpetuate inefficient urban development patterns.

While it is true that the market plays a critical role in shaping urban development patterns, it is not true that sprawl is the work of a neutral invisible hand. Though largely invisible, the hand is by no means neutral. Hidden subsidies and price distortions artificially discount prices for inefficient development (increasing demand and supply) and artificially inflate prices for efficient development (decreasing demand and supply). When efficient development is overpriced and inefficient development underpriced, it is not surprising that we should see more demand for sprawl than we would with accurate price signals.

An unfettered market with accurate price signals would curb sprawl, not create it. Unfortunately, that is not what is in place today. We have a fettered market – one that is highly distorted in favour of sprawl by a wide array of public policies whose consequences are both intended and unintended. What the sprawl advocates are arguing for is really not market forces in their pure sense but, rather, the status quo-distorted market, which favours sprawl. Sprawl defenders further argue that it is pointless to try to curb sprawl because any attempts to do so would be working against the market. As already noted, their market reference point is the current situation, in which planning policies aimed at curbing sprawl are operating at cross-purposes with a distorted market that promotes sprawl. In fact, curbing sprawl would mean removing existing distortions and restoring market neutrality – not working against it but, rather, allowing it to work as it is supposed to.

Clearly, an efficiently operating market for urban goods and services would not result in sprawl. Accurate and transparent price signals would create more efficient use of resources and more efficient urban development patterns. Sprawl is not the result of market forces but, rather, of a particular variety of distorted market forces. Moreover, these distortions emanate largely from public policy. If public policy is the main cause, could it not also be the main solution? Real market-oriented solutions to sprawl have not been implemented as yet and are not what is advocated by the sprawl promoters. Getting the prices right, and getting an unbiased market operating, would go a long way towards curbing sprawl. In short, more accurate price signals will prompt new kinds of decisions, choices, and market responses, shifting demand and supply towards more efficient development patterns.

Finally, the sprawl camp argues that (in the unlikely event it were to occur) curbing sprawl may result in unintended secondary effects that may make people worse off. It is true that curbing sprawl could have distributive impacts that may render some people worse off and others better off compared to their current positions, but who and how much depends on the approach taken. If the approach I've outlined were adopted – that is, if we put in place de-averaged and true cost prices that reflect the costs of development as they vary with place, form, and use – there would indeed be a redistribution of costs. On the one hand, those who previously benefited most from cross-subsidies would likely be faced with higher prices for affected goods, services, and development; on the other hand, those who were previously overcharged would now pay lower prices and be better off. However, in either case, those prices would now reflect their actual cost causation – arguably a fairer situation all round.

Overall, costs for affected network services and infrastructure would be expected to fall as the market would no longer be biased and operating inefficiently, and would now support the efficient allocation of resources rather than over-investment and overspending. In the long run, the expected result would be a redistribution of a lower level of costs. Thus, it is true that the redistribution of costs could result in some people being worse off. But this must be weighed against the current situation in which hidden subsidies and cross-subsidies are haphazard, fraught with unintended consequences, and already making many worse off – principally those who are currently overpaying for services and infrastructure. These people are likely unaware of the degree to which they may be overpaying to cross-subsidize others who have higher levels of consumption and cost causation. It should also be noted that everyone would benefit from the ubiquitous improvements, such as reduced air pollution and reduced GHG emissions, which would come with reduced sprawl.

The Limits to Planning

Despite concerted efforts and the increasing breadth and depth of planning approaches, from growth management to smart growth to new urbanism, there has been limited success in altering the development course of North American cities so as to curb sprawl. This failure is a very expensive proposition, given the considerable resources devoted to this effort compared with the tangible results. In fact, one could say that we have the dubious honour of being blessed with both the costs of planning and the costs of sprawl. Why have we arrived at this point?

First, sprawl has been viewed narrowly within a planning paradigm – as a planning problem that calls for a "planning" solution. The focus has been on solving sprawl with regulatory and design approaches. While these approaches are without question a critical part of the solution to sprawl, the problem is that they have not addressed, nor are they capable of addressing, other critical causes of sprawl, in particular, the mis-pricing issues described in *Perverse Cities*. Unless these causes are addressed directly, sprawl will remain an elusive and intractable problem.

The design solutions have also fallen far short of presenting a credible alternative to everyday sprawl. New urbanism, for example, while perhaps presenting a more pedestrian-friendly urban environment, has not yet provided the kind of structural alteration to urban form that would constitute a different development course for evolving cities. Though allowing somewhat more as-of-right uses than conventional zoning (granny flats, integrated retail uses), its shrink-wrap form regulations are onerous and resistant to further change and evolution. As Sir Peter Hall notes, the emphasis has been too much on form rather than on function:

> What the New Urbanism should be about, but in practice is seldom about, is recapturing not merely the form but also the functioning of the Victorian suburb. New Urbanism should be about ... developments deliberately designed at densities higher than conventional automobile-oriented suburbs, that have shopping and other essential daily services within easy walking distance, and that are above all grouped around good transit. On these clear and unequivocal criteria, few examples so far of the New Urbanism pass the test.[6]

We come full circle when we realize that planning itself has become a significant reason for the prevalence and degree of sprawl. Zoning and other regulations that limit densities or otherwise mandate sprawl and lengthy planning approval processes that make reurbanization difficult are primary causes of sprawl, acknowledged by planners and urban designers alike.

A second issue is that planning approaches have not paid enough attention to the economic context in which urban development occurs. As I keep attempting to show (by now ad nauseam!), planning approaches largely disregard the key role prices play in driving sprawl. Planning approaches are aimed at treating symptoms and do not adequately address the causes of sprawl. Planning is managing a chronic illness rather than offering a cure. I focus on one set of causes – perverse subsidies and poorly designed policies that distort price signals and decision making related to urban goods and services – that plays a significant role in creating inefficient urban development patterns and excessive use of land and buildings, yet has been largely ignored by both the sprawl supporters as well as those aiming to curb sprawl.

Moreover, the economic context imposes constraints upon planning that are not always well recognized or understood. In this global economy, the drivers of urban development often extend well beyond the reach of local regulation. For example, globalization, specialization, and corporate consolidation work together to propel the increasing size and specialization of manufacturing and retail facilities. One need look no farther than the local

20,000-square-foot PetSmart or Golftown or the 100,000-plus-square-foot Walmart for evidence of this trend. These basic retail modules are often difficult to integrate within communities along new urbanist or smart growth lines. Here, planning can try to constrain but cannot necessarily change the standardized development model.

When densification has occurred, it has often been the result of real estate market changes rather than policy. For example, densification in the Toronto suburbs was attributed in large part to a switch in housing type (away from single detached units to more townhouses) that was a response to market demand for more affordable housing. In this case, the role of planning was to not prevent densification from occurring.[7] In other words, economics plays a significant role in determining urban development patterns. Public buildings aside, development only takes place when market conditions make it profitable. Regulation can place boundaries (metaphorical and literal) on development, but it cannot mandate that it occur – that is, it can constrain but not conjure. If the economics do not support higher densities, a minimum density regulation will have little effect, other than perhaps to deflect development to locations without such regulations.

Even where anti-sprawl advocates do try to work with or through the market, by aiming to increase the available supply of alternatives to sprawl (e.g., new urbanism or reurbanization), a lack of consideration of existing price distortions means that their initiatives are price-handicapped and thus may have limited success. The demand for alternatives to sprawl will be artificially lowered if their price on the market is inflated by hidden cross-subsidies and other distortions, while the conventional alternatives continue to enjoy lower than true cost prices from being on the benefiting end of those same subsidies.

Third, there has been little recognition or discussion of the direct and indirect costs that planning approaches can incur. To the extent that they are aimed at correcting a problem that results from distorted market forces, would it not be better to address the distortions directly? For example, greenbelts, and the creation of protected environmental areas at the urban fringe, are often seen as a good approach to curtailing sprawl: "Creative land use planners at the local, regional and state level can use the environmental regulations as an effective technique to manage sprawl. For example, open space acquisitions permanently remove land from the development pool. While this is the most effective deterrent to consumptive land-use practices, wetlands and watershed protection regulations substantially restrict the land uses in the critical environmental areas."[8]

Protecting environmentally sensitive areas is a valid public policy objective in its own right. But the use of this instrument as an urban boundary to control sprawl is questionable. In an urban area with a lot of growth pressure, development can simply leapfrog the protected areas, creating an even less sustainable and more expensive development pattern beyond. This has been the case in the Toronto area, for example, which is now encircled by a greenbelt that protects sensitive lands (even though a substantial supply of developable greenfields lands remain inside the greenbelt perimeter).[9] And it is unlikely that environmentally sensitive areas are located so as to form a boundary that provides just the right amount of containment, neither too much nor too little, in the right locations. Too much containment can create unnecessarily high property prices, while too little will be ineffective.

While well-executed UGBs can be effective, pricing alternatives to these devices deserve more attention and discussion. An analysis by Cheshire and Sheppard, for example, finds that using fiscal instruments, such as a tax on land, could produce the same amount of containment as an urban growth boundary but could do so at much lower social cost.[10]

In relation to sprawl, public policy goals are served by removing existing distortions that promote sprawl, allowing the market to do what it does best: efficiently allocate resources and promote efficient development patterns. This could be supplemented with strategic, coordinated investment or targeted subsidies where warranted but, ideally, not where the effectiveness of investment in one area (e.g., transit) is simply rendered impotent by competing investments (e.g., highways). More regulation is not needed. What *is* needed is different regulation – minimal, flexible, smart, and purposeful land-use regulation.

What Is the Policy Rationale for Subsidizing Sprawl?

It is clear by now that there are myriad subsidies to sprawl, many invisibly bundled in with other public policies or pricing regimes, like average cost prices. Is it possible that there is a legitimate public policy reason for these subsidies to exist? Where a subsidy is created, there should be a public policy rationale. Usually, subsidies compensate for a market failure (e.g., externalities or public goods) or where social equity issues are at stake (e.g., affordable housing for low-income households).

But living in a large house, or on a large lot, or far from affordable services are for the most part personal choices. These personal choices and preferences should not be publicly subsidized. As a society, we don't subsidize other personal choices. If you choose to wear an Armani suit, as long as you can afford it and pay for it yourself, there is no broader issue – no one is made worse off by your choice. Someone who prefers to wear jeans would not be expected to contribute to your Armani purchase. Yet, this is the case with urban sprawl, with those who make efficient development choices subsidizing those who make inefficient ones. Moreover, unlike some personal choices, which have few if any negative public impacts (e.g., wearing an Armani suit), the choice of sprawl has significant social costs attached to it.

This raises the question "What *is* the policy rationale for subsidizing sprawl?" Interestingly, this question is rarely asked. Even putting aside for the moment the equity issue associated with the cross-subsidies involved, sprawl plays a negative role in so many of the key issues of our time – issues for which many millions if not billions of dollars have and will be spent to mitigate its impacts (including the costs of retrofitting suburbs and exurbs). These issues include global warming, water shortages, auto dependence, air pollution, and excessive infrastructure spending. Indeed, as a society, we are spending twice – once to encourage sprawl and once again to mitigate its negative effects.

As a society we are spending twice – once to encourage sprawl and once again to mitigate its negative effects.

One rare explicit rationale for sprawl subsidies occurs with respect to home ownership – namely, that increasing rates of home ownership is a worthwhile public policy objective. Certainly, the wisdom of trying too hard to increase home ownership rates has been called into question by the US mortgage crisis and the subsequent global economic meltdown of 2008, ultimately requiring trillions of dollars of public investment to stem the decline.

But whether or not one shares the view that more home ownership is always desirable, there is no reason that policies to support increased home ownership must also encourage sprawl, as they so often do today. This is simply the result of poorly designed policies. Often these policies are intended to be stimuli to the home-building industry – the GST rebate on newly constructed homes, for example, is hard to rationalize any other way. But again, home building, like home ownership, does not *necessarily* have to involve sprawl and its negative correlates, such as excessive energy consumption and GHG emissions, as it does now.

More precise, surgical policy instruments can be developed and used to avoid unintended negative consequences. And pricing can be much more sophisticated than is currently the case. Anyone who has recently travelled

by air will know the level of sophistication in airline pricing, with many different prices offered even on various flights between the same destinations.
This is a strategic and very calculated use of pricing to deliberately influence
demand (e.g., by placing higher prices on peak period travel and sale prices
for midday travel). There is no reason that more accurate, sophisticated
pricing strategies cannot also be adopted in the public and quasi-public sectors. To quote Wilbur Thompson: "The failure to use price – as an *explicit*
system – in the public sector of the metropolis is at the root of many, if not
most, of our urban problems."[11]

It is hard to conjure up a credible policy rationale for subsidizing sprawl.
This is especially true when one considers that these subsidies support the
creation of negative externalities, not their mitigation, as is generally intended with public subsidies. Indeed, the policy and pricing support it has
received to date has been largely unintended – a by-product of policies that
have failed to consider the urban spatial context in which they operate and
related impacts. In some cases, it may have been
thought that aspatial policies must have aspatial
impacts. But aspatial policies laid down across a
differentiated urban landscape will not have
neutral consequences. As we saw earlier, for example, standard one-size-fits-all policies, average prices, or the use of uniform thresholds in
programs can lead to biases against more expensive but more sustainable urban locations.

> "The failure to use price – as
> an *explicit* system – in the
> public sector of the metrop
> olis is at the root of many, if
> not most, of our urban
> problems."
>
> – *Wilbur Thompson*

As Levine points out, sprawl has become so
commonplace that it is now widely regarded as the norm, from which other
development forms are seen as "alternative" and requiring justification,[12]
when, in fact, it is sprawl that deviates from the norm that would result from
an unbiased market, the perverse result of mis-pricing and misregulation.
Wouldn't it be better to implement accurate direct prices, get the market
working well, and then determine whether there are any explicit subsidies
that are needed and warranted? This might be the case on equity grounds,
regarding affordable housing or other affordability issues for essential services. Subsidies for transit funding are warranted on the grounds of reducing
air pollution and GHG emissions as well as creating equity for those who
cannot drive a car. As is shown above, the use of explicit subsidies is less
costly, as well as more transparent and fair, than the use of implicit subsidies.
Other industries, such as the telephone industry, have been working diligently in this direction, removing implicit, hidden subsidies and replacing

them with much smaller, transparent, targeted subsidies. Why can't the same approach be adopted for pricing around urban development?

Treat the Causes: The Price Is Right

As should be obvious by now, getting the prices right is an absolutely essential part of the solution to sprawl. If the message of prices is "sprawl sprawl sprawl," then sprawl will continue no matter what the planning policy says. While regulation can be effective at limiting density when the economic pressure exists, regulation cannot mandate denser development if the economics do not support it. This planning problem cannot be solved by planning solutions alone.

The first and most powerful thing to do to change urban development patterns is to create accurate price signals. At a minimum, governments should look within their own organizations and that of their agencies and regulated entities to:

- adopt true cost prices for all urban infrastructure and related services, regardless of the pricing mechanism: DCs, property taxes, user fees, and utility rates
- unbundle prices for bundled goods, such as parking and local roads
- where direct subsidies are needed and warranted (e.g., investment in infrastructure), adopt criteria to ensure that they are effective and as non-distortionary as possible, and avoid the "double subsidy" dilemma
- remove distortionary subsidies, such as selective tax breaks that subsidize sprawl and excessive car use
- introduce pricing for infrastructure and services that are currently non-priced, such as road use
- remove spatial biases from programs, such as home ownership programs
- fix policy mis-incentives, such as mortgage loan insurance for second homes or market value-based property tax
- ensure that prices are transparent and apparent.

Introducing prices for externalities, such as a carbon tax on fuels to compensate for GHG emissions and air pollution-related costs, can also form an important part of the repertoire.

Once an identification of the price and policy distortions that most contribute to sprawl has been undertaken, reforms can be prioritized for implementation. But even individual actions can have a significant positive and immediate impact. For example, restructuring to true cost-based DCs would have an immediate and significant impact on the nature of new development. To date, curbing sprawl has meant planning solutions that have ignored the key role that mis-pricing plays in driving sprawl. A lot more attention must be paid to the pricing issue if there is to be hope of solving the sprawl problem. It cannot be solved without addressing the kind of mis-pricing and mis-incentives described above. Getting the prices right and fixing policy biases are necessary and fundamental to the solution.

But prices cannot solve sprawl single-handedly. The other causes of sprawl must also be addressed, and planning plays an important role. This means, for example, removing the many policy and regulatory obstacles that currently prevent more efficient development patterns from occurring. This could include changes to planning policies and zoning regulations, streamlining planning approval processes, and revising engineering standards to allow more mixing of uses, higher densities, and connected and appropriately engineered street patterns. Better urban design must be encouraged and permitted. Regional coordination for greenspace systems and transportation infrastructure investments is needed. When undertaken in conjunction with true cost pricing, these reforms and measures can reduce the costs of planning while improving its effectiveness.

The key is to have planning and pricing work together as complementary components of a single, unified, and coherent anti-sprawl strategy rather than to have pricing and policy mis-incentives that undermine planning objectives, as is the current situation. Implementing a true cost pricing regime would establish a different set of price signals for urban goods and services, and this would lead homebuyers and business operators to make different, more efficient development choices regarding location, amount of land and building, and transportation. This, in turn, would lead to more efficiency in development patterns, use of land, and transportation.

Correcting existing pricing and policy biases would not lead to an upending of property markets and prices. Property prices will continue to be higher in more central and accessible locations, and in locations with higher amenity, than they will in more distant and less amenity-rich areas – as they should in a fair market. The policies I propose will not alter this overall pattern. But these corrections would eliminate the financial penalties that put efficient development at a relative price disadvantage in the market in relation to inefficient development. Prices for urban goods and services – such as telephone, water, or property taxes – would become cheaper in more efficient urban locations and for more efficient development types and would increase for locations with inefficient development.

Large lots, low densities, car travel, and other elements usually associated with urban sprawl would not be eliminated. They will still occur. However, if true cost prices are in effect, no market distortions will occur, and, significantly, those who choose these options will pay their real costs. According to my definition – that sprawl is an inefficient development pattern that results when prices do not reflect marginal costs as they vary with location, density, land use, and other urban form factors – so long as true costs were (truly!) in effect, such types of development would not be considered "sprawl." However, in practice, the implementation of true cost pricing for urban goods and services would shift prices such that the demand for the kinds of urban forms we normally associate with sprawl would be significantly reduced, while the demand for efficient development – more compact development or reurbanization, for example – would be significantly increased.

Making It Happen

There are myriad opportunities and an infinite variety of ways to establish good price signals and policy that create efficiency and fairness and that support compact urban development patterns. Outlined above are just a few of the possibilities. The specific set of instruments used in any one place will depend on local objectives and conditions, and the creativity and determination of those involved. Clearly, there is no shortage of options for introducing efficient pricing and better urban policy: a wide array of financial tools exists, and these tools can be tweaked or introduced to support the evolution of efficient urban development patterns.

The remaining challenge is not a lack of policy options but, rather, how to get these tools adopted in the political arena and implemented. As in cases of all changes to the status quo, opposition will arise. Strategies will be required to deal with citizen groups, bureaucrats and policy advisors, and reluctant politicians. While there is no magic wand that can be waved to smooth the adoption of new or reformed policies, there are a few considerations that can help in developing an implementation agenda.

The first is that the basic research must be done within the given context – municipal, state, provincial, or federal. Existing financial instruments and other policies must be inventoried, and the key instruments that are harbouring the wrong incentives and disincentives must be identified before they can be addressed (this is the aforementioned "consistency audit"). In making the case, it would be useful to have access to research that assesses the impact of these flawed instruments on urban development patterns and the ability to achieve planning objectives, on infrastructure costs, on external costs (e.g., pollution, loss of farmland, and congestion), or on double-whammy spending on program costs (e.g., in which financial instruments undermine other programs and policies). An assessment of the public (and private) costs to be saved and objectives achieved by adopting better-designed financial tools would also be useful.

Second, planners and other non-finance urban professionals must be educated so that they understand the importance of financial drivers in shaping urban form. If planners are aware of the hidden dynamics of financial instruments that affect city form, they can better act as advocates for sustainable development patterns by promoting more sophisticated urban fiscal policy. Similarly, municipal finance personnel – as well as those at other levels of government whose policies affect urban development – need to be made aware of the impacts that the policies and instruments they develop can have on urban development patterns. The establishment of multi-disciplinary policy development teams within government bureaucracies would also help to ensure a greater synergy in the policy, programs, and instruments that are adopted.

Third, citizens must also be brought into the equation, with awareness campaigns regarding the costs of sprawl and how they vary with urban form, and the role that financial tools and policy play in promoting inefficient and costly development patterns. They should also be made aware of the embedded subsidies and cross-subsidies that are inherent in many of these tools – subsidies whose existence is not widely recognized or understood. Those constituents who are currently penalized by existing financial tools (i.e., the subsidizers rather than the subsidizees) would no doubt be particularly interested in these revelations. They could form a coalition of the overcharged – raising the flawed instruments as a political issue and putting pressure on politicians to react. This coalition could also include developers and builders aiming to produce a more efficient and affordable product that is currently overcharged or otherwise penalized by blunt one-size-fits-all financial instruments. An important question for these groups to ask recalcitrant staff or politicians is the one raised above: "What is the policy rationale for subsidizing sprawl?" Politicians must be made aware of the issues inherent in fiscal policy as it relates to urban sprawl and the linkages between the design of financial instruments, the efficiency of urban development patterns, and the broader costs.

Finally, the way in which new or reformed instruments are introduced is crucial and must be thoroughly considered. Tools designed to reflect actual costs – as they vary with density, location, local context, land use, or other urban form factors – will by definition level the playing field so that the normal financial incentives to more efficient urban forms and disincentives to less efficient ones that would be present in an unbiased market will exist. Reforms or new tools are best implemented as part of a comprehensive package, structured so that citizens benefit tangibly by reduced taxes or fees if "efficient" actions are taken. Such a program can be phased in over time. In some cases, it may be easier to begin with amending existing tools before introducing new.

This analysis suggests that sprawl is first and foremost the result – intended or, more likely, unintended – of public policy. While it is unfortunate to have been brought to this point by government actions, the good news is that this makes the issue much more tractable than do some of the other alleged but non-causes of sprawl, such as population growth or "technology." Public policy can be changed, providing the will exists. If we choose not to implement price and other necessary reforms now, altering the form of cities fifty or even twenty years from now will be a much more difficult and expensive proposition.

Notes

CHAPTER 1: THE PRICE OF SPRAWL

1 Statistics Canada, *Portrait of the Canadian Population*, 22.
2 Ibid., 23.
3 Malenfant et al., *Demographic Changes*, 7.
4 Statistics Canada, "Loss of Dependable Agricultural Land," 5.
5 Motor vehicles include passenger vehicles, large and small trucks, and buses. The source for 1975 data is Statistics Canada, *Historical Statistics of Canada*. Data for 2004 is from Statistics Canada, *Canadian Vehicle Survey*, 21.
6 IBI Group, *Toronto-Related Region*, 100.
7 Environment Canada, *Canada's National Environmental Indicator*.
8 St. Lawrence, "Demand Perspective," Table 3.
9 Jonathan Rose Companies, *Developing Times*, Newsletter 6, Winter 2004, 7.
10 Canada Mortgage and Housing Corporation, "Greenhouse Gas Emissions." In isolating the effect of urban form and location, this analysis keeps urban form constant, assuming a suburban development form in an inner location, something that would not likely occur in reality. This would also tend towards an underestimation of potential reductions in emission associated with a central location.
11 See, for example, Duany et al., *Suburban Nation*; Calthorpe and Fulton, *Regional City*.
12 See, for example, Holcombe and Staley, *Smarter Growth*; Bruegmann, *Sprawl*; Gordon and Richardson, "Compact Cities."
13 Bruegmann, *Sprawl*.
14 Holcombe and Staley, "Policy Implications," in *Smarter Growth*, 252.
15 Ibid., 257.
16 Ibid., 260.

17 Bruegmann, *Sprawl*.
18 Canada Mortgage and Housing Corporation, *Canadian Housing Observer 2007*, 38 and 40.
19 US Census Bureau, Table A-1, Annual Geographic Mobility Rates, by Type of Movement: 1947-2006, http://www.census.gov/.
20 This will be shown in detail in subsequent chapters.
21 Development charges, known as impact fees in the United States, are charges levied on new development to cover the costs of infrastructure associated with new growth, including roads, water and sewer networks, transit, and community facilities. Whether and how the amount of the charge is passed on to the buyer and included in the price of the house – the "incidence" of the charge – is discussed in greater detail in Chapter 7.
22 A note on the use of metric and imperial measurements. Imperial units are used when an original source uses them, when their use is not technical, and when it is common in planning and real estate circles, such as regarding density, lot size, and floor area. In all other instances, metric measurements are used.
23 Will Dunning Inc., *Economic Influences*.
24 Definitions based, in part, on those found in Myers and Kent, *Perverse Subsidies*, 3-5.
25 Levine, *Zoned Out*.

CHAPTER 2: SPRAWL

1   Galster et al., "Wrestling Sprawl," 682-83.
2   See, for example, Gillham, *Limitless City*, 3-8.
3   Ewing et al., *Measuring Sprawl*, 3.
4   Galster et al., "Wrestling Sprawl," 685.
5   Duany et al., *Suburban Nation*.
6   Gillham, *Limitless City*, 8.
7   Ewing et al., *Measuring Sprawl*, 3.
8   Duany et al., *Suburban Nation*, x.
9   See, for example, Duany et al., *Suburban Nation*.
10 Knaap et al., *Government Policy and Urban Sprawl*; Burchell et al., *Sprawl Costs*; Gillham, *Limitless City*.
11 Ewing, "Los Angeles-Style Sprawl."
12 Duany et al., *Suburban Nation*; Burchell et al., *Sprawl Costs*.
13 Pendall, "Land Use Controls."
14 Razin and Rosentraub, "Fragmentation and Sprawl."
15 Knaap, "Sprawl of Economics."
16 Gillham, "Limitless City," 10-11.
17 Gillham, "Limitless City"; Ewing, "Los-Angeles-Style Sprawl."
18 CNU Charter, *Congress for the New Urbanism*, http://www.cnu.org/.
19 From the Smart Growth Network, http://www.smartgrowth.org/.
20 Nelson, "How Do We Know," 86.
21 For a sampling, see Gillham, *Limitless City*, 157. Nelson, "How Do We Know," also provides a good review of smart growth in theory and practice.
22 Smart Growth Network at http://www.smartgrowth.org/.

23 Nelson, "How Do We Know," 87.
24 For a useful summary of the approach, see Duany and Talen, "Transect Planning." Note that the SmartCode was revised in 2005.
25 American Planning Association, *Planning for Smart Growth.*

CHAPTER 3: THE COSTS AND BENEFITS OF SPRAWL

1 American Rivers et al., *Paving Our Way.*
2 John Ibbitson, "The Dehydrated States of America," *Globe and Mail,* 23 June 2007.
3 Ewing et al., *Measuring Sprawl.* For a review of the evidence on sprawl and its impact on travel, see Burchell et al., *Costs of Sprawl – Revisited.*
4 Ewing et al., *Measuring Sprawl.*
5 Ibid., 18-19.
6 Miller et al., *Travel and Housing Costs,* 29.
7 On fatal crashes, see Ewing et al., *Measuring Sprawl.* See also McCann and Ewing, *Measuring the Health Effects.*
8 Ewing et al., *Measuring Sprawl.*
9 Bray et al., *Report on Public Health.*
10 Ibid.
11 See, for example, Fischel, *Economics of Zoning Laws;* or Levine, *Zoned Out.*
12 See, for example, Wheaton and Schussheim, *Cost of Municipal Services;* Isard and Coughlin, *Municipal Costs and Revenues;* Real Estate Research Corporation, *Costs of Sprawl.*
13 Wheaton and Schussheim, *Cost of Municipal Services.*
14 Findings summarized in Burchell et al., *Costs of Sprawl – Revisited,* Table 4, 19.
15 Findings summarized in Burchell et al., *Costs of Sprawl – Revisited,* Table 8, 48.
16 Center for Energy and Environment et al., *Two Roads Diverge,* 23.
17 Blais, *Economics of Urban Form.*
18 A synthesis of the Duncan study, the Frank study, and the Burchell studies, presented in Burchell et al., *Costs of Sprawl – Revisited,* Table 9, 49.
19 Burchell et al., *Costs of Sprawl – 2000,* 272-75.
20 Ibid.
21 Sierra Club, *Sprawl Costs Us All.*
22 Fodor, "Cost of Growth," iii.
23 Governor Kitzhaber's Task Force, *Growth and Its Impacts,* iv.
24 Center for Energy and Environment et al., *Two Roads Diverge,* 23.
25 Essiambre et al., *Infrastructure Costs,* 30.
26 American Farmland Trust, *Density-Related Public Costs,* Washington, DC, 1986, quoted in Mazza and Fodor, *Taking Its Toll,* 7.
27 Included are Peter Gordon and Harry Richardson, Wendell Cox, Samuel Staley, and Randal O'Toole.
28 Gordon and Richardson, "Compact Cities," 99.
29 Peiser, "Does It Pay."
30 Ibid., 424.
31 Ladd, "Population Growth."
32 Cox and Utt, "Costs of Sprawl Reconsidered."

33 Cox, *Myths about Urban Growth*, 15.
34 Lawrence, "Food Study."
35 Ewing et al., *Measuring Sprawl*, 20.
36 Cox, *Myths about Urban Growth*, 17.
37 Gordon and Richardson, "Compact Cities," 98.
38 Ewing et al., *Measuring Sprawl*, 18.
39 Cox, *Myths about Urban Growth*, 22.
40 Ibid., 37.
41 Hobbs and Stoops, *Demographic Trends*, 33.
42 See, for example, Gordon and Richardson, "Compact Cities"; or Cox, *Myths about Urban Growth*; or Staley, *Sprawling of America*.
43 Gordon and Richardson, "Compact Cities."
44 Mills, "Truly Smart," 4.
45 Miller et al., *Travel and Housing Costs, Report Highlights*.
46 Ibid., *Travel and Housing Costs, Technical Report*, viii.
47 Burchell et al., *Costs of Sprawl – 2000*, ch. 14.

CHAPTER 4: THE COSTS AND BENEFITS OF PLANNING

1 Cervero, "Efficient Urbanization."
2 Ibid., 1.
3 Ibid., 18. Regarding Paris and London, see Prud'homme and Lee, "Size, Sprawl, Speed."
4 Ciccone and Hall, "Productivity."
5 See Florida, *Rise of the Creative Class*; and Florida, *Flight of the Creative Class*.
6 One exception is the work of Prud'homme, which estimates the labour productivity benefits delivered by transportation investments. Prud'homme found that increasing the speed of travel within a city by 10 percent increases productivity by 2.9 percent. Based on this, in the case of Paris, he found that transportation investments between 1983 and 1991 of 45 billion francs resulted in an increase in output of 29 billion francs, a 64 percent immediate return. See Prud'homme and Lee, "Size, Sprawl, Speed."
7 United Kingdom, Office of the Deputy Prime Minister, *Economic Consequences*. Data are for 1996/97.
8 Other direct costs are sometimes discussed in the literature, including costs associated with "planning delay" as well as impact fees or development charges. I do not deal with these in any detail here. In the case of planning delay, it is difficult to actually measure its costs as it is difficult to measure delay itself – that is, to judge what is a "reasonable" amount of time for the planning process. Impact fees and development charges, insofar as they are charges for the provision of physical infrastructure, are costs of *development* rather than of planning.
9 More detail on whether these and other charges, such as development charges, are passed forward – the "incidence" of the charge – is found in the discussion of development charges (see Chapter 7).
10 A summary of recent US analyses of the impact of a wide range of regulatory barriers on housing supply and affordability is contained in US Department of Housing and

Urban Development, "Why Not in Our Community?" An overview of UK research can be found in Roger Tym and Partners, *Planning and Competitiveness.*

11 For further reading on this view, see http://www.demographia.com, one anti-smart growth consultant's website.

12 Brueckner, "Government Land-Use Interventions."

13 See, for example, Cox, "Trouble."

14 Phillips and Goodstein, "Growth Management."

15 Downs, "Housing Prices." See other articles in this issue as well as an earlier forum that appears in vol. 8, no. 1 (1997) of the same journal.

16 Nelson, *Housing Price Effects* (referred to in Downs, "Housing Prices").

17 Cheshire and Sheppard, "Land Markets."

18 Ibid.

19 Allmendinger and Ball, *Rethinking.*

20 Cheshire and Sheppard, "Land Markets."

21 United Kingdom, Office of the Deputy Prime Minister, *Economic Consequences.*

22 Quoted in ibid.

23 Roger Tym and Partners, *Planning and Competitiveness.*

24 McKinsey, *Driving Productivity Growth.*

25 Ibid., page 2 of Food Retailing case study.

26 The measure used for output in this case is total gross margin, defined as sales less cost of goods sold.

27 McKinsey, *Driving Productivity Growth* (page 10 of Food Retailing case study).

28 Ibid., page 10 of Food Retailing case study.

29 Cheshire and Sheppard, "Welfare Economics."

30 Ibid., 243.

31 This in the case where the costs of planning are compared against the least-constrained planning scenario examined in the study.

32 Brueckner, "Government Land-Use Interventions."

33 Cheshire and Sheppard, "Land Markets," paraphrasing Chris Riley, "Comments on Mills and Evans."

34 Cheshire and Sheppard, "Welfare Economics," 264.

CHAPTER 5: HOW DO OUR CITIES GROW?

1 Ewing et al., *Growing Cooler,* 1.

2 Ontario, *Places to Grow,* 9.

3 Metropole Consultants, *Growth Opportunity.*

4 Ibid., 19.

5 Sierra Club, *Dark Side.*

6 H.C. Planning Consultants et al., *Costs of Suburban Sprawl,* 8.

7 Ontario, *Places to Grow.*

8 Urban Strategies Inc., *Application.*

9 Ewing et al. *Growing Cooler,* 2.

10 Holtzclaw, *Using Residential Patterns.*

11 Ibid.

12 Ewing and Cervero, "Travel and the Built Environment."

13 Ibid.
14 Ibid.
15 See, for example, Newman and Kenworthy, *Cities and Automobile Dependence*; Newman and Kenworthy, *Sustainability and Cities*.
16 Ewing and Cervero, "Travel and the Built Environment."
17 Ibid.
18 Transit Cooperative Research Program, "Evaluation."
19 Birch, *Who Lives Downtown*?
20 Cooperative Research and Policy Services, *Smart Growth in Canada*. One exception is noted in some suburban municipalities in the Vancouver region.
21 Urban Strategies Inc., *Application*.
22 Canada Mortgage and Housing Corporation and Ministry of Municipal Affairs and Housing, *2000 GTA*; ibid., *2001 GTA*; and ibid., *2003 GTA*. The 3 percent figure is calculated from the table in Appendix V. These figures only count development that occurs on a site that has been previously in urban use and, therefore, excludes sites within an urban boundary that have not been previously urbanized. This definition may account for some of the discrepancy in figures.
23 Greater Vancouver Regional District, *Livable Region*.
24 Greater Vancouver Regional District, *2005 Annual Report*.
25 Urban Strategies Inc., *Application*.
26 Statistics Canada, "Loss of Dependable Agricultural Land," 5.
27 Malenfant et al., *Demographic Changes*, 7.
28 1971 data are from Statistics Canada, *Econnections* 2000. Urban population data for 2001 are from the Census of Canada, http://www.statcan.ca/; data for urban land area are from Statistics Canada, "Loss of Dependable Agricultural Land," 7, fig. 3. An urban land area figure of 30,941 square kilometres was provided by Doug Trant, Chief, Spatial Analysis Section, Statistics Canada.
29 Bunting et al., "Density Gradients," Table 1.
30 Fulton et al., *Who Sprawls Most?*
31 Kolankiewicz and Beck, *Weighing Sprawl Factors*.
32 Fulton et al., *Who Sprawls Most?*
33 Ibid., 5.
34 Ibid.
35 Bunting et al., "Density Gradients"; and Cooperative Research and Policy Services, *Smart Growth in Canada*.
36 Bunting et al., "Density Gradients," tables 4 and 5. The weighted mean for inner cities is 4,556 persons per square kilometre in inner cities, compared to 2,317 persons per square kilometre in suburban areas.
37 Blais, *Inching toward Sustainability*.
38 Gordon and Vipond, "Gross Density and New Urbanism."
39 Taylor, *Analysis of Existing Urban Areas*.
40 Ibid., 35.
41 Hernandez and Simmons, "Evolving Retail Landscapes," 468.
42 Jones and Doucet, "Big-Box Retailing," 234.
43 Hernandez and Simmons, "Evolving Retail Landscapes," 470.

44 Ibid., 473.
45 International Council of Shopping Centers, *ICSC Shopping Center Definitions*, http://www.icsc.org/.
46 Hernandez and Simmons, "Evolving Retail Landscapes," 474.
47 Ibid., 480.
48 Jones and Doucet, "Big Box, the Flagship," 502.
49 International Council of Shopping Centers, *ICSC*.
50 Pardy, *USA's Largest Retail Centers*.
51 Ewing et al., *Measuring Sprawl*.
52 See, for example, Metropole Consultants, *Growth Opportunity*.
53 Taylor, *Shaping the Toronto Region*, 70.
54 Garreau, *Edge Cities*.
55 Ewing et al. *Measuring Sprawl*.
56 Glaeser et al., "Job Sprawl."
57 Statistics Canada, *Where Canadians Work*.
58 Blais, *Inching toward Sustainability*; Canadian Urban Institute, *GTA Urban Structure*; Filion, *Urban Growth Centres*.
59 Filion, *Urban Growth Centres*.
60 Cooperative Research and Policy Services, *Smart Growth in Canada*, 221.
61 Data cited in this paragraph are from Environment Canada, *Canada's National Environmental Indicator Series 2003*.
62 Cooperative Research and Policy Services, *Smart Growth in Canada*, 33 and 214.
63 Ibid., 120. Transit includes local transit and GO train.
64 Motor vehicles include passenger vehicles, large and small trucks, and buses. Source for 1975 data: Statistics Canada, *Historical Statistics*. Data for 2004 are from Statistics Canada, *Canadian Vehicle Survey*, 21.
65 IBI Group, *Toronto-Related Region*, 100.
66 US Department of Transportation, Bureau of Transportation Statistics, Table 1-11: Number of US Aircraft, Vehicles, Vessels, and Other Conveyances, http://www.bts.gov/. Numbers quoted include passenger cars and other two-axle, four-tire vehicles.
67 Ibid., Table 1-37M: US Passenger-Kilometres, http://www.bts.gov/. Numbers quoted include passenger cars and other two-axle, four-tire vehicles.
68 Ibid., Table 1-32: US Vehicle-Miles, http://www.bts.gov/. Numbers quoted include passenger cars and other two-axle, four-tire vehicles.
69 Ewing et al., *Growing Cooler*, Executive Summary, 2.
70 US Department of Transportation, Bureau of Transportation Statistics, Table 1-33: Roadway Vehicle-Miles Travelled (VMT) and VMT per Lane-Mile by Functional Class, http://www.bts.gov/.
71 Ibid.
72 Polzin and Chu, "Closer Look," 2.
73 Ibid.
74 Ibid.
75 Ibid.
76 Ibid. For the United States, times series data are not available for transit person-miles travelled as a share of urban-only person-miles travelled.

CHAPTER 6: PRICES DRIVE SPRAWL

1 Gottlieb, "Do Economists Have Anything"; Mills, "Truly Smart."
2 See, for example, Brueckner, "Urban Sprawl: Diagnosis"; Mills, "Truly Smart."
3 Telecommunications technology is sometimes seen as a factor in increasing decentralization, though other evidence suggests that things are much more complex than this as it has both centralizing and decentralizing effects, depending on factors such as type of industry or work. See Blais, "Shape of the Information City."
4 Mieszkowski and Mills, "Causes of Metropolitan Suburbanization."
5 Ibid., 137.
6 Brueckner, "Urban Sprawl: Diagnosis," 161.
7 Ibid.," 163.
8 Brueckner, "Urban Sprawl: Lessons." Farm subsidies are noted as providing subsidies that work in the opposite direction, bolstering the agricultural use of land.
9 Mills, "Comments"; and Mills, "Truly Smart," 5.
10 Fischel, "Zoning and Land Use," 421; Mills, "Comments," 91; Mills, "Truly Smart."
11 Brueckner, "Urban Sprawl: Diagnosis," 163.
12 Mills, "Truly Smart," 1.
13 Wassmer, "Economic Perspective," 4.
14 Ibid., 8.
15 Ibid.
16 Mills, "Comments," 92.
17 Brueckner, "Urban Sprawl: Diagnosis," 167.
18 Mills, "Comments," 91.
19 Dewees, "Pricing Municipal Services," 587.
20 Renzetti, "Municipal Water Supply," quoted in Kitchen, "Municipal Finance," 14.
21 Oates, "Local Property Taxation."
22 Thompson, "City as Distorted Price."
23 Mills, "Comments," 90.

CHAPTER 7: MUNICIPAL SERVICES

1 All of these figures exclude stormwater management costs, which are levied on a per net hectare basis at $50,988.62. Charges as of 1 February 2006.
2 These figures also exclude stormwater management costs of $50,988.62 per net hectare.
3 In Ontario, for example, the Development Charges Act mandates that capital costs be based on levels of service that were in place for the previous ten years. Improvements to standards cannot be financed through the development charge. Also, only 90 percent of the capital costs can be recovered through the development charge for a number of types of infrastructure and services.
4 City of Ottawa, Information on City of Ottawa Development Charges Bylaw 2004-298, http://ottawa.ca/. These amounts were in effect from 1 April 2008 to 31 March 2009.
5 Canada Mortgage and Housing Corporation, *CHS*, Table 13.
6 Regional Municipality of York, *2007 Development Charge.*
7 Such as the Region of York, discussed in more detail in Chapter 11.

8 Huffman et al., "Who Bears the Burden."
9 Ibid., 54.
10 Skaburskis, "Burden of Development Impact Fees," 181.
11 Ihlanfeldt and Shaughnessy, "Effects of Impact Fees."
12 See Burge et al., "Effects of Proportionate-Share," for an excellent review of the research.
13 Skaburskis and Qadeer, "Empirical Investigation."
14 This explanation was provided to me by a land developer.
15 Kitchen, "Financing City Services."
16 Association of Ontario Municipalities, "Ontario's $3 Billion."
17 City of Toronto, "2006 City Operating Budget."
18 Kitchen, "Financing City Services," 6.
19 Ibid.
20 This calculation is based on a house price of $335,000, which was the median house price in the Toronto Real Estate Board's Central District as of February 2007. City of Toronto tax rates used are for 2006.
21 Kitchen, "Canadian Municipalities."
22 Skaburskis, "Consequence of Taxing."
23 Shoup, "Effect of Property Taxes."
24 Grieson, "Economics of Property Taxes." This and the Shoup study are cited in Nowlan, "Local Taxation."
25 Brueckner and Kim, "Urban Sprawl."
26 Rates quoted are for 2005 and do not include education taxes. Rates other than the City of Toronto (which is a single-tier government) are the sum of municipal and regional tax rates. See City of Toronto, *Economic Development Survey*.
27 Assuming a property value of $350,000.
28 Canadian Federation of Independent Business, "Overtaxing Peter to Subsidize Paul," 4.
29 Kitchen and Slack, "Business Property Taxation," quoted in Kitchen, "Canadian Municipalities."
30 KPMG, *Study of Consumption of Tax Supported City Services*, report prepared for the City of Vancouver, 1995, quoted in Kitchen, "Canadian Municipalities."
31 City of Toronto, "Enhancing Toronto's Business Climate," Final Recommendations.
32 With some modifications, the rates reflect the various rates that school boards imposed in 1998, which were in effect when the province took over education funding.
33 Tomlinson, *Level Playing Field*.
34 For a review of studies on this issue, see Tomlinson, *Level Playing Field*.
35 City of Toronto, "Enhancing Toronto's Business Climate," presentation.
36 See, for example, City of Toronto, "Enhancing Toronto's Business Climate," final recommendations; and Canadian Urban Institute, "Business Competitiveness in the GTA."
37 City of Toronto, *Economic Development Survey*.
38 Slack, "Municipal Finance."
39 Ontario Ministry of Finance, *2006 Ontario Economic Outlook*.
40 See Province of Ontario. Ministry of Revenue, http://www.rev.gov.on.ca/.

CHAPTER 8: NETWORK SERVICES

1 Aside from the specific references in this section, most of the cost-of-sprawl studies reviewed in Chapter 3 include an analysis of water and sewer costs and the impact of urban form.

2 More so than the other two factors studied, namely, dispersion (or discontiguity of the urban fabric) and distance to the treatment plant.

3 Speir and Stephenson, "Does Sprawl Cost Us All?" This study looks at capital and energy costs associated with water and sewer infrastructure.

4 Speir and Stephenson, "Does Sprawl Cost Us All?" 59. See also Engel-Yan et al., "Toward Sustainable Neighbourhoods," 49.

5 Natural Resources Defense Council, *Another Cost of Sprawl*.

6 Environment Canada, *Municipal Water Pricing*, 4.

7 Ibid., 10.

8 Ibid., 5.

9 Steven Renzetti, "Municipal Water Supply," quoted in Kitchen, "Municipal Finance."

10 Natural Resources Defense Council, *Another Cost of Sprawl*, Part 2.

11 In the case of flat rates, low-volume users also subsidize high-volume users.

12 Statistics Canada, *Spending Patterns in Canada – 2005*. Catalogue 62-202-XIE, December, 2006, Table 9.

13 See, for example, Yatchew, "Economic and Regulatory Consequences"; and Camfield, "Findings and Recommendations."

14 Yatchew, "Scale Economies."

15 Salvanes and Tjotta, "Productivity Differences"; and Filippini, "Municipal Electricity Distribution Utilities."

16 The methodology and calculations used to establish RPP prices are set out in Ontario Energy Board, *Regulated Price Plan*. This report is updated annually.

17 Ontario Clean Air Alliance, *Tax Shift*.

18 Hydro One Networks website, http://www.hydroone.com. Hydro One Networks – Customers – Residential – Rates and Pricing.

19 Estimated using monthly prices and thresholds in effect for 1 November 2006 to 30 April 2007 and based on usage of 1,000 kilowatt hours. Percentages are for distribution costs only and do not include transmission or other delivery costs.

20 Adams and Bertolotti, "What Happened."

21 Ontario Energy Board, *EB-2005-0317*, 2-3.

22 The default meter reading factors the OEB has presented represent very rudimentary classifications, essentially only distinguishing between urban and rural for residential uses. Rural is given a factor of 2.00, compared to a factor of 1.00 for urban, suggesting that meter-reading costs in rural areas are twice those in urban areas. See Ontario Energy Board, *EB-2005-0317*.

23 This includes $127 million available for 2005, plus $21 million for Hydro One Remote Communities (for 2006, as identified in OEB Decision RP-2005-0020, EB-2005-0511), as per Ontario Regulation 442/01.

24 Ontario Energy Board, *Ontario Energy Board Electricity Distribution*.

25 Bernard et al., "Marginal Cost."

26 Guldmann, "Modeling the Structure."

27 Ibid., 314.

28 Bernard et al., "Marginal Cost."

29 A third, smaller utility is also regulated: Natural Resource Gas Limited.

30 Ontario Energy Board, *Natural Gas Regulation*, 58.

31 The customer charge also includes customer services, such as billing, but these costs are not related to urban form.

32 Union Gas, "Frequently Asked Questions."

33 Price ranges are based on usage thresholds.

34 Price discrimination is said to occur when the ratios of price to marginal cost vary within and across rate classes (i.e., some classes are charged more relative to costs than others).

35 Guldmann, "Capacity Cost Allocation."

36 Bernard et al., "Marginal Costs."

37 Ontario Energy Board, *Natural Gas Regulation*.

38 US Congress, *Technological Reshaping.*

39 Weinhaus et al., "What Is the Price."

40 Ibid., figs. 3 and 4.

41 Ibid., figs 7 and 19.

42 CRTC, Telecom Decision CRTC 99-16, *Telephone Service to High-Cost Serving Areas*, Ottawa, 19 October 1999.

43 The cross-subsidy issue is complex. There was also a subsidy from business customers (who have historically paid prices higher than costs) to residential customers and from long-distance service to local service.

44 CRTC, Decision CRTC 2000-745, *Changes to the Contribution Regime*, Ottawa, 30 November 2000.

45 For 2006, the contribution rate was set at 1.03 percent of contribution-eligible revenues. See Telecom Decision CRTC 2005-68, *Final 2005 Revenue-Percent Charge and Related Matters*, Ottawa, 10 November 2005.

46 The Public Notice for the CRTC hearing on band restructuring states: "ILEC's proposals to restructure bands must be based on costs. The structure of each band should be based on costs which are as homogeneous as possible. Each band must also have unambiguous and clearly identifiable boundaries." See CRTC Public Notice 2000-27, paragraph 6.

47 CRTC, Decision CRTC 2000-745, *Changes to the Contribution Regime*, as described in Telecom Decision CRTC 2005-4, *Implementation of Competition in the Local Exchange and Local Payphone Markets in the Territories of Société en commandite Télébec and the former TELUS Communications (Quebec) Inc.*, Ottawa, 31 January 2005.

48 As adopted in CRTC, Decision CRTC 2001-238, *Restructured Bands, Revised Loop Rates and Related Issues*, Ottawa, 27 April 2001.

49 CRTC, Telecom Decision CRTC 2005-68, *Final 2005 Revenue-Percent Charge and Related Matters*, Ottawa, 10 November 2005.

50 Bell Canada, letter to CRTC, 31 March 2005, re Decision 2002-34: Total Subsidy Requirement Filing, http://www.crtc.gc.ca/.

51   SaskTel letter to CRTC, 31 March 2005, re SaskTel – 2005 Total Subsidy Requirements (TSR) Calculation, http://www.crtc.gc.ca/.

52   CRTC, Telecom Decision CRTC 2005-68, *Final 2005 Revenue-Percent Charge and Related Matters,* Ottawa, 10 November 2005.

53   Ibid.

54   Public Interest Advocacy Centre, "Eliminating Phonelessness."

55   Bell Canada, Island Telecom Inc., Maritime Tel & Tel Limited, MTS Communications Inc., NBTel Inc., and NewTel Communications Inc., "Restructured Bands, Revised Local Loop Rates and Related Issues," submission re Telecom Public Notice CRTC 2000-27, 30 June 2000.

56   Bell Canada, Response to Interrogatory, Bell (CRTC)19Jun98-1204 HCSA, abridged, 28 August 1998, re Public Notice 97-42, High Cost Serving Areas, http://www.crtc. gc.ca/.

57   Source for population density figures: Bell (CRTC)19June98-1201 HCSA Attachment 3. Population density figures cited are those given by Bell for the entire wire centre area, derived from StatsCan data. They include enumeration areas (EAs) identified by Bell as high cost (i.e., those with densities less than 35 persons per square kilometre, primarily more rural areas surrounding towns) and the remaining lower-cost EAs within the towns. Bell's proposal was to extract the high-cost EAs from all the relevant wire centres and put them in separate high-cost bands. This proposal was not adopted (in favour of the Band definition described in Chapter 6).

58   This was prior to the establishment of the current system of explicit subsidies targeting high-cost areas. The request was denied as, "given that the banding approach approved by the Commission used to allocate the residential subsidy requirement is based on rate and cost averaging, it would not be appropriate to exclude subsets of NAS (lines) within a band" (CRTC Decision 98-2).

59   CRTC, Decision CRTC 98-2, *Implementation of Price Cap Regulation and Related Issues,* Ottawa, 5 March 1998.

60   Telecommunications Policy Review Panel, *Final Report 2006,* http://www. telecomreview.ca/.

61   CRTC, Telecom Decision CRTC 2005-27, *Review of Price Floor Safeguards for Retail Tariffed Services and Related Issues,* Ottawa, 29 April 2005; and CRTC, Telecom Decision CRTC 2005-69, *Extension of the Price Regulation Regime for Aliant Telecom Inc., Bell Canada, MTS Allstream Inc., Saskatchewan Telecommunications and TELUS Communications Inc.,* Ottawa, 16 December 2005.

62   Bell Canada, Island Telecom Inc., Maritime Tel & Tel Limited, MTS Communications Inc., NBTel Inc., and NewTel Communications Inc., "Restructured Bands, Revised Local Loop Rates and Related Issues," Submission re Telecom Public Notice CRTC 2000-27, 30 June 2000, p. 9; and Bell Canada, Response to Interrogatory, Bell (CRTC)19Jun98-1204 HCSA, abridged, 28 August 1998, re Public Notice 97-42, High-Cost Serving Areas, 4.

63   Bell Canada, Bell (CRTC)19Jun98-1204 HCSA, 28 August 1998, 4.

64   Statistics Canada, *Spending Patterns in Canada,* Table 6.

65   Ibid.

66 From company websites for Rogers, Shaw, Cogeco, and Videotron (viewed 1 February 2007).
67 Organization for Economic Cooperation and Development, Broadband Statistics to June 2006, http://www.oecd.org/.
68 Statistics Canada, Survey of Household Spending, *The Daily*, Tuesday, 12 December 2006.
69 OECD, Broadband Statistics to June 2006.
70 From Rogers and Shaw websites (viewed 30 January 2007).
71 See, for example: Organization for Economic Cooperation and Development, *Regulatory Reform*.
72 NERA Economic Consulting, *Economics of Postal Services*.
73 Ibid., 151. This finding is for the original fifteen EU member states. In the new member states, costs would increase by 5.6 percent.
74 NERA Economic Consulting, *Economics of Postal Services*.
75 Ibid., 154. This figure is for original member states. For new member states, the cost increase was 5.8 percent.
76 Cazals et al., "Analysis," cited in NERA, *Economics of Postal Services*, 105.
77 Bernard et al., "Delivery Cost," cited in NERA, *Economics of Postal Services*.
78 NERA Economic Consulting, *Economics of Postal Services*, 126.
79 Ibid., 129.
80 Royal Mail, "Application under Licence Condition 21 for Approval to Offer Geographic Zonal Prices for Bulkmail Services," 5 July 2006, 21, http://www.psc.gov.uk/.
81 Iacobucci et al., "Rerouting the Mail."
82 Ibid., 8.
83 In fact, given the methodology used, cost differentials are likely to be understated. See Royal Mail, "Application," 10.
84 Though agreeing that the zonal pricing system proposed for those select retail bulk mail services was cost-reflective, in 2007 the regulator rejected the proposal. However, a separate agreement was reached to allow a new 4-zone pricing structure for certain wholesale mail services (see http://www.royalmail.com/).

CHAPTER 9: HOUSING, INFRASTRUCTURE, AND ENERGY

1 Harris, *Creeping Conformity*.
2 Hayden, *Field Guide to Sprawl*.
3 Goldsmith, "Resisting the Reality of Race."
4 Cooperative Research and Policy Services, "Ten Steps."
5 Miller et al., *Travel and Housing Costs, Technical Report*, 29.
6 Hollingworth et al., *Greenhouse Gas Emissions*, cited in Miller et al., *Travel and Housing Costs, Technical Report*, 29.
7 Ibid.
8 Miller et al., *Travel and Housing Costs, Technical Report*, 68.
9 Ibid., calculated from data in Table 9.1, p. 68. Transportation costs in Miller et al. are personal expenditures on transportation, including expenditures on new and used vehicles, fuels and lubricants, maintenance and repairs, insurance and intra-city transit.

10 Based on Canadian Automobile Association estimates of driving costs associated with a Chevy Cavalier driven 18,000 kilometres per year.

11 Department of Finance Canada, *Tax Expenditures and Evaluations 2009*, p. 18, http://www.fin.gc.ca/. The Finance Department provides two alternatives for calculating the tax expenditure: one assuming that 100 percent of the capital gains would normally be subject to taxation ("full inclusion") and therefore 100 percent of revenues foregone with the exemption; the other assumes that only 50 percent of capital gains would normally be taxed, thus only 50 percent of revenues foregone. The figures cited are based on the full inclusion rate; if the partial inclusion rate is assumed, the tax expenditures would be half those cited above.

12 Only a "substantial renovation" is eligible for the rebate – that is, a renovation affecting 90 percent or more of the building.

13 Canada Mortgage and Housing Corporation and Ontario Ministry of Municipal Affairs and Housing, *2001 Residential Land Inventory Survey*. Calculated from data in Appendix V.

14 Department of Finance Canada, *Tax Expenditures and Evaluations 2009*, p. 29, http://www.fin.gc.ca/.

15 Starting in April 2007.

16 Natural Resources Canada, "ecoENERGY Efficiency."

17 Ontario Ministry of Finance, *2006 Ontario Economic Outlook*.

18 Ibid., Annex V.

19 Department of Finance Canada, "Oil and Gas Prices."

20 Ibid.

21 Ibid.

22 Infrastructure Canada website is http://www.infrastructure.gc.ca.

23 Ontario Ministry of Finance, *2007 Ontario Budget: Budget Papers*, p. 94. The program began in 2004, with 1¢ per litre, rising to 1.5¢ in 2005, and 2¢ beginning in 2006.

24 Office of the Auditor General of Canada, *Report of Commissioner*, 3-17 – 3-18.

25 Ibid., 3-20.

26 Ibid.

27 Pembina Institute, *Submission to Standing Committee*.

28 Only employees with a dedicated parking space were taxed for this benefit. It is estimated that 80 percent of employee parking space is not dedicated (see IBI Group, *Transportation and Climate Change*).

29 Ontario Ministry of Finance, *2006 Ontario Economic Outlook*, Annex V.

30 Ontario Ministry of Finance, *Automobile Insurance Affordability Plan*.

31 Figures from the Infrastructure Canada website, http://www.infrastructure.gc.ca/.

32 Ontario Ministry of Public Infrastructure Renewal, *ReNew Ontario*.

33 Ontario Ministry of Finance, *2006 Ontario Budget;* and Ontario Ministry of Finance, *Strengthening Ontario's Transportation Infrastructure*.

34 Pembina Institute, *Building Sustainable Urban Communities*.

35 Delucchi and Murphy, *Motor Vehicle Goods*, Table 6.1.

36 Victoria Transport Policy Institute, *Transportation Cost and Benefit Analysis – Parking Costs*, updated December 2006, http://www.vtpi.org/.

37 US Department of Transportation, Federal Highway Administration, State Motor Vehicle Registrations – 2003, http://www.fhwa.dot.gov/.

38 Statistics Canada, Motor Vehicle Registrations by Province and Territory, 2005, http://www.statcan.ca/.

39 Both figures based on data from the 1990 *Nationwide Personal Transportation Study*, US Department of Transportation, Washington DC, and quoted in Shoup, "Opportunity to Reduce."

40 Victoria Transport Policy Institute, *Transportation Cost*, 5.4-8.

41 Ibid., 5.4-9, http://www.vtpi.org/.

42 Delucchi and Murphy, *Motor-Vehicle Goods*, Table 6.1 and Table 6.6. The numbers quoted represent the annual cost of all offstreet non-residential parking spaces from Table 6.1, not excluding the cost of priced parking plus the costs of residential parking from Table 6.6.

43 Victoria Transport Policy Institute, *Transportation Cost*, 5.4-8.

44 There may be issues of cross-subsidy within a given residential building or new development, depending on how exactly house prices reflect parking costs, but I leave this issue aside.

45 These figures are based on a revision of an estimate provided in Shoup, *High Cost of Free Parking*, Table 7.1. Shoup estimates that only 1 percent to 5 percent of parking is paid for. But his calculations double-counted some costs, which I exclude, and include residential parking, which I assume to be paid for by residents, and exclude municipal and institutional parking revenues, which I include.

46 For an excellent analysis of this cycle, and all other matters related to pricing of parking, see Shoup, *High Cost of Free Parking*. Much of the discussion in this section of parking pricing and its relationship to urban form is drawn from this book.

47 For a good summary of the research, see US Transportation Research Board, *Parking Pricing and Fees*.

48 Delucchi and Murphy, *Motor Vehicle Goods*, 30.

49 Ibid., Table 6.12, 83.

CHAPTER 10: DRIVING SPRAWL

1 *The Economist*, Online Dictionary, http//www.economist.com/. For further definitions and typologies, see Myers and Kent, *Perverse Subsidies*.

2 Ralph, "Cross-Subsidy."

3 Ralph, "Cross-Subsidy," quoting Faulhaber, "On Subsidization."

4 Beato, "Cross Subsidies in Public Services," 5.

5 InfoDev and International Telecommunications Union, *ICT Regulation Toolkit, Module 2 Competition and Price Regulation*, last updated 19 January 2007, http://www.infodev.org/.

CHAPTER 11: PRINCIPLES FOR A MARKET-ORIENTED APPROACH

1 Levine, *Zoned Out*.

2 Bosquet, "Environmental Tax Reform."

3 Nowlan, "Economic Implications," 16-18.

4 The tax was implemented in 2008, at slightly reduced rates, and with concessions for first-time home buyers.

CHAPTER 12: A TOOLBOX OF MARKET-ORIENTED INSTRUMENTS

1 Kitchen, "Municipal Finance."
2 Bird and Tsiopoulos, "User Charges for Public Services," 56.
3 Ibid., 60.
4 Interestingly, this came about as the result of a development industry appeal of the DC bylaw.
5 Town of Markham, *Development Charges Information Package*, http://www.markham. ca/. Rates as of 1 July 2009.
6 The 2007 Region of York *Development Charges Background Study* (p. 89), for example, notes that, in that region, single and semi-detached houses average 3.6 persons per unit, compared to 2.9 for townhouses, 2.1 for larger apartments, and 1.5 for smaller apartments.
7 One potential tweak is that some of the townwide hard costs charged on a per unit basis are related to the road network and might better be charged on a land-area basis.
8 Duff, "Benefit Taxes and User Fees," 393.
9 Bird and Tsiopoulos, "User Charges for Public Services," quoted in Duff, "Benefit Taxes and User Fees," 393.
10 Duff, "Benefit Taxes and User Fees," 393.
11 Kitchen, "Municipal Finance," 5.
12 See Zodrow, "Property Tax as a Capital Tax," 140-41 for a summary.
13 McCluskey and Franzsen, "Land Value Taxation," 75.
14 Netzer, "Land Value Taxation."
15 Lusht, "Site Value Tax," 13-14.
16 McCluskey and Franzsen, "Land Value Taxation," 37.
17 Australian Government, Productivity Commission, *Assessing Local Government Revenue Raising Capacity*, Productivity Commission Research Report, April, 2008, Fig. 2, p. xxi, http://www.pc.gov.au/.
18 Ibid.
19 City of Sydney, *Corporate Plan 2008-2011*, pp. 77-86, http://www.cityofsydney.nsw. gov.au/.
20 Oates and Schwab, "The Impact of Urban Land Taxation," Table 2.
21 See, for example, Cord, "Taxing Land More Than Buildings"; Bourassa, "Land Value Taxation and New Housing Development in Pittsburgh."
22 Hughes, "Why So Little Georgism in America?"
23 Banzhaf and Lavery, "How 'Smart.'"
24 Oates and Schwab, "Impact of Urban Land Taxation," 22.
25 In addition, Oates and Schwab point out that, in the Pittsburgh case, there were additional taxes levied on land (e.g., county and school district taxes).
26 The annual budget of the Municipal Property Assessment Corporation for 2006, *MPAC 2006 Annual Report*, http://www.mpac.ca/.

27 See Chapter 7. The figure for Ontario is 30 percent, due to higher mandated levels of social spending in Ontario municipalities.

28 Though, strictly speaking, market value is a poor reflection of cost causation even for these services. It is more justified as an ability-to-pay approach, with households with higher-value homes seen as being more able to pay than those with lower-value homes, though this is a questionable assumption.

29 Bird and Tsiopoulos, "User Charges for Public Services," quoted in Duff, "Benefit Taxes and User Fees," 393.

30 Duff, "Benefit Taxes and User Fees," 394.

31 Bird, "Threading the Fiscal Labyrinth," 212.

32 Kitchen, "Financing City Services."

33 Litman, *Socially Optimal Transport Prices*, 9.

34 This is not to say that cost of the treatment plant itself cannot vary according to where it is situated within the service area – of course it can, depending on variations in land prices and other factors. The point here is that, whatever the cost of the treatment facility, its cost should be allocated to consumers on the basis of water usage level rather than according to the location of the consumer (or other urban form characteristics of the consumer). Also, the discussion above assumes one treatment plant services the entire billing area. If more than one treatment plant is used, then the costs *can* vary by location and should be reflected in prices. For example, in an expanding municipality, new development in older areas may be serviced by a treatment plant with existing capacity, while new suburban growth requires a new facility. In this case, usage charges should reflect differences in serving the two areas – that is, they should be higher in the suburban area so as to account for the new facility required.

35 For further details on pay-as-you-drive insurance, see Victoria Transport Policy Institute, Pay-As-You-Drive Vehicle Insurance, *TDM Encyclopedia*, updated 4 September 2007, http://www.vtpi.org/.

36 See, for example, Shoup, *High Cost of Free Parking;* Litman, *Parking Taxes;* Litman, *Parking Management Best Practices;* Vaca and Kuzmyak, "Parking Prices and Fees."

37 California Legislative Analyst's Office, "A Commuter's Dilemma."

38 US and Australian examples from Litman, *Parking Taxes*, 3-4.

39 Ibid., 9.

40 Canadian Automobile Association. *Driving Costs, 2007 Edition*, http://www.ama. ab.ca/.

41 McClanaghan and Associates, *Location-Based Mortgages.*

42 National Resources Defense Council, *Location Efficient Mortgages*, http://www. nrdc.org/.

43 Canada, NRTEE, *Environmental Quality in Canadian Cities.*

44 Go to http://www.dft.gov.uk/ for further information.

45 For more information, see http://www.usgbc.org/.

46 Bird and Tsiopoulos, "User Charges."

CHAPTER 13: PERVERSE SUBSIDIES, PERVERSE CITIES

1 Levine, *Zoned Out*, 3.

2 Knaap, "Sprawl of Economics," 12.
3 Razin and Rosentraub, "Are Fragmentation and Sprawl Interlinked?"
4 Brueckner, "Urban Sprawl."
5 Holcombe and Staley, "Policy Implications," in *Smarter Growth*, 252.
6 Hall, "Retro Urbanism," 125.
7 Blais, *Inching toward Sustainability.*
8 Soule, "Defining and Managing Sprawl," in Soule, *Remaking American Communities*, 9.
9 Birnbaum et al., *Simcoe County.*
10 Cheshire and Sheppard, "Taxes versus Regulation."
11 Thompson, "City as a Distorted Price System," 28.
12 Levine, *Zoned Out.*

Bibliography

Abeles, Ethan C. "Analysis of Light-Duty Vehicle Price Trends in the US." Institute of Transportation Studies, University of California, Davis, June 2004, UCD-ITS-RR-04-15.

Adams, Tom, and Alfredo Bertolotti. "What Happened to My Electricity Bill?" *Energy Probe*, 31 March 2005, http://energy.probeinternational.org/.

Allmendinger, Phil, and Michael Ball. *Rethinking the Planning Regulation of Land and Property Markets, Final Report*. New Horizons Research Program, Great Britain, Office of the Deputy Prime Minister, April 2006. http://www.rmd.communities.gov.uk/.

American Planning Association. *Planning for Smart Growth: 2002 State of the States*. Chicago, February 2002. http://www.planning.org/.

American Rivers, Natural Resources Defense Council and Smart Growth America. *Paving Our Way to Water Shortages: How Sprawl Aggravates Drought*, 2002. http://www.smartgrowthamerica.org/.

Association of Ontario Municipalities. "Ontario's $3 Billion Provincial Municipal Fiscal Gap." August 2005. http://www.amo.on.ca/.

Banzhaf, H. Spencer, and Nathan Lavery. "How 'Smart' Is the Split-Rate Property Tax? Evidence from Growth Patterns in Pennsylvania." Cambridge, MA, Lincoln Institute of Land Policy, Working Paper, 2008. http://www.lincolninst.edu/.

Beato, Paulina. "Cross Subsidies in Public Services: Some Issues." Sustainable Development Department, Technical Papers Series. Washington, DC: Inter-American Development Bank, January 2000. http://www.iadb.org/.

Bernard, Jean-Thomas, D. Bolduc, and A. Hardy. "The Marginal Cost of Natural Gas Distribution Pipelines: The Case of Société en Commandite Gaz Métropolitain (SCGM)." *Energy Economics* 24, 5 (2002): 425-38.

Bernard, Stephane, R. Cohen, M. Robinson, B. Roy, J. Toledano, J. Waller, and S. Xenakis. "Delivery Cost Heterogeneity and Vulnerability to Entry." In *Postal and Delivery Services: Delivering on the Competition*, ed., M.A. Crew and P.R. Kleindorfer, 169-84. Boston: Kluwer Academic Publishers, 2002.

Birch, Eugenie. *Who Lives Downtown*. Washington, DC, Brookings Institution, Living Cities Census Series, November 2005. http://www.brookings.edu/.

Bird, Richard M. "Threading the Fiscal Labyrinth: Some Issues in Fiscal Decentralization." *National Tax Journal* 46, 2 (1993): 207-27.

Bird, Richard M., and Thomas Tsiopoulos. "User Charges for Public Services: Potentials and Problems." *Canadian Tax Journal* 45, 1 (1997): 25-86.

Birnbaum, Leah, Lorenzo Nicolet, and Zack Taylor. *Simcoe County: The New Growth Frontier*. Toronto: Neptis Foundation, 2004.

Blais, Pamela. "The Economics of Urban Form." Paper prepared for the Greater Toronto Area Task Force, January 1996.

–. *Inching toward Sustainability: The Evolving Urban Structure of the Greater Toronto Area*. Toronto: Neptis Foundation, March 2000.

–. "The Shape of the Information City: Understanding the Impacts of the Information Revolution on City Form." *Plan Canada* 38, 5 (1998): 8-11.

Bosquet, Benoit. "Environmental Tax Reform: Does It Work? A Survey of the Empirical Evidence." *Ecological Economics* 34 (2000): 19-32.

Bourassa, S.C. "Land Value Taxation and New Housing Development in Pittsburgh." *Growth and Change* 18, 4 (1987): 44-56.

Bray, Riina, Catherine Vakil, and David Elliot. *Report on Public Health and Urban Sprawl in Ontario: A Review of the Pertinent Literature*. Environmental Health Committee, Ontario College of Family Physicians, January 2005. http://www.ocfp.on.ca/.

Brueckner, Jan K. "Government Land-Use Interventions: An Economic Analysis." Paper presented at the 4th Annual Urban Research Symposium, World Bank, Washington, DC, February 2007. http://www.worldbank.org/.

–. "Urban Sprawl: Diagnosis and Remedies." *International Regional Science Review* 23, 2 (2000): 160-71.

–. "Urban Sprawl: Lessons from Urban Economics." *Brookings-Wharton Papers on Urban Affairs* (2001): 65-97.

Brueckner, Jan K., and Hyun-A Kim. "Urban Sprawl and the Property Tax." *International Tax and Public Finance* 10, 5 (2003): 5-23.

Bruegmann, Robert. *Sprawl: A Compact History*. Chicago: University of Chicago Press, 2005.

Bunting, T., P. Filion, and H. Priston. "Density Gradients in Canadian Metropolitan Regions, 1976-96: Differential Patterns of Central Area and Suburban Growth and Change." *Urban Studies* 39, 13 (2002): 2531-52.

Burchell, Robert, Anthony Downs, Barbara McCann, and Sahan Mukherji. *Sprawl Costs: Economic Impacts of Unchecked Development*. Washington, DC: Island Press, 2005.

Burchell, Robert W., George Lowenstein, William R. Dolphin, Catherine C. Galley, Anthony Downs, Samuel Seskin, Katherine Gray Still, and Terry Moore. *Costs of*

Sprawl – 2000. TCRP Report 74, Transit Cooperative Research Program, Transportation Research Board, National Research Council. Washington, DC: National Academy Press, 2002.

Burchell, Robert W., Naveed A. Shad, David Listokin, Hilary Phillips, Anthony Downs, Samuel Seskin, Judy S. Davis, Terry Moore, David Helton, and Michelle Gall. *The Costs of Sprawl – Revisited.* TCRP Report 39, Transit Cooperative Research Program, Transportation Research Board, National Research Council. Washington, DC: National Academy Press, 1998.

Burge, Gregory S., Arthur C. Nelson, and John Matthews. "Effects of Proportionate-Share Impact Fees." *Housing Policy Debate* 18, 4 (2007): 679-710.

California Legislative Analyst's Office. "A Commuter's Dilemma: Cash or Free Parking?" Prepared for the LAO by Rebecca Long. Sacramento: LAO, 19 March 2002. http://www.lao.ca.gov/.

Calthorpe, Peter, and William Fulton. *The Regional City: Planning for the End of Sprawl.* Washington, DC: Island Press, 2001.

Camfield Robert. "Findings and Recommendations: Comparators and Cohorts for Electricity Distribution Rates." Paper prepared for the consideration of the Ontario Energy Board, December 2004. http://www.oeb.gov.on.ca/.

Canada. National Roundtable on the Environment and the Economy (NRTEE). *State of the Debate on the Environment and the Economy: Environmental Quality in Canadian Cities – The Federal Role,* 2003. http://www.nrtee-trnee.ca/.

Canada Mortgage and Housing Corporation. *Canadian Housing Observer 2007.* http://www.cmhc-schl.gc.ca/.

–. *CHS: Residential Building Activity, Dwelling Starts, Completions, under Construction and Newly Completed and Unabsorbed Dwellings – 2007.* Table 13, April 2008. http://www.cmhc-schl.gc.ca/.

–. "Greenhouse Gas Emissions from Urban Travel: Tool for Evaluating Neighbourhood Sustainability." *Research Highlights,* Socio-Economic Series, issue 50, revision 2, 2000. http://www.cmhc-schl.gc.ca/.

Canada Mortgage and Housing Corporation and Ontario Ministry of Municipal Affairs and Housing. *The 2000 GTA Residential Land Inventory.*

–. *The 2001 GTA Residential Land Inventory.*

–. *The 2003 GTA Residential Land Inventory.*

Canadian Federation of Independent Business. *Overtaxing Peter to Subsidize Paul: Business Property Tax Unfairness in Ontario,* October 2006. http://www.cfib-fcei.ca/.

Canadian Urban Institute. "Business Competitiveness in the GTA: Why Toronto Is Losing Ground – Final Report." Prepared for the Toronto Office Coalition, June 2005. http://torontoofficecoalition.com/.

–. *GTA Urban Structure: An Analysis of Progress towards the Vision.* Toronto: 1997.

Cazals, C., J. Florens, and B. Roy. "An Analysis of Some Specific Cost Drivers in the Delivery Activity." In *Future Directions in Postal Reform,* ed. M.A. Crew and P.R. Kleindorfer, 197-212. Boston: Kluwer Academic Publishers, 2001.

Center for Energy and Environment, Minnesotans for an Energy-Efficient Economy, and 1000 Friends of America. *Two Roads Diverge: Analyzing Growth Scenarios for the Twin Cities Region,* June 1999. http://www.mncee.org/.

Centre for Sustainable Transportation. *Sustainable Transportation Performance Indicators (STPI) Project.* Report on Phase 3, 31 December 2002. http://www.centreforsustainabletransportation.org/.

Cervero, Robert. "Efficient Urbanization: Economic Performance and the Shape of the Metropolis." Lincoln Institute of Land Policy, Working Paper, 2000. http://www.lincolninst.edu/.

Cheshire, Paul, and Stephen Sheppard. "Land Markets and Land Market Regulation: Progress toward Understanding." *Regional Science and Urban Economics* 34 (2004): 619-37.

–. "Taxes versus Regulation: The Welfare Impacts of Policies for Containing Sprawl." *LSE Research Papers in Environmental and Spatial Analysis* 75 (July 2002). http://www.lse.ac.uk/.

–. "Welfare Economics of Land Use Regulation." *Journal of Urban Economics* 52 (2002): 242-69.

Ciccone, Antonio, and Robert E. Hall. "Productivity and the Density of Economic Activity." *American Economic Review* 86, 1 (1996): 54-70.

City of Toronto. "2006 City Operating Budget of $7.6 Billion Approved by Council." *Backgrounder,* 11 April 2006. http://www.toronto.ca/.

–. *Economic Development Survey of Local Municipalities.* http:// www.toronto.ca.

–. "Enhancing Toronto's Business Climate: It's Everybody's Business." Final Recommendations, 26 October 2005. http://www.toronto.ca/.

–. "Enhancing Toronto's Business Climate." Presentation of Final Recommendations to Joint Meeting of Policy and Finance Committee and Economic Development and Parks Committee, 20 October 2005. http://www.toronto.ca/.

Cooperative Research and Policy Services. *Smart Growth in Canada: Implementation of a Planning Concept.* Canada Mortgage and Housing Corporation, Research Report, August 2005. http://www.cmhc-schl.ca/.

–. "Ten Steps to a Cooler Planet." *CMHC Research Highlights,* Technical Series 00-146, 2000.

Cord, Steven. "Taxing Land More Than Buildings: The Record in Pennsylvania." *Proceedings of the Academy of Political Science* 35, 1 (1983): 172-97.

Cox, Wendell. *Myths about Urban Growth and the Toronto "Greenbelt."* Fraser Institute Digital Publication, December 2004. http://www.fraserinstitute.org/.

–. "Trouble in Smart Growth's Nirvana." *Planetizen,* 30 June 2002. http://www.planetizen.com/.

Cox, Wendell, and Joshua Utt. "The Costs of Sprawl Reconsidered: What the Data Really Show." *Backgrounder* 1770, Heritage Foundation, 25 June 2004. http://www.heritage.org/.

Delucchi, Mark, and James Murphy. *Motor Vehicle Goods and Services Bundled in the Private Sector.* Report no. 6 in the series Annualized Social Cost of Motor-Vehicle Use in the United States. Institute of Transportation Studies, University of California at Davis, June 1998 (rev. November 2004). http://www.its.ucdavis.edu/.

Department of Finance Canada. "Oil and Gas Prices, Taxes and Consumers." *Backgrounder,* July 2006. http://www.fin.gc.ca/.

Dewees, Donald N. "Pricing Municipal Services: The Economics of User Fees." *Canadian Tax Journal* 50, 2 (2002): 586-99.

Downs, Anthony. "Have Housing Prices Risen Faster in Portland Than Elsewhere?" *Housing Policy Debate* 13, 1 (2002): 7-13.

Duany, Andres, Elizabeth Plater-Zyberk, Jeff Speck. *Suburban Nation: The Rise of Sprawl and the Decline of the American Dream.* New York: North Point Press, 2000.

Duany, Andres, and Emily Talen. "Transect Planning." *Journal of the American Planning Association* 68, 3 (2002): 245-66.

Duff, David G. "Benefit Taxes and User Fees in Theory and Practice." *University of Toronto Law Journal* 54 (2004): 391-447.

Duncan Associates. *The Search for Efficient Urban Growth Patterns.* Tallahassee: Florida Department of Community Affairs, 1989.

Engel-Yan, Joshua, Chris Kennedy, Susana Saiz, and Kim Pressnail. "Toward Sustainable Neighbourhoods: The Need to Consider Infrastructure Interactions." *Canadian Journal of Civil Engineering* 32 (2005): 45-57.

Environment Canada. *Canada's National Environmental Indicator Series 2003: Passenger Transportation.* http://www.ec.gc.ca/.

–. *Municipal Water Pricing 1991-1999.* Minster of Public Works and Government Services, 2001. http://www.ec.gc.ca/.

Essiambre Phillips Desjardins Associates Ltd., *Infrastructure Costs Associated with Conventional and Alternative Development Patterns, Summary Report.* Ottawa: Canada Mortgage and Housing Corporation, June 1995.

Evans, Alan W. "Building Jerusalem: Can Land Use Planning Affect Economic Growth?" Lincoln Institute of Land Policy, conference paper, 2002. http://www.lincolninst.edu/.

Ewing, Reid. "Is Los Angeles-Style Sprawl Desirable?" *Journal of the American Planning Association* 63, 1 (1997): 107-26.

Ewing, Reid, Keith Bartholomew, Steve Winkelman, Jerry Walters, and Don Chen. *Growing Cooler: The Evidence on Urban Development and Climate Change.* Washington, DC: Urban Land Institute, Smart Growth America, Center for Clean Air Policy, National Center for Smart Growth, 2007.

Ewing, Reid, and Robert Cervero. "Travel and the Built Environment: A Synthesis." *Transportation Research Record* 1780 (2001): 87-114.

Ewing, Reid, Rolf Pendall, and Don Chen. *Measuring Sprawl and Its Impact.* Smart Growth America, 2002. http://www.smartgrowthamerica.org/.

Faulhaber, G.R. "On Subsidization: Some Observations and Tentative Conclusions." Paper delivered at Conference on Communication Policy Resources, Washington, DC, Office of Telecommunication Policy Resources, 1972.

Filion, Pierre. *The Urban Growth Centres Strategy in the Greater Golden Horseshoe: Lessons from Downtowns, Nodes and Corridors.* Toronto: Neptis Foundation, 2007.

Filippini, M. "Are Municipal Electricity Distribution Utilities Natural Monopolies?" *Annals of Public and Cooperative Economics* 69, 2 (1998): 157-74.

Fischel, William A. *The Economics of Zoning Laws: A Property Rights Approach to American Land Use Controls.* Baltimore: Johns Hopkins University Press, 1985.

—. "Zoning and Land Use Regulation." In *Encyclopaedia of Law and Economics.* Vol. 2: *Civil Law and Economics,* ed. Boudewijn Bouckaert and Gerrit De Geest, 403-42. Cheltenham: Edward Elgar, 2000. http://encyclo.findlaw.com/.

Flaherty, John, and Kenneth M. Lusht. "Site Value Taxation, Land Values and Development Patterns." Institute for Real Estate Studies Working Paper 96-05, Pennsylvania State University, Smeal College of Business, October 1996.

Florida, Richard. *The Flight of the Creative Class: The New Global Competition for Talent.* New York: Harper Collins, 2005.

—. *The Rise of the Creative Class: And How It's Transforming Work, Leisure, Community and Everyday Life.* New York: Basic Books, 2002.

Fodor, Eben V. "The Cost of Growth in Oregon, 1998 Report: Executive Summary." Fodor and Associates. http://www.fodorandassociates.com/.

Fulton, William, Rolf Pendall, Mai Nguyen, and Alicia Harrison. *Who Sprawls Most? How Growth Patterns Differ across the US.* Washington, DC: Centre for Urban and Metropolitan Policy, the Brookings Institution, July 2001.

Frank, James E. *The Costs of Alternative Development Patterns: A Review of the Literature.* Washington, DC: Urban Land Institute, 1989.

Galster, George, Royce Hanson, Michael R. Ratcliffe, Harold Wolman, Stephen Coleman and Jason Freihage. "Wrestling Sprawl to the Ground: Defining and Measuring an Elusive Concept." *Housing Policy Debate* 12, 4 (2001): 681-717.

Garreau, Joel. *Edge Cities: Life on the New Frontier.* New York: Anchor Books, 1991.

Gillham, Oliver. *The Limitless City: A Primer on the Urban Sprawl Debate.* Washington, DC: Island Press, 2002.

Glaeser, Edward L., Matthew Kahn, and Chenghuan Chu. *Job Sprawl: Employment Location in US Metropolitan Areas.* Washington, DC: Brookings Institution, Center on Urban and Metropolitan Policy, May 2001.

Goldsmith, William W. *Resisting the Reality of Race: Land Use, Social Justice, and the Metropolitan Economy.* Cambridge, NJ: Lincoln Institute of Land Policy, 1999.

Gordon, David, and S. Vipond. "Gross Density and New Urbanism: Comparing Conventional and New Urbanist Suburbs in Markham, Ontario." *Journal of the American Planning Association* 71, 1 (2005): 41-54.

Gordon, Peter, and Harry W. Richardson. "Are Compact Cities a Desirable Planning Goal?" *Journal of the American Planning Association* 63, 1 (1997): 95-106.

Gottlieb, Paul D. "Do Economists Have Anything to Contribute to the Debate on Urban Sprawl? (And Would Anybody Listen to Them if They Did?" *Forum for Social Economics* 28, 2 (1999): 51-64.

Governor Kitzhaber's Task Force on Growth in Oregon. *Growth and Its Impacts in Oregon.* Salem, OR, January 1999. http://www.econw.com/.

Greater Vancouver Regional District. *2005 Annual Report: Livable Region Strategic Plan.* http://www.metrovancouver.org/.

—. *Livable Region Strategic Plan.* Policy and Planning Department, 1999. http://www.metrovancouver.org/.

Grieson, Ronald E. "The Economics of Property Taxes and Land Values: The Elasticity of Supply of Structures." *Journal of Urban Economics* 1 (1974): 367-91.

Guldmann, Jean-Michel. "Capacity Cost Allocation in the Provision of Urban Public Services: The Case of Gas Distribution." *Growth and Change* 20, 2 (1989): 1-18.

—. "Modeling the Structure of Gas Distribution Costs in Urban Areas." *Regional Science and Urban Economics* 13 (1983): 299-316.

Hall, Peter. "Retro Urbanism: The Once and Future TOD." In *Sprawl and Suburbia*, ed. William S. Saunders, 122-29. Minneapolis: University of Minnesota Press, 2005.

Harris, Richard. *Creeping Conformity: How Canada Became Suburban, 1900-1960.* Toronto: University of Toronto Press, 2004.

Hayden, Dolores. *A Field Guide to Sprawl.* New York: W.W. Norton and Company, 2004.

H.C. Planning Consultants Inc., and Planimetrics, LLP. *The Costs of Suburban Sprawl and Urban Decay in Rhode Island.* Executive Summary. Prepared for Grow Smart Rhode Island, December 1999. http://www.growsmartri.com/.

Hernandez, Tony, and Jim Simmons. "Evolving Retail Landscapes: Power Retail in Canada." *Canadian Geographer* 50, 4 (2006): 465-86.

Hobbs, Frank, and Nicole Stoops. *Demographic Trends in the 20th Century.* US Census Bureau, Census 2000 Special Reports, November 2002. http://www.census.gov/.

Holcombe, Randall G., and Samuel R. Staley. "Policy Implications." In *Smarter Growth: Market-Based Strategies for Land-Use Planning in the 21st Century,* 251-65. Westport, CT: Greenwood Press, 2001.

—. *Smarter Growth: Market-Based Strategies for Land-Use Planning in the 21st Century.* Westport, CT: Greenwood Press, 2001.

Hollingworth, B., A. Pushkar, and E.J. Miller. *Greenhouse Gas Emissions from Urban Travel: Tool for Evaluating Neighbourhood Sustainability.* Research Report, Healthy Housing and Communities Series. Ottawa: Canada Mortgage and Housing Corporation, 2000.

Holtzclaw, John. *Using Residential Patterns and Transit to Decrease Auto Dependence and Costs.* San Francisco: Natural Resources Defense Council, 1994.

Huffman, Forrest E., Arthur C. Nelson, Marc T. Smith, and Michael Stegman. "Who Bears the Burden of Development Impact Fees?" *Journal of the American Planning Association* 54, 1 (1988): 49-55.

Hughes, Mark Allen. "Why So Little Georgism in America? Using the Pennsylvania Case Files to Understand the Slow, Uneven Progress of Land Value Taxation." Lincoln Institute of Land Policy, Working Paper, July 2007. http://www.lincolninst.edu/.

Iacobucci, Edward M., Michael J. Trebilcock, and Tracey D. Epps. "Rerouting the Mail: Why Canada Is Due for Reform." *C.D. Howe Institute Commentary* 243 (2007). http://www.cdhowe.org/.

IBI Group. *Toronto-Related Region Futures Study, Interim Report: Implications of Business-as-Usual Development.* Toronto: Neptis Foundation, 2002.

—. *Transportation and Climate Change: Tax Exempt Status for Employer-Provided Transit Passes.* Prepared for the Passenger (Urban) Sub-Group of the Transportation Table on Climate Change, June 1999.

Ihlanfeldt, Keith R., and Timothy M. Shaughnessy. "An Empirical Investigation of the Effects of Impact Fees on Housing and Land Markets." *Regional Science and Urban Economics* 34, 6 (2004): 639-61.

Isard, Walter, and Robert E. Coughlin. *Municipal Costs and Revenues Resulting from Community Growth*. Wellesley, MA: Chandler-Davis, 1957.

Jones, Ken, and Michael J. Doucet. "The Big Box, the Flagship, and Beyond: Impacts and Trends in the Greater Toronto Area." *Canadian Geographer* 45, 4 (2001): 494-512.

–. "Big-Box Retailing and the Urban Retail Structure: The Case of the Toronto Area." *Journal of Retailing and Consumer Services* 7 (2000): 233-47.

Kiefer, Matthew J. "Suburbia and Its Discontents: Notes from the Sprawl Debate." In *Sprawl and Suburbia*, ed. William S. Saunders, 34-43. Minneapolis: University of Minnesota Press. (Harvard Design Magazine Reader 2 [2005]: 34-43.)

Kitchen, Harry. "Canadian Municipalities: Fiscal Trends and Sustainability." *Canadian Tax Journal* 50, 1 (2002): 156-80.

–. "Financing City Services: A Prescription for the Future." Paper no. 3 of the AIMS Urban Futures Series, Atlantic Institute for Market Studies, September 2004. http://www.aims.ca/.

–. "Municipal Finance in a New Fiscal Environment." *C.D. Howe Institute Commentary* 147 (November 2000). http://www.cdhowe.org/.

Kitchen, Harry M., and Enid Slack. "Business Property Taxation." Government and Competitiveness Project Discussion Paper No. 93-24 (1993): 24-30.

Kolankiewicz, Leon, and Roy Beck. "Weighing Sprawl Factors in Large US Cities: Analysis of U.S. Bureau of the Census Data on the 100 Largest Urbanized Areas of the United States." *Numbers USA*, 19 March 2001. http://www.numbersusa.com/.

Knaap, Gerrit-Jan. "The Sprawl of Economics: A Response to Jan Brueckner." Lincoln Institute of Land Policy Working Paper, 2007. http://www.lincolninst.edu/.

Knaap, Gerrit, Emily Talen, Robert Olshansky, and Clyde Forrest. *Government Policy and Urban Sprawl*. Report prepared for the Illinois Department of Natural Resources, 2000. http://dnr.state.il.us/.

Ladd, Helen. "Population Growth, Density and the Costs of Providing Public Services." *Urban Studies* 29, 2 (1992): 273-95.

Lawrence, Felicity. "Food Study Reveals Hidden £9 Bn Costs of Transport." *Guardian*, 15 July 2005.

Levine, Jonathan. *Zoned Out: Regulation, Markets, and Choices in Transportation and Metropolitan Land Use*. Washington, DC: Resources for the Future, 2006.

Litman, Todd. *Parking Management Best Practices*. Chicago: APA Planners Press, 2006.

–. *Parking Taxes: Evaluating Options and Impacts*. Victoria Transport Policy Institute, 29 May 2006. http://www.vtpi.org/.

–. *Socially Optimal Transport Prices and Markets: Principles, Strategies and Impacts*. Victoria Transport Policy Institute, 2 December 2007. http://www.vtpi.org/.

Lusht, Kenneth. *The Site Value Tax and Residential Development*. Cambridge, MA: Lincoln Institute of Land Policy, 1992.

Malenfant, Eric Caron, Anne Milan, Mathieu Charron, and Alain Belanger. *Demographic Changes in Canada from 1971 to 2001 across an Urban-to-Rural Gradient.* Statistics Canada Research Paper, cat. no. 91F0015 MIE–No. 008.

Mazza, Patrick, and Eben Fodor. *Taking Its Toll: The Hidden Costs of Sprawl in Washington State.* Olympia, WA: Climate Solutions, 2000.

McCann, Barbara A., and Reid Ewing. *Measuring the Health Effects of Sprawl.* Smart Growth America, Surface Transportation Policy Project, September 2003. http://www.smartgrowthamerica.org/.

McClanaghan and Associates. *Location-Based Mortgages: Feasibility Study and Business Case.* Prepared for Ministry of Community Services, Coast Capital Savings, Greater Vancouver Regional District, October 2006.

McCluskey, William J., and Riel C.D. Franzsen. "Land Value Taxation: A Case Study Approach." Lincoln Institute of Land Policy Working Paper, 2001. http://www.lincolninst.edu/.

McKinsey Global Institute. *Driving Productivity Growth in the UK Economy,* October 1998. http://www.mckinsey.com/.

Meen, Geoffrey, and Mark Andrew. "Land Regulation, Fiscal Incentives and Housing Segmentation." Lincoln Institute of Land Policy, conference paper, 2002. http://www.lincolninst.edu/.

Metropole Consultants. *The Growth Opportunity: Leveraging New Growth to Maximise Benefits in the Central Ontario Zone.* Toronto: Neptis Foundation, 2003.

Mieszkowski, Peter, and Edwin S. Mills. "The Causes of Metropolitan Suburbanization." *Journal of Economic Perspectives* 7, 3 (1993): 135-47.

Miller, Eric J., Matthew J. Roorda, Murtaza Haider, Abolfazl Mohammadian, Jonathan Ross, and Winnie W.L. Wong. *Travel and Housing Costs in the Greater Toronto Area: 1986-1996, Report Highlights.* Toronto: Neptis Foundation, 2004.

–. *Travel and Housing Costs in the Greater Toronto Area: 1986-1996, Technical Report.* Vols. 1 and 2. Toronto: Neptis Foundation, 2004.

Mills, Edwin. "Comments on Jan K. Brueckner, 'Urban Sprawl: Lessons from Urban Economics.'" *Brookings-Wharton Papers on Urban Affairs* (2001): 90-94.

–. "Truly Smart 'Smart Growth.'" *Illinois Real Estate Letter* (Summer 1999). Office of Real Estate Research, University of Illinois at Urbana-Champaign. http://www.business.uiuc.edu/.

Mitchell, William J. "Electronic Cottages, Wired Neighborhoods and Smart Cities." In *Smart Growth: Form and Consequences,* ed. Terry S. Szold and Armando Carbonell, 66-81. Cambridge, MA: Lincoln Institute of Land Policy, 2002.

Myers, Norman, and Jennifer Kent. *Perverse Subsidies: How Tax Dollars Can Undercut the Environment and the Economy.* Washington, DC: Island Press, 2001.

Natural Resources Canada. "ecoENERGY Efficiency Initiative: Using Less, Living Better." *Backgrounder* (21 January 2007). http://www.ecoaction.gc.ca/.

Natural Resources Defense Council. *Another Cost of Sprawl: The Effects of Land Use on Wastewater Utility Costs,* 1998, Part 2. http://www.nrdc.org/.

Nelson, Arthur C. *Housing Price Effects of Landowner Behavior: Implications of Urban Containment.* Report on the Symposium of Housing Price and Landowner Behavior Effects of Urban Containment. Cambridge, MA: Lincoln Institute of Land Policy and Fannie Mae Foundation, 2000.

–. "How Do We Know Smart Growth When We See It?" In *Smart Growth: Form and Consequences*, ed. Terry S. Szold and Armando Carbonell, 82-101. Cambridge, MA: Lincoln Institute of Land Policy, 2002.

NERA Economic Consulting. *Economics of Postal Services: Final Report*. A Report to the European Commission DG-MARKT, July 2003. London, UK, July 2004. http://ec.europa.eu/.

Netzer, Dick. "Land Value Taxation: Could It Work Today?" *Land Lines* 10, 2 (1998): 1-3.

Newman, Peter W.G., and Jeffrey R. Kenworthy. *Cities and Automobile Dependence: An International Sourcebook*. Brookfield, VT: Gower Publishing, 1989.

–. *Sustainability and Cities: Overcoming Automobile Dependence*. Washington, DC: Island Press, 1999.

Nowlan, David M. "Economic Implications of the Proposed City of Toronto Land Transfer Tax," 6 July 2007. http://www.toronto.ca/.

–. "Local Taxation as an Instrument of Policy." In *The Changing Canadian Metropolis*. Vol. 2: *A Public Policy Perspective*, ed. Frances Frisken, 799-841. Berkeley/Toronto: Institute of Governmental Studies Press/Canadian Urban Institute, 1994.

Oates, Wallace E. "Local Property Taxation: An Assessment." Cambridge, MA, Lincoln Institute of Land Policy, May 1999. http://www.lincolninst.edu/.

Oates, Wallace E., and Robert M. Schwab. "The Impact of Urban Land Taxation: The Pittsburgh Experience." Cambridge, MA: Lincoln Institute of Land Policy, 1996. http://www.lincolninst.edu/.

Office of the Auditor General of Canada. *Report of the Commissioner of the Environment and Sustainable Development, 2000*. http://www.oag-bvg.gc.ca/.

Ontario. *Places to Grow: Growth Plan for the Greater Golden Horseshoe*. Ministry of Public Infrastructure Renewal, 2006. https://www.placestogrow.ca/.

–. Office of the Greater Toronto Area. *Urban Density Study, General Report*. March 1995.

Ontario Clean Air Alliance. *Tax Shift: Eliminating Subsidies and Moving to Full Cost Electricity Pricing*. Ontario Clean Air Alliance Research Inc., 3 March 2008. http://www.cleanairalliance.org/.

Ontario Energy Board. *EB-2005-0317, Cost Allocation Review, Board Directions on Cost Allocation Methodology for Electricity Distributors*, 29 September 2006. http://www.oeb.gov.on.ca/.

–. *Natural Gas Regulation in Ontario: A Renewed Policy Framework*. Report on the Ontario Energy Board Natural Gas Forum, 30 March 2005. http://www.oeb. gov.on.ca/.

–. *Ontario Energy Board Electricity Distribution Rate Handbook*, 9 March 2000. http://www.oeb.gov.on.ca/.

–. *Regulated Price Plan, Price Report, November 1, 2009 to October 31, 2010*, 15 October 2009. http://www.oeb.gov.on.ca/.

Ontario Ministry of Finance. *2006 Ontario Budget: Building Opportunity.* http://www.fin.gov.on.ca/.

–. *2006 Ontario Economic Outlook and Fiscal Review.* Annex V, Transparency in Taxation. http://www.fin.gov.on.ca/.

–. *2007 Ontario Budget: Budget Papers.* http://www.fin.gov.on.ca/.

–. *Automobile Insurance Affordability Plan for Ontario: Next Steps.* White Paper, July 2003. http://www.fin.gov.on.ca/.

–. "Strengthening Ontario's Transportation Infrastructure." *Backgrounder.* http://www.fin.gov.on.ca/.

Ontario Ministry of Public Infrastructure Renewal. *ReNew Ontario 2005-2010, Strategic Highlights*, 2005. http://www.mei.gov.on.ca/.

Organization for Economic Co-operation and Development. *Regulatory Reform in the Telecommunications Industry.* OECD Reviews of Regulatory Reform, Regulatory Reform in Canada from Transition to New Regulation Challenges, 2002. http://www.oecd.org/.

Palameta, Boris, and Ian Macredie. "Property Taxes Relative to Income." *Perspectives.* Statistics Canada, cat. no. 75-001-XIE, March 2005.

Pardy, Sasha M. *USA's Largest Retail Centers under Construction Defy Definition.* CoStar Realty Information, 10 October 2007. http://www.costar.com/.

Peiser, Richard B. "Does It Pay to Plan Suburban Growth?" *Journal of the American Planning Association* 50, 4 (1984): 419-33.

Pembina Institute, *Building Sustainable Urban Communities in Ontario: A Provincial Progress Report*, September 2006. http://communities.pembina.org/.

–. *Submission to the Standing Committee on Finance*, February 2007. http://www.pembina.org/.

Pendall, Rolf. "Do Land Use Controls Cause Sprawl?" *Environment and Planning B: Planning and Design* 26, 4 (1999): 555-71.

Phillips, Justin, and Eban Goodstein. "Growth Management and Housing Prices: The Case of Portland, Oregon." *Contemporary Economic Policy* 18, 3 (2000): 334-44.

Polzin, Steven E., and Xuehao Chu. "A Closer Look at Public Transportation Mode Share Trends." US Department of Transportation, Bureau of Transportation Statistics. *Journal of Transportation and Statistics* 8, 3 (2005). http://www.bts.gov/.

Prud'homme, Rémy, and Chang-Woon Lee. "Size, Sprawl, Speed and the Efficiency of Cities." *Urban Studies* 36, 11 (1999): 1849-58.

Public Interest Advocacy Centre. "Eliminating Phonelessness in Canada: Possible Approaches," March 2002. http://www.piac.ca/.

Ralph, Eric. "Cross-Subsidy: A Novice's Guide to the Arcane." Duke University, 27 July 1992. http://www.ekonomicsllc.com/.

Razin, Eran, and Mark S. Rosentraub. "Are Fragmentation and Sprawl Interlinked? North American Evidence." *Urban Affairs Review* 35, 6 (2000): 821-36.

Real Estate Research Corporation. *The Costs of Sprawl: Environmental and Economic Costs of Alternative Residential Development Patterns at the Urban Fringe.* Washington, DC: US Government Printing Office, 1974.

Regional Municipality of York. *2007 Development Charge Background Study as Approved by Regional Council*, 24 May 2007. http://www.york.ca/.

Renzetti, Steven. "Municipal Water Supply and Sewage Treatment: Costs, Prices and Distortions." *Canadian Journal of Economics* 32 (1999): 688-704.

Riley, Chris. "Comments on Mills and Evans." Lincoln Institute of Land Policy, conference paper, 2002. http://www.lincolninst.edu/.

Roger Tym and Partners. *Planning and Competitiveness: A Selective Literature Review.* Prepared for the British House of Commons Select Committee of the Office of the Deputy Prime Minister (Housing, Planning, Local Government, and the Regions), December 2002.

Salvanes, K., and S. Tjotta. "Productivity Differences in Multiple Output Industries." *Journal of Productivity Analysis* 5 (1994): 23-43.

Shoup, Donald C. "The Effect of Property Taxes on the Capital Intensity of Urban Land Development." In *Metropolitan Financing and Growth Management Policies,* ed. George F. Break, 105-32. Madison, WI: University of Wisconsin Press, 1978.

–. *The High Cost of Free Parking.* Washington, DC: APA Planners Press, 2005.

–. "An Opportunity to Reduce Minimum Parking Requirements." *Journal of the American Planning Association* 61 (1995): 14-28.

Sierra Club. *The Dark Side of the American Dream: The Costs and Consequences of Suburban Sprawl,* 1998. http://www.sierraclub.org/.

–. *Sprawl Costs Us All: How Your Taxes Fuel Suburban Sprawl,* 2000. http://www.sierraclub.org/.

Skaburskis, Andrejs. "The Burden of Development Impact Fees." *Journal of Property Research* 7, 3 (1990): 173-85.

–. "The Consequence of Taxing Land Value." *Journal of Planning Literature* 10, 1 (1995): 3-21.

Skaburskis, Andrejs, and Mohammed Qadeer. "An Empirical Estimation of the Price Effects of Development Impact Fees." *Urban Studies* 29, 5 (1992): 653-67.

Slack, Enid. *Municipal Finance and the Pattern of Urban Growth.* C.D. Howe Institute Commentary 160 (February 2002), http://www.cdhowe.org/.

Soule, David C., ed. *Remaking American Communities: A Reference Guide to Urban Sprawl.* Lincoln and London, Nebraska: University of Nebraska Press, 2007.

Speir, Cameron, and Kurt Stephenson, "Does Sprawl Cost Us All?" *Journal of the American Planning Association* 68, 1 (2002): 56-70.

Staley, Samuel R. *The Sprawling of America: In Defense of the Dynamic City.* Reason Public Policy Institute, Policy Study No. 251, January 1999. http://reason.org/.

Statistics Canada. *Canadian Vehicle Survey, Annual 2004.* Cat. no. 53-223-XIE, October 2005.

–. *Historical Statistics of Canada.* Section T, Transportation and Communications. Cat. no. 11-516-XIE, ser. T147-194, Motor Vehicle Registrations by province, 1903 to 1975.

–. *Econnections: Linking the Environment and the Economy, Indicators and Detailed Statistics 2000.* Cat. no. 16-200-XKE, February 2001.

–. "The Loss of Dependable Agricultural Land in Canada." *Rural and Small Town Canada Analysis Bulletin* 6, 1 (January 2005). Ottawa: Statistics Canada. Cat. no. 21-006-XIE.

—. *Portrait of the Canadian Population in 2006: 2006 Census*. Cat. no. 97-550-XIE, March 2007.

—. *Spending Patterns in Canada*. Cat. no. 62-202-XIE, December 2006.

—. *Where Canadians Work and How They Get There*. Analysis Series, 2001 Census. Cat. no. 96F0030XIE2001010, 11 February 2003.

St. Lawrence, Joe. "A Demand Perspective on Greenhouse Gas Emissions." *Enviro-Stats* 1 (2), Statistics Canada, cat. no. 16-002-XIE, Fall 2007.

Taylor, Zack, with planningAlliance Inc. *Urban Form and Density Study. Part 1: Analysis of Existing Urban Areas in the Toronto Region*. Toronto: Neptis Foundation, 2006.

Taylor, Zack, with John van Nostrand, planningAlliance, Inc. *Shaping the Toronto Region, Past, Present, and Future*. Toronto: Neptis Foundation, September 2008.

Thompson, Wilbur. "The City as a Distorted Price System." *Psychology Today* 2, 3 (1968): 28-33.

Tomlinson, Peter. *A Level Playing Field by 2009: Achieving Property Tax Parity for Toronto Businesses*. Report prepared for the Toronto Office Coalition, January 2006. http://torontoofficecoalition.com/.

Transit Cooperative Research Program. "An Evaluation of the Relationships between Transit and Urban Form." *Research Results Digest* 7 (June 1995). http://www.tcrponline.org/.

Union Gas. "Frequently Asked Questions about the October 2006 Rates." http://www.uniongas.com/.

United Kingdom. Office of the Deputy Prime Minister. *The Economic Consequences of Planning to the Business Sector*. 1999.

Urban Strategies Inc. *Application of a Land-Use Intensification Target for the Greater Golden Horseshoe*. Prepared for the Ontario Growth Secretariat, Ministry of Public Infrastructure Renewal, Winter 2005. http://www.mei.gov.on.ca/.

US Congress. Office of Technology Assessment. *The Technological Reshaping of Metropolitan America*, OTA-ETI-643. Washington, DC: US Government Printing Office, September 1995.

US Department of Housing and Urban Development. *"Why Not in Our Community?" Reviewing Barriers to Affordable Housing*, February 2005. http://www.huduser.org/.

US Transportation Research Board. *Parking Pricing and Fees*. TCRP Report 95. Washington, DC: Transit Cooperative Research Program, 2005.

Vaca, Erin, and J. Richard Kuzmyak. "Parking Pricing and Fees." *Traveler Response to Transportation System Changes*, chap. 13, TCRP Report 95. Washington, DC: Transit Cooperative Research Program, Transportation Research Board, 2005. http://www.trb.org/.

Wassmer, Robert W. "An Economic Perspective on Urban Sprawl: With an Application to the American West and a Test of the Efficacy of Urban Growth Boundaries," September 2002. http://www.csus.edu/.

Weinhaus, Carol, Sandra Makeeff, Peter Copeland, et al. "What Is the Price of Universal Service? Impact of Deaveraging Nationwide Urban/Rural Rates." Paper presented at the July 1993 National Association of Regulatory Utility Commissioners (NARUC) meeting, San Francisco, CA, 26 July 1993. http://www.convergingindustries.org/.

Wheaton, William M., and Morton J. Schussheim. *The Cost of Municipal Services in Residential Areas.* Washington, DC: US Department of Commerce, 1955.

Will Dunning Inc. *Economic Influences on Population Growth and Housing Demand in the Greater Golden Horseshoe.* Neptis Foundation: Neptis Studies on the Toronto Metropolitan Region, January 2006.

World Commission on Environment and Development. *Our Common Future.* Oxford: Oxford University Press, 1987.

Yatchew, Adonis. "Economic and Regulatory Consequences of the Creation of New Embedded Distributors." Evidence of Adonis Yatchew, PhD, before the Ontario Energy Board, RP-2003-0044, 27 November 2003. http://www.oeb.gov.on.ca/.

–. "Scale Economies in Electricity Distribution: A Semiparametric Analysis." *Journal of Applied Econometrics* 15 (2000): 197-210.

Yinger, John. "The Incidence of Development Fees and Special Assessments." *National Tax Journal* 51, 1 (1998): 23-41.

Zodrow, George R. "The Property Tax as a Capital Tax: A Room with Three Views." *National Tax Journal* 54, 1 (2001): 139-55.

Index

Printed and bound in Canada by Friesens

Set in Futura Condensed, Warnock, and Meta
by Artegraphica Design Co. Ltd.

Text design: Irma Rodriguez

Copy editor: Joanne Richardson

Proofreader and indexer: Dianne Tiefensee